For Michael and Carolyn Eggor—
Dear friends whose
love and support make
this work possible.
Shalom—
Joe Fogle

LAST RIGHTS

JOSEPH B. INGLE
LAST RIGHTS

13
Fatal
Encounters
with the
State's
Justice

ABINGDON PRESS
Nashville

LAST RIGHTS:
THIRTEEN FATAL ENCOUNTERS WITH THE STATE'S JUSTICE

Copyright © 1990 by Joseph B. Ingle

This book is printed on acid-free paper.

Library of Congress Cataloging-in-Publication Data

Ingle, Joseph B. (Joseph Burton), 1946–
    Last rights : thirteen fatal encounters with the state's justice /
Joseph B. Ingle.
      p. cm.
    ISBN 0-687-21124-7 (alk. paper)
    1. Capital punishment—United States. I. Title.
HV8699.U5I53   1990
364.6'6'0973—dc20   89-78112
                                                          CIP

Scripture quotation on pp. 19-20 is from the King James Version of the Bible.

All Scripture quotations are from *The Jerusalem Bible,* copyright © 1966 by Darton, Longman & Todd, Ltd. and Doubleday & Company, Inc. Used by permission of the publisher.

Excerpts from *The Cunning Use of History* by Richard L. Rubenstein, copyright © 1975 by Richard L. Rubenstein. Reprinted by permission of Harper & Row, Publishers, Inc.

Excerpts from *Obedience to Authority* by Stanley Milgram, copyright © 1974 by Stanley Milgram. Reprinted by permission of Harper & Row, Publishers, Inc.

Excerpts from "Ministering to the Condemned: A Case Study," in *Facing the Death Penalty* edited by Michael Radelet, reprinted by permission of Temple University Press.

Excerpts from *Democracy in America* by Alexis de Tocqueville, copyright 1945 and renewed 1973 by Alfred A. Knopf, Inc. Reprinted by permission of the publisher.

MANUFACTURED IN THE UNITED STATES OF AMERICA

For *Becca,* my love, and *Amelia,* my light

ACKNOWLEDGMENTS

In the aftermath of John Spenkelink's electrocution by the state of Florida in 1979, I received a version of the chaotic events involved in that story from David Kendall, John's lawyer. Reading the personal recounting of John's story from David's perspective helped me to realize it was healing to see the story on paper beyond our subjective experiences. In the spring of 1980 I began writing of my relationship with John. I found the experience to be cathartic for me emotionally, and healing for me personally. Little did I realize the next ten years would be spent working with eighteen people who would be victims of the executioner and that thirteen of those stories would be recorded in a book.

Not having written a book before, I turned to friends for assistance, and I have been abundantly blessed. Tony Dunbar and John Egerton offered criticisms and suggestions that pointed the way for this becoming a book. Charles Merrill and Anne Allen were equally helpful after reading the manuscript. Each chapter has been reviewed by a participant in the events described. I am thankful to everyone who read and commented on these sections. I would like to mention a few of those whose suggestions have made this a better book: Dick Burr, Nancy Goodwin, Henry Hudson, Marie Deans, Mike Radelet, Lloyd Snook, and David Kendall. I am especially grateful to Margaret Vandiver because her editorial remarks have strengthened this work considerably, and her participation in many of the events described herein was a blessing.

The work of typing a manuscript is a labor of love indeed. I am thankful for Zel Morris and Judy Gower for their efforts in this regard.

I am in debt to the good folks at Abingdon Press who helped me work this manuscript into a book.

Finally, I would like to express my appreciation and gratitude to the friends whose story is recorded in these pages. The public needs to see them for who they were and how their love enriched my life. To their memories and for those who loved them, I offer their stories to the world.

"They have healed the wound of my people lightly, saying, 'Peace, peace,' when there is no peace."

THE BOOK OF JEREMIAH 6:14

CONTENTS

I know a young woman in her late twenties who happened by chance to be in Orlando, Florida, on the night before the famous serial killer Ted Bundy was executed not far away in the state prison. In the early evening hundreds of jubilant people, many of them quite drunk, marched past her motel with shouts of "Kill! Kill!" and other celebratory sounds; Bundy's approaching death had created a circus atmosphere, and the young woman was shocked and horrified. She is not a religious person, and while opposed in principle to the death penalty, she has never regarded it as being at the top of her list of moral wrongs; she had also been violently repelled by Bundy and his savage crimes. She is highly intelligent and poised and not given to perverse fantasies. Nonetheless, that night she was possessed by an astonishing dream; she saw herself bathing Bundy, cleansing him with water, bathing him over and over again in some helpless enactment of solace and redemption.

I have been haunted by this story for a couple of reasons. The spontaneous and innocent compassion at its heart evokes a kind of awe. But the rowdy celebration, which no doubt prompted the dream, tells us much about recent public attitudes toward legalized murder. When I was a young boy growing up in Virginia in the 1930s—at a time when American executions were at their apex, during a single year claiming close to one life every other day—the state's killing of a man (and occasionally a woman) was carried out with extreme solemnity. While the more notorious cases attracted considerable attention in the media, as they do now, there was a funereal mood attached to the ceremony, and the idea of any jubilant mass demonstration would have been unthinkable.

Perhaps the contrast between that time and the present signifies little—a gruesome delight, after all, has been part of the public contemplation of executions throughout history—but this new clamor for vengeance, so open and unabashed, does at least seem to indicate an outspoken manifestation of what the polls tell us: The overwhelming majority of Americans favors the death penalty. They appear to favor it with a vehement passion, even though the statistics tend to demonstrate a grave dichotomy at the core of that passion. Why, with over two thousand people on Death Row nationwide, should executions not only fail to increase in number but to decline precipitously from their horrendous peak in the 1930s, to the point where during some recent years only a relative handful of the condemned actually goes to the gas chamber or the electric chair?

Could it be that, despite the bloodthirsty enthusiasm expressed by much of the public, there really exists a powerful (perhaps subconscious) revulsion and shame, so that the death penalty in the United States will wither away through attrition or be killed by legislation, as it has in virtually all the advanced countries in the Western world? The complex political structure of the United States, with its multitude of jurisdictions, makes it difficult to conceive of any abrupt and decisive abolition, such as happened for example in France, where after nearly two hundred years of the guillotine the newly elected administration of François Mitterrand swiftly seized the moral high ground and summarily abolished the death penalty—this in a nation which like ours had expressed an avid popular desire for blood. If however, for whatever reason, this historical decline continues to hold true in the United States as it has elsewhere, its culmination—total abolition—will still come about only through the dedication of opponents who ceaselessly fight for the wretched minority of the condemned: those so ill-favored in the lottery of capital punishment as to finally come face to face with the executioner.

For many years Joe Ingle has been at the forefront of this struggle, and has done as much as any single person to stir the consciousness of the public, especially in the South, which is America's chief killing ground. He has valiantly gone about the region and elsewhere, spreading the hard facts about this blight upon our democracy—the truth being that the death penalty almost never deters a criminal, that it is visited overwhelmingly on the indigent and those disadvantaged by race and class (and too often, unbearably, on minors and the mentally retarded), that it is applied with callous inequity to the point of randomness, and that a significant number of those who are later proved innocent go to their doom. No sentimentalist, Joe Ingle is not an adversary of punishment and its reasonable necessities, only of the single punishment which is final and irrevocable. To the list of reasons that makes the death penalty an intolerable wound on the body of a free society he would add finally, I'm sure, the simple one over which Christians and secular people of good will find no conflict: If it is wrong to destroy a human life, vengeance compounds the wrong. The wrong of the crime of killing is in no way redressed by the state's own vengeful murder.

Not long ago Joe Ingle was nominated for the Nobel Peace Prize, and this is a tribute which anyone who is moved by his advocacy for justice would feel well-earned. But for Ingle the fight against the death penalty has not been an intellectual abstraction; as the present book demonstrates, his ministry among the condemned has been unceasingly active, passionate, and so arduous at times as to require the superhuman defense against fatigue that perhaps only the greatest faith can procure. Whatever animates Joe Ingle, his service in the cause of the abolition of the death penalty—one of the purest of all moral missions—has been steadfast and sometimes heroic, and his work will deserve honor long after that day when the hand of the executioner is finally stilled.

—WILLIAM STYRON

CHAPTER ONE

Richmond to New York

It was a gray and chilly day in late November as I walked across the campus of the Union Theological Seminary in Richmond, Virginia. When I opened my mailbox and read the note written on seminary letterhead the day seemed to grow grayer and chillier still.

The note from one of my theology professors instructed me to make an appointment to see him right away. I knew this was bad news. Though I had been one of the fair-haired boys of the seminary when I first arrived at Union in 1969, I now found myself out of step with many of my fellow seminarians and most of the faculty—including the professor who had summoned me to his office.

I had spoken out against the Vietnam War and marched in an anti-war demonstration in Washington, D.C. I had helped start an alternative newspaper on campus. The erstwhile fair-haired boy had begun to be seen as a radical peacenik by a seminary establishment that considered itself liberal by denominational—Southern Presbyterian—standards. I was part of a group of Union students who sought to learn more about the Christian faith without committing ourselves to serving the institutional church. Our doubts, our concerns, and our questions were perceived as threatening by some students and faculty members. Our challenges to the status quo at Union generated many discussions, some controversies, and more than a little paranoia on the part of the more traditional students and professors.

As my political activity increased, as I struggled more and more with the question "What does it mean to be a Christian in 1969?" my relationship with the theology professor who summoned me to his office had deteriorated. The nadir came when he assigned all his graduate seminary students to memorize the Nicene Creed ("We believe in one God, the Father, the Almighty, maker of heaven and earth, of all that is, seen and unseen . . .") and write it from memory.

Like my fellow students, I had already earned a bachelor's degree.

Mine was in philosophy and religion from St. Andrews Presbyterian College in Laurinburg, North Carolina. It seemed silly to me to assign graduate students the kind of rote memory work usually reserved for elementary school students. I told the professor in advance that I refused to do the assignment, but that I would write an alternate assignment. He warned me that he would drop my semester grade by one letter if I did so. In lieu of regurgitating the Nicene Creed on cue, I wrote a paper rooted in my educational philosophy, a paper explaining why graduate students working toward advanced degrees in religion and divinity shouldn't be treated like Sunday school students being drilled on Bible memory verses to earn gold stars. I made an appointment to see the professor the next day.

As I sat down in his office he looked across the desk at me.

"Mr. Ingle, I have never been so insulted in my life," he said in his raspy voice. "Your attack on my person was uncalled for. I demand an apology."

I replied, "I'm sorry if I upset you, but I honestly don't recall writing anything in my paper which was meant as a personal attack. I really don't remember anything in the paper intended to be an insult to you."

"Mr. Ingle, I know that young people have different ideas as to what is proper these days. But I don't think using an obscenity directed at a professor in an assignment is proper by anyone's standards."

I couldn't believe this charge! I *was* upset when I wrote my paper, but I certainly hadn't written any obscenities.

"Professor, would you please tell me what obscenity I wrote in my paper?"

"I won't repeat the word."

"Would you please show me the paper?"

"I don't have it here."

"Maybe we could meet again when you have the paper. I don't recall using an obscenity, but my handwriting is difficult to read. Maybe you misunderstood."

We agreed to meet again the following afternoon. I left his office feeling a combination of relief and anxiety.

I spent a sleepless night struggling to remember what I could have said that might have offended him. I began to wish I had simply memorized the Nicene Creed and coughed it up for him.

As I knocked on the professor's office door the next afternoon, I felt as though it should have borne the inscription posted above the entry to Dante's *Inferno*: "All hope abandon, ye who enter here."

He told me to come in, and I sat down.

"Here's your paper, Mr. Ingle," he said, shoving it across his desk at me.

I slowly read the front and back page of my paper.

"I know my handwriting is hard to read, but I don't see an obscenity. Would you tell me where it is?"

"The front page!" he said in a raspy bark.

I combed through the first page. Nothing.

"Would you please tell me precisely where the word is located or just tell me the word?"

"I won't repeat such a word!"

"Well, could you tell me just the first letter of the word?"

He seemed to consider the question carefully before he said softly, "F."

I was shocked that he would suspect me of using the infamous "F word" to insult him. I anxiously perused the front page again and found nothing.

Baffled, I asked him, "Where on the front page did I write the word?"

"You abbreviated the word. You only used the first letter, 'F.' I know what it means and so do you."

As I re-read the page yet again, I felt a surge of relief as I figured out what had happened.

"Professor, I think there's a misunderstanding here. What you took for the letter 'F' is really my abbreviation for the word 'and.' As you can see I've used it several times in this paper. If you substitute the word 'and' wherever you see the symbol, I think you'll agree the sentence makes sense."

I handed the paper back to him. He read the front and back of the paper slowly and carefully. Finally, without looking up, he muttered, "That will be all, Mr. Ingle."

The absurdity of my encounter with my theology professor was just one of the events that made the world seem like something viewed through a series of fun-house mirrors. The more I spoke out against the Vietnam War, the more I saw the hostility galvanized in people who supported the war. My struggles at Union, my anti-war activism, my work on the alternative newspaper, all seemed to drain my energy and my spirit. I was actually told by a fellow student that as far as America and Union Theological Seminary were concerned I should "Love it or leave it." If I couldn't love my country and the establishment church—and love them uncritically, unthinkingly—then I should go to Russia. I was worn down from constantly defending my position against attacks by students and professors. John Kennedy, Robert Kennedy, and Martin Luther King, Jr., had all been assassinated. The war was escalating and race riots were breaking out throughout the country. I was considering abandoning my studies for the ministry and working in community organizing.

By the spring semester, when the Union community passed a resolution protesting the invasion of Cambodia and President Nixon's broadening of the war, I was too dispirited to care. I had reached a dead end. I felt alienated at Union and decided to leave as soon as I could.

The summer of 1970 was hot and humid in Richmond. My field placement for Union was a temporary job as tutor in the black community of Churchill. The burden of anxieties and frustrations grew day by day. Every day I slipped deeper and deeper into depression.

One afternoon I returned to the rented house I shared with some other Union students. I slumped in the kitchen chair, leaned over the table, and cradled my head in my arms. I was just too weary of life to continue. I just couldn't go on any more. There seemed no way out—except one.

The gas oven seemed to be the simplest way. I rose slowly from my chair and began shutting the kitchen windows to keep the gas in the room until it had done its work.

Before I could turn on the gas I heard the front door open. "Anybody home?" called Jim, one of my roommates. As I pondered what to say, the first bars of the Fifth Dimension's soulful "By the Riverside" wafted in from the next room. In spite of myself, a grim chuckle welled within me. Jim had switched on the stereo and played the song he always played when *he* was depressed. I opened the windows to the still and sweltering air. I walked out into the living room to talk with Jim.

The oppressive heat wore on into July. Each day of existence seemed tedious, meaningless, empty. Concerned that my despair might bring me to the point of suicide again, I telephoned the Reverend Jim Forbes. Jim was the minister of a small Pentecostal church in the Churchill community where I worked. He had preached at Union one Sunday, and I had never heard a more powerful sermon. His face, like Moses leaving the tent of meeting, radiated the presence of God. I turned to him because he was the one man I knew who had been touched by God.

I met him at his church the next day. He took me into his "office": an open area with a desk, a chair, and a telephone.

I stumbled through an introduction and tried to describe the spiritual malaise that gripped my soul. He rested his chin on his folded hands and listened. Then he asked me, "Have you prayed, Joe? I mean, lately, have you prayed?"

"Jim, I can't pray anymore," I said, shaking my head. "There are no words. It just seems empty inside."

He unfolded his hands and leaned toward me across his desk.

"Do you mind if I read a little scripture which has meant much to me in my low points?" he asked me. "And then I would like us to pray together. Is that okay?"

I nodded and sat back in my folding chair as he opened his Bible, found his place, and began to read the 139th Psalm:

> O LORD, thou hast searched me and known me! Thou knowest when I sit down and when I rise up; thou discernest my thoughts from afar. Thou searchest out my path and my lying down, and art acquainted with all my ways. Even before a word is on my tongue, lo, O LORD, thou knowest it altogether. Thou dost beset me behind

and before, and layest thy hand upon me. Such knowledge is too wonderful for me: it is high, I cannot attain it.

Whither shall I go from thy Spirit? Or whither shall I flee from thy presence? If I ascend to heaven, thou art there! If I make my bed in Sheol, thou art there! If I take the wings of the morning and dwell in the uttermost parts of the sea, even there thy hand shall lead me, and thy right hand shall hold me. If I say, 'Let only darkness cover me, and the light about me be night,' even the darkness is not dark to thee, the night is bright as the day; for darkness is as light with thee.

For thou didst form my inward parts, thou didst knit me together in my mother's womb. I praise thee, for thou art fearful and wonderful. Wonderful are thy works! Thou knowest me right well; my frame was not hidden from thee, when I was being made in secret, intricately wrought in the depths of the earth. Thy eyes beheld my unformed substance; in thy book were written, every one of them, the days that were formed for me, when as yet there was none of them. How precious to me are thy thoughts, O God! How vast is the sum of them! If I would count them they are more than the sand. When I awake, I am still with thee.

O that thou wouldst slay the wicked, O God, and that men of blood would depart from me, men who maliciously defy thee, who lift themselves up against thee for evil! Do I not hate them that hate thee, O Lord? And do I not loathe them that rise up against thee? I hate them with perfect hatred; I count them my enemies. Search me, O God, and know my heart! Try me and know my thoughts! And see if there be any wicked way in me, and lead me in the way everlasting.

With the Bible open in front of him, Jim Forbes bowed his head in prayer, and I joined him. His prayer was like a song, with a cadence that rose and fell, the words and rhythm merging into a caressing embrace of my soul. I, who had for months been unable to pray, was lifted and transported by this prayer.

Forbes said, "Amen." I rose, shook his hand, and walked out into the afternoon light. For the first time in weeks, I knew that I would survive tomorrow.

— ▼ —

My encounter with Jim Forbes supported me and undergirded me for a few days. But I knew it wouldn't sustain me indefinitely, especially while my future was so uncertain. I began praying, asking for a sign, desperately fighting off the return of despair.

There is much in life that can be seen as either coincidental or providential. At age twenty-three I had reached what seemed to be a dead end. Then something happened that made me realize that my life had reached not an ending, but a turning—not a dead end, but a crossroads.

I received a letter from the president of New York Theological Seminary in New York City. In his letter he apologized for taking so long to respond to my letter inquiring about studying at the seminary. (I had forgotten writing the letter.) He said he had recently assumed the presidency of the seminary and had been immersed in work. He asked if I was still interested in studying in their East Harlem Urban Year Program, a program which combined theological training with inner-city ministry. He said the seminary would accept me if I still wanted to come.

My hand trembled after I read the letter. A long-forgotten letter to a seminary about which I knew little had resulted in an invitation to study and work in the North: a region which to me, a lifelong Southerner, seemed as alien as a distant planet. I believed a sign had been given to me. I sat down and wrote a letter saying I wanted to come but I had no money. Ten days later he wrote back saying money was not a problem and that I would be expected to begin at New York Theological Seminary in September.

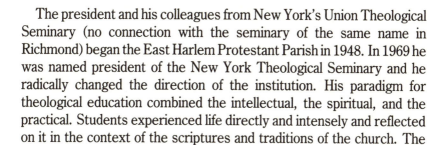

The president and his colleagues from New York's Union Theological Seminary (no connection with the seminary of the same name in Richmond) began the East Harlem Protestant Parish in 1948. In 1969 he was named president of the New York Theological Seminary and he radically changed the direction of the institution. His paradigm for theological education combined the intellectual, the spiritual, and the practical. Students experienced life directly and intensely and reflected on it in the context of the scriptures and traditions of the church. The

East Harlem Urban Year Program was just one of many educational experiences that enabled seminary students to put their faith to work facing the problems of people living in the inner city.

This promised to be an experience very different from the arid and depressing scholastic environment at Union in Richmond.

The president of the seminary was always on the move, brimming with ideas he was eager to share. A trim five feet ten inches, he generated an invigorating energy devoted to taking theology out of the dusty library and putting it to work in the streets.

He suggested I contact a fellow student living in East Harlem, Doug Magee for housing and job information. He also told me about possible internships for the year.

The common denominator in East Harlem in 1969 was poverty. The square-mile neighborhood included about 215,000 people. (That was almost as many people as lived in Charlotte, the largest city in my home state of North Carolina.) One block in East Harlem—100th Street between First and Second Avenues—was home to more than 4,000 people. I knew of many towns in North Carolina with fewer people than that one East Harlem block.

East Harlem included Puerto Ricans (about 45 percent), blacks (about 45 percent), Italian-Americans, Chinese-Americans, and whites. Central Harlem, farther uptown, was a racial ghetto comprising mostly black people. Central Harlem had a sizable black middle class. East Harlem was an economic ghetto comprising the poor of all races. East Harlem had no middle class to speak of. Virtually everybody was poor.

East Harlem suffered the usual urban ills—unemployment, drug abuse, street crime, inadequate housing, and other symptoms of the underlying disease, the cause of the suffering: poverty—deep, grinding poverty. But even though they endured this suffering, most of the residents of East Harlem worked hard to improve their lives. Many of them raised their families in the community with a joy and delight in life. I was grateful to learn about their living experience through the East Harlem Urban Year.

It was as though somebody had erected an invisible barrier along 96th Street from the East River to Central Park, then declared that the poor people would live north of that line and everybody else could live south of the line.

The East Harlem Urban Year gave students the chance to integrate the study of the Christian faith with the living of it. We lived and worked in the project of our choice in East Harlem. Some of us were social workers. Some led church youth groups. Others worked with autistic children. We studied theology, the scriptures, church history, and other disciplines while experiencing the life of the poor in the ghetto. This brand of "doing theology" attracted students who were searching for ways to live a meaningful Christian life in a chaotic world. We believed the abstract academic studies of conventional seminaries to be unrelated to the real world of our day. The combination of studying theology and doing theology was a rich and powerful mixture.

We met as a group twice a week and met as smaller groups to study and discuss specific areas of interest. We also audited courses at Union Theological Seminary in Manhattan. It was there that an Old Testament professor showed us the power, the poetry, and the music of the Psalms, Isaiah, and Job. I often left his class intoxicated by the beauty of the scriptures. My theology professor prodded us to do our best work and conveyed his expectations in a manner that was as affable as it was demanding. After just a few classes, I knew he was the teacher I wanted to work with on my senior thesis.

Strong friendships grew among the students working with the poor in East Harlem. Doug Magee and his wife, Kathie, had come to East Harlem so he could work in the Metropolitan Urban Student Training (MUST) program. They introduced me to a MUST student from Pampa, Texas. He and I roomed together. We started off in a small tenement apartment across the street from the Elite Linen Service, whose delivery trucks roared out of the garage—and by the sound of them, were headed straight into our living room—promptly at 3:30 every morning. We later found a railroad apartment on 102nd Street and traded the daily assault of laundry trucks for Sunday morning loudspeakers shouting the Spanish language service of the Pentecostal Holiness Church across the street. We both believed it was a good trade.

Southerners in New York shared an instant kinship that knew no barriers of race or class, a bond forged by the simple fact that you were from "down home." Many blacks in East Harlem had come from the South or had family whom they visited whenever they could. This bonding between black and white in a poor section of New York shattered my stereotype of "black and poor" and taught me the humanity of us all. I could identify with black people who had been forced northward seeking jobs that weren't available in the South, for I had made the journey seeking a kind of learning that I couldn't get in the South. Witnessing the suffering of many blacks from the South caused me to ache as I saw what their life was like in East Harlem. The friendships that emerged from our shared experience taught me lessons about life that I could never have learned in a university.

One Yankee friend in the East Harlem Urban Year Program said: "I wondered how you could survive in such a place when it was clear from the color of your skin and your accent that you didn't belong. Then I began to realize there was something to this 'Southern' thing. There seemed to be a warmth of feeling between black and white which puzzled me. It was difficult for me to understand that a white Southerner, with all that racial baggage, could fit more easily into an urban ghetto than those of us who grew up in the North and tried to help all along."

I learned a lot from watching people wrestle with the problems in East Harlem. Tim, a student from St. Andrews (my alma mater), came to live in the ghetto to organize and reeducate the people, to make them ready for "the revolution." When he described his plan to sell his Marxist newspaper on the streets of East Harlem, I had to brief him on the politics of the street corner.

"Tim," I said, "there are several things that could happen to you selling papers on the street. First, you could get busted for not having a permit. Second, you might get extremely bored standing there trying to sell your papers. Third, if you *do* sell any papers you might get mugged because somebody will figure you have some money. Finally, and most likely, I don't think folks give a damn about what your newspaper says no matter how fervently you believe they should. People are too busy trying to survive. This is a ghetto, Tim, not a college campus."

When I saw Tim the next evening his chipper, upbeat tone led me to conclude he hadn't spent the day selling his newspapers on the corner of 105th Street and Second Avenue.

"Joe," he said, "after talking it over with my political comrades, we decided I would be more successful on a college campus in Brooklyn. So I took the subway over there and had an amazingly successful day selling the paper and talking politics on campus. I have decided to spend my month commuting to Brooklyn and selling the paper. I think I will be quite helpful in bringing about the revolution that way."

The irony of Tim coming to East Harlem to live in order to "experience the plight of the poor" and then spending his days selling a revolutionary newspaper on a Brooklyn college campus illustrated the disconnectedness of most Marxist groups with the poor. Marxist rhetoric was often appealing on a college campus, but it remained basically unrelated to the poor and working class people in East Harlem and throughout the country.

My experience of poverty and life in the ghetto stripped me of any pretensions I might have had of finding facile political solutions for deeply rooted social problems. I was truly a student, learning from neighbors and acquaintances, learning through the friendships with people I dwelled among. Living among the poor of the neighborhood taught me humility as I daily saw them struggle bravely, sustained by their own resourcefulness, determination, and abiding faith in God. My own theology began to develop from the concrete soil of the ghetto as I witnessed the Christian faith emerging in people for whom life was hard and often cruel. The domesticated, middle-class trappings of religion were unknown to these souls. Jesus Christ was real in their lives daily. Even amidst the violence, many people relied on faith to persevere in East Harlem.

I had yet to decide on my work project for my second year in East Harlem. I had spent the first year working with youth in the Church of the Good Neighbor. I didn't want to go into a parish ministry after I graduated, so interning in a church again made no sense. As I was casting about for a solution to the problem, the answer presented itself.

In upstate New York, near a little town called Attica, a dramatic series of events began to unfold in September of 1971. In the nearby state prison, also called Attica, inmates protesting conditions in the prison rebelled against the administration and took over the prison and held some guards as hostages.

For days the tension mounted as prisoners demanding better living conditions and prison officials demanding the release of the hostages worked with a civilian negotiation team to resolve the crisis. Governor Nelson Rockefeller called out the National Guard.

As I followed the Attica story in the *New York Times* and on television news, I realized I knew next to nothing about prisons. I was impressed by the powerful and articulate statements of the prisoners. As the crisis dragged on, I had a sense of foreboding. Attica seemed to be a symbol for our divided country in the late sixties and early seventies. The chasm between political leaders who talked about the need for law and order and many citizens who wanted their leaders to think in terms of justice and even mercy, stretched before us all. The crisis of mistrust and misunderstanding came to a head at Attica. Full of fear and dread, I watched the Attica crisis build to its climax.

In mid-September of 1971, Highway Patrol officers and selected prison guards stormed the prison. The casualty report read like the results of a Vietnam firefight. Thirty-nine people killed, another hundred injured. News reports implied that the "good guys" were victorious against the "bad guys." But when the prison was stormed on September 13, all thirty-nine people killed were shot by the bullets or buckshot utilized by those retaking the prison. Ten hostages and twenty-nine prisoners were killed. As one relative of a dead hostage put it, her loved one had been killed by "a bullet that had the name Rockefeller on it."[1]

— ▼ —

The Attica rebellion was crushed by a slaughter that left me sick at heart, even though it accomplished the prison authorities' goals and may have boosted the political career of Governor Rockefeller.

I began to wonder what life was like inside a prison. I had never visited a jail or prison, much less been locked up in one. After Attica I felt compelled to learn about these places and the people who were locked up in them. I decided to make it my nine-month seminary project to visit prisoners in the Bronx House of Detention. I made the necessary arrangements through the school.

As I drove my little blue Toyota up to the Bronx I had no idea what to expect. My orientation from the chaplain at the jail had been thorough, but I was anxious and apprehensive about this first visit. Tension knotted inside me as I parked my car and walked inside.

I showed my I.D. card at the entrance and rode the elevator to the sixth floor. I showed my I.D. to the guard and followed him around the huge barred cage that was the cellblock—"the walk"—containing the individual cells. The doors to the cellblock were closed and locked, but the doors of the individual cells were open so the prisoners could move around in the walk. My hands were sweaty. As we neared the corner of the rectangular cellblock, the guard motioned to a room on the left.

"You can visit in here," he told me.

I stood for a moment, silent.

"I'd like to get in the cellblock and talk with the men."

He looked at me askance, shrugged his shoulders, and opened the door leading into the cellblock. I stepped through. The door slammed shut behind me. The crash of the steel-bar door shook me and rang in my ears.

My mind surged with fear. "Oh, God! What am I doing here? I'm locked in here with all these criminals, with all these animals!" I stood frozen.

"Man, what are you doing here?"

I looked over toward the sound. In the cell on my right a young man was looking up at me from where he sat on his bunk.

Laughing nervously and with relief, I explained to him that I was there to visit with anyone on the walk who wanted to talk and that I'd be coming back to visit regularly until June. He invited me to sit down on his bunk, and we chatted for a while. Then he took me around the walk and introduced me to the men in each cell.

Two hours later I left the Bronx House of Detention, climbed into my car, and started the ten-minute drive back to East Harlem. I tried to sort through myriad thoughts and feelings. Those two hours had completely changed my perception of jails. With one exception, every one of the twenty-four or so men I talked with was black or Puerto Rican. Some of the people there had been convicted of crimes and were serving their sentences. Others were there because they had been arrested and charged but couldn't post bond. A man who couldn't make bail could expect to wait an average of eighteen months before he would go to trial.

I felt that I had just visited a different world. I was shocked and ashamed to realize that my own socialization process had conditioned me so that my first reaction, when the cellblock door slammed behind me, was to fear these men and see them all as animals. Gradually I began to understand why the prisoners at Attica had rebelled. I was stunned.

As the weeks passed, I struggled with my visits to the Bronx House of Detention. I discussed my work with others in the Urban Year Program. Their support and our meetings for group sharing and reflection helped me in my struggles to find a Christian response to the jail system. As the months passed, a framework of faith slowly emerged from my experiences and my studies.

I had always taken the Bible seriously as the basic tool for understanding the Christian faith. What the Bible has to say about prisons and jails is striking. Jeremiah, John the Baptist, Joseph, Paul, Peter, and Jesus had all been in jail. These men were not criminals. Each was a man acting on his understanding of what God called him to be and do. Yet they suffered the common lot of ordinary criminals.

Theologian Karl Barth said that the first Christian community did not arise following the Pentecost experience, but comprised the two thieves who were crucified with Jesus. It was a crucified thief who confessed Jesus was Lord when almost everyone had deserted Jesus. The first confessing Christian community was on Golgotha.

As I studied the scriptures I realized that the law, whether it be the Hebrew Torah or the Pax Romana, could not deal with the reality of the Spirit of God moving individuals in ways incomprehensible to the cold, rational juggernaut of the judiciary system. This was equally true of the Pax Americana as it locked up thousands of civil-rights demonstrators and war protesters in the nation's jails and prisons. The law, which society conceived as its absolute guide to human behavior, should be merely a tool for the furtherance of the will of God. When the tool proved useless, God summoned someone to direct the people on the path of righteousness. Many times, from the time of Jeremiah to the time of Martin Luther King, Jr., this path led through conflict with the traditions embodied in the law of the time.

But how did all this apply to a bunch of "common criminals" I visited each week in the Bronx? Each had either been convicted of a crime or arrested and accused of a crime; this fact alone made it hard to see them in the same category as the prophets and apostles who went to jail.

My study of the scriptures and my experiences in the jail led me to reevaluate the meaning of "righteousness." When that cellblock door slammed behind me I thought of those men as "animals" not so much because of what they had done or were accused of having done, but because I believed I was better than they were because of what I had *not* done. I was self-righteous. To regard them as animals, I had to see myself as superior to these criminals, these sinners. It was this position of moral superiority that I found conspicuously absent in the biblical studies of the prophets and disciples.

Indeed, I found Jesus himself giving definitive instruction about judgment and punishment in the eighth chapter of the Gospel of John. Not only did Jesus forgive a woman accused and confessed of a capital crime, but he posed a dilemma for her accusers who wanted to carry out the death sentence then and there.

"Let him who is without sin among you be the first to throw a stone at her," Jesus said.

Jesus not only forgave the woman charged with the crime, but he also questioned the authority of those who sought to condemn her and execute her.

Clearly, I was among those willing to cast the first stone when I reacted as I did to that cellblock door slamming behind me for the first time. Yet I knew I certainly was not without sin.

That particular gospel story was part of a pattern of Jesus urging followers to turn the other cheek, to fulfill the law by transcending it, to render evil for evil to no one, to the constant forgiveness of people regardless of who they were or what they had done.

This teaching led me to see that the law as I knew it, the law that locked people up in the jails and prisons of our country, was rooted in a presumption of moral judgment, which functioned to maintain law and order in society, but which had little to do with what Jesus was calling people toward in discipleship. What Jesus taught was antithetical to the values of any earthly society, be it Marxist or American Christian, because his message was and is scandalous to those who desire to dwell and rule in any earthly domain.

Slowly, I came to see the men at the Bronx House of Detention as my brothers in Christ. I went to them simply as a friend, not as someone who had all the answers or who could even really help them in a material way. All I could offer was the little things: to contact their families, to give them postage stamps when I could afford them, to telephone their lawyers. I was the one with the seminary education and the minister's I.D. card, but I soon began to wonder who was ministering to whom. I discovered that even as I tried to minister to the men in jail, they were also ministering to me. Within those concrete walls and behind those steel bars the Spirit of Christ was manifest. Jesus taught us that whenever we served "the least of these" we were serving him. These men locked in the cages of the Bronx House of Detention helped me to see that God was calling me to minister to people locked up in jails and prisons.

In 1973 I received my master of divinity degree and was ordained a minister in the United Church of Christ. I had entered seminary to study religion and philosophy. Deciding to be ordained was a long, slow process for me. I knew I wasn't meant to be a parish pastor. My year's work with the men at the Bronx House of Detention had convinced me that I should be working in prison ministry.

I also knew that New York was not the place for me to work. As much as I loved New York, it was not home. I was a Southerner who yearned to return to the South.

My old friend Bob Pryor, whom I had known years before when I worked as a camp counselor, was now directing a camp for fifth-graders for the Richmond Public Schools. He asked me to come down and work with him.

It was a steamy day in August when I packed my two suitcases and my trunk, loaded them into my Toyota, and got ready to leave. I walked back upstairs to make sure I'd gotten everything.

As I looked around the empty apartment one last time I was hit by a flood of memories of my friends in East Harlem.

Big, lovable James, who lived around the corner on 105th Street, had a disarming wit and as sunny a disposition as could be found on this earth. One day I asked a neighbor about James's whereabouts and learned that James had found his wife with another man. The man ran away and James went looking for him. The man was waiting for James and stabbed my friend James to death. . . .

Marie was a former nun who lived on East 118th Street. She invited me to a champagne party one evening on the ocean liner the *S.S. France*. I knew neither of us could afford a party on a luxury cruise ship. But Marie had discovered that if you learned when a cruise ship was sailing you could dress up, board the ship, mingle with the departing passengers and their invited guests, and party for a couple of hours before the final whistle blew and you had to go ashore. Marie always had a scheme for having a good time. . . .

Big Tom was from Richmond, Virginia. We became friends while he was held in the Bronx House of Detention awaiting trial on a murder rap. He swore he didn't do it. He and I talked regularly, reminiscing about Richmond. The last time I visited him he was still awaiting trial. . . .

I remembered how my roommate and I had furnished our apartment by borrowing a friend's van and taking off on "The Manhattan Midnight Furniture Run" to pick up pieces of furniture and mattresses that people had set out for the garbage trucks. . . .

I remembered friendly football games on Ward's Island. . . .

I remembered Hal Eads's storefront arts ministry that brought artists and actors to East Harlem to teach the children and that took children down to Lincoln Center to see theater, dance, and music. That small storefront ministry brought a vision of new opportunities and new worlds to the eager children of East Harlem. I would miss it and the children always clustered about the place, learning of new and wonderful things in life. . . .

I remembered a lovely woman about fifteen years older than I who tutored neighborhood kids at the East Harlem Protestant Parish. From the first day I picked up my mail at the parish, she had been gracious and kind to me. We enjoyed teasing and joking with each other. The goodness in that woman shone out all around her, lighting up the lives of everyone she met. . . .

As the memories washed through me I felt a wrenching sadness. I would miss these people, this neighborhood, this city. I looked around the room one last time, turned, walked out of the apartment and down the stairs.

As I drove out of East Harlem, headed for the George Washington Bridge, the sadness faded. New York had given me much, and I was grateful for my two years there. But I would remain her distant lover, always remembering and cherishing my time in the City.

As I headed the Toyota south on the New Jersey Turnpike, I took one last look at the New York skyline as I pulled away from the first toll booth.

NOTE

1. Tom Wicker, *A Time to Die* (New York: Times Book Company, 1975), p. 301.

CHAPTER TWO

Nashville

Finding myself unsatisfied with Richmond, and in love with a woman in Nashville, I decided to make the Tennessee capital my home. I moved to Nashville in 1974.

I wanted to get started in a prison ministry but wasn't sure how to begin. I telephoned Will Campbell.

The Reverend Will Campbell was the director of the Committee of Southern Churchmen. He lived in Mt. Juliet, Tennessee, near Nashville. I had met Campbell when I was at St. Andrews Presbyterian College. I had visited the Campbells' farm during my travels. Campbell was an itinerant preacher, ordained by the Southern Baptists but belonging only to God, who roamed through the South among Ku Klux Klansmen, rednecks, black militants, civil-rights activists, and anybody else who needed him. Campbell's message was simple and was summed up in the Greek title of the Committee of Southern Churchmen's magazine, *Katallagete*: be reconciled. Jesus has reconciled humans one to another, and we should live out our lives grounded in the free grace Jesus has given through his life, death, and resurrection.

Will answered the phone. "Will, this is Joe Ingle. I was wondering if you knew anybody in prison ministry. I'm looking for a job in that area and thought I'd call to see if you had any ideas."

Will told me to call Tony Dunbar, director of the Southern Prison Ministry, who lived just north of Nashville in Madison.

Tony told me that after *Katallagete* published an issue focusing on prisons and prisoners, the Committee received enough donations to start the Southern Prison Ministry. He and I talked and agreed that I would become the Tennessee director for the ministry and that I would be paid $50 a week.

Later that year we were able to get the foundation grants we needed to expand our work to serve prisoners throughout the South. In June of 1974 we gathered at Will Campbell's farm for the first meeting of the

Southern Coalition on Jails and Prisons (SCJP). We decided to set up shop in six states: North Carolina, South Carolina, Georgia, Mississippi, Alabama, and Tennessee. Our headquarters would be in Nashville, but each SCJP state project would be rooted in its own community and linked to the regional headquarters by quarterly staff meetings. Tony Dunbar would serve as coordinator. I would direct the Tennessee project. We had raised only enough money to operate for six months, but we had faith we could raise what we needed to keep going.

As I visited prisoners throughout Tennessee, I became convinced of the need for a prisoners' organization through which inmates—especially those serving long sentences—could voice their concerns to prison administrators. After much discussion among prisoners and "free-world" people, we decided to form the Lifer's Club. The Lifer's Club was open to any prisoner serving a sentence of at least twenty years.

The Lifer's Club idea was well received by the prisoners, but not by the Tennessee Department of Corrections. It took a year—and three changes of correction department commissioners—before the Lifer's Club was established within the Tennessee State Prison for Men in Nashville.

We had to move carefully since a recent U.S. Supreme Court decision, *Jones* v. *North Carolina Prisoners Union*, said that prisoners had no right to organize. In doing away with the Prisoners Union structure established by the North Carolina SCJP project, the court struck a blow against the prisoners' rights in such fundamental areas as mail, freedom of association, and visitation.

We tried to organize the Lifer's Club in Tennessee so that prison officials wouldn't perceive it to be a "union." The club held weekly meetings, invited outside guests, and spoke out for one of its members when he was unjustifiably placed in administrative segregation.

In the early summer of 1975 an acting warden was named as head of the Tennessee State Prison. He adopted a "tough but fair" policy, which the prisoners perceived as simply "get tough." Among the changes he made in the prison routine was stopping the established practice of letting inmates meet with their visitors in the prison picnic area. What had been common practice was now a privilege that the inmates would have to earn. This seemingly small change, coupled with other changes the prisoners saw as arbitrary and harsh, slowly raised the temperature at the prison to the boiling point. Men in the Lifer's Club predicted the prison would erupt in violence. As the summer weather cooled, I was relieved that tempers inside the prison cooled down too.

I had just returned home from the office on September 11 when the telephone rang. It was the associate warden at the prison.

"Joe, we're having a little problem and the prisoners would like you to come out."

"What kind of problem?"

"I'll tell you about it when you get here."

"I'll be right there."

It took me fifteen minutes to drive across town to the old prison, which always looked to me like the castle in Walt Disney's Magic Kingdom. But there was no magical kingdom inside those walls.

As I pulled up to the prison I saw a crowd of reporters and television broadcast vans. A reporter friend told me no one was being allowed to enter the prison.

"I'm going in," I said. I identified myself at the checkpoint and was allowed to enter. I walked immediately to Operations, the nerve center of the prison. The Operations room window looked out into the yard. I saw about fifteen prisoners, several of whom I knew through the Lifer's Club, pressed up against the Operations window and calling for me. I asked the associate warden if anyone had called the commissioner of corrections. The associate warden said he had called him. I walked over to the Operations window, opened it, and the prisoners told me what had happened.

An inmate who celled in Unit Two had gone to chow with his unit earlier that evening. Unit Two was served last, as they had been for the past two weeks. Once again the cafeteria ran out of the meat they were serving (pork chops on that night), and once again they gave the men on Unit Two bologna. The inmate told the cafeteria servers he was tired of eating last and always being given the scraps. He said he was going to wait to get a pork chop just like the other men had gotten. A guard walked over. Words were exchanged. Blows were struck. The cafeteria erupted in a melee of flying trays, tumbling bodies, and people scurrying for cover. More guards were dispatched to quell the disturbance.

It appeared to me that the fifteen men in front of the Operations window were all that remained of that skirmish. They pressed against the wall facing the acting warden and his riot squad and yelled at me through the open window of the Operations center.

The acting warden and the commander of the riot squad carried rifles. The rest of the squad were armed with billy clubs and wore helmets with plastic visors pulled down over their faces.

The prisoners asked me to call in other "free-world" people. I picked up the phone and was dialing the first number when shots rang out from the yard.

I looked up quickly. No one seemed to be hurt. They must have fired warning shots into the air to intimidate the prisoners. The effect was like throwing gasoline on a smoldering fire.

"Okay, you want to murder us, murder us!" shouted one prisoner.

"We aren't moving unless you kill us!" yelled another.

The riot squad had overplayed their hand. They had crossed the line and turned a manageable situation into a confrontation. Firing warning shots was a bluff, and the prisoners had called the bluff. By showing they were not afraid to die, the prisoners had taken control of the situation.

After the standoff in the yard, the prisoners began assembling a negotiating team to meet with prison officials and outside observers. I worked with the prisoners to formulate their demands while other convict leaders secured the release of the guard hostages and tried to calm the prisoners who were raising hell in the cellblocks. Later I borrowed a bull horn from the prison guards and went from cellblock to cellblock trying to calm things down, but it was futile. The long hot summer of oppression was erupting as some prisoners set fires and tore up equipment in the cells and in the mail room. They vented their rage and frustration with small fires and property destruction, but they did not set fire to any of the prison industries. One burning match thrown into the prison furniture shop would have ignited the flammable varnishes and lumber and would have turned the whole prison into an inferno. The prisoners were angry, but their leaders managed to keep the anger within bounds.

The negotiations began at about 10:00 P.M. in the prison basement and lasted through the night. Shortly before dawn we reached an agreement that all parties felt they could live with. As I was leaving I was impressed by the fact that the tension-filled negotiations had resulted in a settlement despite the atmosphere of hostility and mistrust. I left the prison exhausted and went home.

The major concessions won by the inmates included:

1. No reprisal or retaliation against any prisoner as a result of the rioting.
2. A promise to disband an inmate council appointed by penitentiary officials and permit the prisoners to elect the council members.
3. Discontinuation of the present requirements limiting visitation rights in the prison's picnic area, returning to an earlier program which suspends an inmate's use of the area if convicted of a rules infraction or an escape attempt.
4. A return to the practice of allowing prisoners permission to change cellmates.
5. A review of disciplinary procedures.
6. A review of the present operation of the institution's honor dormitory, a minimum security area where inmates enjoy a setting of relaxed regulations. (Complaints had come from inmates not having these benefits.)
7. The suspension of a guard pending investigation into the Thursday night dining room melee that sparked later rioting. It was also agreed that if the guard was found guilty of misconduct, a recommendation would be made that he be discharged.

Early the following morning I got a telephone call from the prisoners asking me to come back to witness how the authorities had restored order during the long night before. I was stunned as I walked through the hospital and learned what had happened the night before while we sat in the basement of the prison trying to resolve the conflict. The prisoners had entered the negotiations assuming no action would be taken against their fellow prisoners while the negotiations were under way. But while we talked, prison guards, Nashville police officers, Highway Patrol officers, and members of the Tennessee National Guard assembled outside the prison walls. As we talked deep in the basement about peaceful ways to resolve the situation, we didn't know what was happening above. The assembled police had stormed the prison with guns, clubs, and dogs.

As I walked through the cellblocks that morning I saw the aftermath of their assault. Walls were pocked with holes left by shotgun pellets. Cell walls were smeared with blood. Blood-spattered sheets covered the bunks. When I got to the prison hospital I saw men literally beaten black and blue, men with broken arms, men with cuts and bruises, men with legs lacerated by dog bites.

The disturbance and protest at the prison had been started by the prisoners, but the bloody riot had been aggravated by the police.

In the aftermath of the September 11 rebellion, the lawyers of the Southern Prisoners' Defense Committee, the SCJP-created law project, brought damage suits on behalf of the prisoners against the Nashville police, the Tennessee Highway Patrol, and correctional officers. The National Prison Project of the ACLU and Legal Services of Middle Tennessee filed a class-action suit aimed at remedying the barbaric conditions in Tennessee prisons. Each of these suits would ultimately be successful, but they did little to erase the horror of what happened on September 11, 1975, at the Tennessee State Prison.

Within a week of the disturbance three other people and I were barred from the prison. Prison officials said that the prisoners had been perfectly happy before the "outside agitators" came to the prison to cause trouble. This was the same tactic that had been used by the authorities who had opposed the civil-rights movement in the South: "Our colored people were happy as could be until these outsiders came and stirred up trouble." I was labeled an agitator, a troublemaker. The acting commissioner of corrections sent me a letter expressing his intention of prosecuting me for first-degree murder as a conspirator in the riot, which had resulted in the death of one prisoner. (They didn't follow up on this threat.) Not until January of 1976, when Will Campbell intervened with the newly inaugurated governor, was I able to reenter the prison.

Neither I nor the other three people barred from the prison were the cause of the riot. The shortage of pork chops was not the real problem either. The problem was that in 1975 there were 1,800 prisoners housed in the Tennessee State Penitentiary. The prison was built to hold 800 men. The basic cause of the riot was overcrowding and idleness. The courts later found the overcrowding of the state penitentiary to be unconstitutional as a result of the lawsuit filed on behalf of the prisoners.

In 1976 Tony Dunbar decided to move to North Carolina to finish writing a book. He asked me to succeed him as coordinator of the SCJP. I agreed to be a candidate and was elected at the spring SCJP meeting in Atlanta. At that meeting the SCJP, fearing that the U.S. Supreme Court would soon open the door to reinstating the death penalty, decided to work to block the states from killing prisoners. Since most of the condemned prisoners in the United States were in Southern prisons, we decided to focus on working with prisoners on Death Row.

That winter I had met with Death Row prisoners in Tennessee and set up a visitation program for them. As I got to know those men I realized they were no different from any other prisoners, except that they were generally better behaved and were more serious about their religious inclinations.

In July of 1976 the U.S. Supreme Court upheld the death penalty in Texas, Georgia, and Florida while striking it down in North Carolina, Louisiana, and Oklahoma. Only time would tell how this would affect the men on Death Row in the states where the court had said it was constitutional to kill prisoners.

As I traveled back to Nashville after visiting prisoners on North Carolina's Death Row, I thought about what it meant to be a Christian in a country determined to legally kill people. It was only a matter of time before executions were resumed with a vengeance across the United States. As I prayed and reflected on the scriptures I felt called by the Lord to fast.

Every day I got up, took a shower, read the scriptures, meditated, prayed, and then went to work. I visited various Southern prisons and all of the SCJP projects.

After two weeks I had broken the American eating routine of three meals a day. I no longer desired food. I ceased to be hungry. The fruit-juice-and-water diet kept me from dehydrating, and my energy level remained good. I understood the fast to be a symbol, the will of the Lord of life, not death. I had no intention of starving myself to death.

In the twenty-fifth day of the fast I was surprised to find myself experiencing a spiritual joy. I felt freer than I had ever felt in my life, yet also totally dependent on God. The morning spiritual exercise often left me feeling contented and fulfilled in ways I couldn't describe.

I flew to Oregon to stay with friends of mine from seminary. On the fortieth day of the fast we hiked out to a promontory that jutted far out into the Pacific. Standing on the tip of that rocky point, the wind whistling around me, surrounded by the ocean, I felt as though I could spread my arms and dissolve into the wind, floating over the ocean. I stood there a long time, feeling the Spirit upon me in a way I had not dreamed was possible. I was at one with all about me. I physically experienced what the Christian faith calls atonement.

In the fall of 1976 the SCJP staff met at Highlander Center in New Market, Tennessee, in the foothills of the Smoky Mountains. We didn't know how quickly the courts would act in resuming executions, but we organized the Witness Against Execution demonstration for the spring and planned how we would work directly with condemned prisoners. We now had SCJP projects in nine Southern states.

The end of 1976 brought the bizarre story of Gary Gilmore to the nation's attention. Gary Mark Gilmore had committed a murder in Utah. He was convicted of murder and sentenced to death. He moved to dismiss his appeals so the authorities could go ahead and execute him. It appeared that this articulate, angry, and determined man would be the first person executed under the death penalty laws currently held constitutional.

As winter spread its cold and gray around Nashville I decided to stop fasting after 134 days. Physical exhaustion had taken over my body. I had to lie down while in the office. I realized that if I didn't resume eating I'd be bedridden and unable to work. I understood my calling to be that of a servant, not a martyr. The fasting was simply offering myself as a sign that the Lord's will would be served, not denied for the false gods of political expediency that I believed drove the advocates of the death penalty. When it became clear to me that my choice was either to become sick and die or to resume eating, the choice was obvious. After prayer and meditation, I decided to end the fast.

On a cold November night (all nights seem cold when you're fasting) a few friends gathered at Becca Joffrion's house for the breaking of the fast. Becca had prepared some mild soup and bread. Will Campbell led the group in communion. It was a special night as I shared a cup of soup with friends who had supported me, encouraged me, and worried about me on this spiritual pilgrimage. It was a quiet time of rejoicing. The warm soup tasted good and felt good as it rolled down my gullet.

Other friends took up the fast and witness, first Don Beisswenger, then John Lozier, who worked with me in Tennessee. So as the execution of the first prisoner killed in the country in a decade drew nearer, a small witness continued against the madness of state-sanctioned killing.

— ▼ —

In January of 1977, Tony Dunbar, John Lozier, and I flew to Salt Lake City to bear witness against the state of Utah for killing Gary Gilmore. We stood with other protesters in an all-night vigil that ended when the state's executioners raised their rifles and shot Gary Gilmore to death.

In the spring more than 3,000 people gathered in Atlanta for the Witness Against Execution. We marched from the Martin Luther King, Jr., Center to the Georgia Capitol. Though the number of participants may have seemed small, their message was clear: Abolish the death penalty.

I visited prisoners on Death Row in all the states with SCJP projects: North Carolina, South Carolina, Georgia, Florida, Mississippi, Alabama, Kentucky, Tennessee, and Louisiana. The face-to-face encounters with these condemned men and women were crucial to me. Some of my colleagues from outside the SCJP states, who saw the death penalty as a legal or philosophical issue, often spoke about capital punishment from an intellectual point of view. Their abstract arguments maintained that the state execution of individuals degraded all the people in the state. I agreed with them, but for me the death penalty was a personal struggle, a spiritual question.

I had visited every Death Row in the South several times. A network of friendships had formed between the folks working with the SCJP and the men and women who sat in cells across the South waiting to be killed. These men and women on Death Row were not just rap sheets or mug shots or court cases or death warrants. They were human beings I had talked with and had gotten to know as individuals. We kept in touch with one another by letters. I had made many friendships through my prison visits, and I desperately wanted to keep my friends alive.

Some of my friends had in the past committed horrible crimes, and I could understand the states' desire to punish these people and remove them from society. But for me, the issue was how we as a society would respond to these crimes and how we would treat the people convicted of these crimes. The original murder was terrible. Should we compound the tragedy by killing again in the name of justice? Is murder—the premeditated taking of a human life—any less coldblooded when carried out by employees of the state following the instructions of government officials? When the state executes a human being, the men who do the killing are our servants. They are killing in our names. Are we prepared to personally accept the responsibility for that killing?

For me, capital punishment is a spiritual question. I view the death penalty through the eyes of a Christian. I cannot imagine that Jesus of Nazareth could condone or permit the killing of any child of God, no matter how terrible the crimes he or she had committed.

CHAPTER THREE

JOHN SPENKELINK
Florida
May 25, 1979

The autumn of 1977 brought the first real test of the new death penalty laws passed in the wake of the U.S. Supreme Court's capital punishment decisions. Florida Governor Ruben Askew signed the death warrant for a prisoner named John Spenkelink. Everyone waited anxiously as the lawyers raced to court to stop the execution. The lawyers got a stay of execution.

I decided to visit John Spenkelink. I wrote to him, and he wrote back. I marvelled at his tiny but meticulous handwriting. He explained that while in solitary confinement, when the only paper he had was toilet paper, he had learned to write in a tiny but legible hand so he could squeeze as many words as possible onto the paper. He wrote that he would be more than happy for me to visit him.

Florida State Prison lay sprawled like a prehistoric monster on flat fields cut out of the piney woods of north central Florida near the town of Starke. The pale green, three-story building stood behind double chain-link fences topped with barbed wire and interrupted by guard towers. Guard dogs patrolled between the fences. Stretching out from the spine of the beast were the wings in which twelve hundred men were locked in the cages of the maximum security prison.

The wings labelled *P, Q, R, S,* and *T* held the men convicted of murder and condemned to death. These were the men the state of Florida wanted to kill. This was Death Row.

After the governor of Florida—acting in the name of the people of Florida—signs a prisoner's death warrant, the condemned prisoner is transferred to *Q* wing and the holding cells near the room that contains Florida's electric chair. These cells hold the men under death warrant who are waiting and hoping for a reprieve through a stay of execution from the courts. For many of these men the waiting and hoping would end when they were taken to the death chamber at the end of Q wing. In that chamber the death squad straps the condemned man into the electric chair and throws the switch that sends 2,200 volts of electricity through his body.

I parked my car outside the administration building, which lies outside the prison gates. I walked to the main prison gate and picked up the black telephone mounted on a post. The guard in the tower above me answered the phone and looked down on me. He checked with the control room, verified that I was on the list of scheduled visitors, and told me that I could enter. The first of the chain-link gates squeaked as it opened. The emaciated German shepherd barked and growled at me behind the wire fence. I walked on through the second sliding gate and up to the door of the prison. A barred gate opened and the guard behind the glass wall in the control room motioned me into the room where he sat. The door lock buzzed and I pushed the heavy steel door open.

"So you're from Tennessee, huh?" he said.

"Yes, I am."

He nodded and motioned with a gnarled hand toward the visitors' log book. I noted the time, my home address, and purpose for visit.

The guard told me to go through the metal detector in front of the control room. I removed every bit of metal I had. Coins, belt (the buckle was metal), eyeglasses, shoes (the shoelace grommets were metal), even the Committee of Southern Churchmen medallion I wore around my neck. I walked through the metal detector without setting off the alarm, then went back through to reclaim my possessions.

The guard escorted me down the corridor to the visiting area known as "the Colonel's room": a large room subdivided into cubicles, each with two chairs and a table, where the condemned men meet with their lawyers, the press, and their ministers. The guard left, and I sat down in one of the cubicles.

A few minutes later the door to the Colonel's room opened and a guard brought in a handcuffed man. He was a lean, smooth-faced man, about twenty-three years old, with prematurely gray hair that was almost white through the middle of the wave he combed back from his forehead. He wore the uniform of Death Row inmates: jeans, a t-shirt, and a prison jacket with his name stencilled on the pocket. The guard removed the handcuffs and left the room. The prisoner and I looked straight into each other's eyes—both of us were about six feet tall. I reached out my hand.

"I'm Joe Ingle."

We shook hands.

"I'm John Spenkelink."

With his thumb he pointed to the nametag on his prison jacket. On it was written, "SPINKELLINK."

"They've misspelled my name in this prison, in the courts, and in the newspapers. It's really easy, though. It's S-P-E-N-K-E-L-I-N-K."

We joked about the fact that a criminal justice system that was so certain of its work in condemning a man to death couldn't even spell his name right. It seemed to me that a government so eager to kill a man ought to at least be competent enough to spell his name.

John Spenkelink and I talked for a while, getting to know each other. His life had narrowed to a forked road. If the state had its way, he would be put to death in the electric chair. If we were successful in getting his death sentence commuted, he would spend twenty-five years of his life in prison.

But somehow Spenkelink was able to talk easily, even to joke, about the absurdity of life on Death Row. He told me about the endless hours in his six-by-eight-foot cell, the prison routine, the twice-weekly exercise period, the trips to the prison library. Perhaps he had to make jokes and laugh to keep from crying. Perhaps he had to fend off the absurdities with humor to keep them from driving him crazy.

After a while John Spenkelink began to tell me about the long road that had led him to Death Row.

— ▼ —

John Spenkelink was born in Iowa, and later moved with his family to southern California. He was bright, inquisitive, playful, close to his parents. His was a childhood much like that of millions of other American children. Then one day, when John was twelve years old, that childhood was shattered.

When John walked into the closed-up garage that day, he found the family car running and the garage full of exhaust fumes. His father lay sprawled on the floor dead.

Shortly after his father's suicide, the teenaged John Spenkelink began to get involved in petty crimes such as vandalism. He was in and out of trouble with the law and as a result was placed in juvenile correctional institutions in California. At the age of eighteen, strung out on speed, he held up six stores one night. He was convicted to serve an indeterminate sentence in the California adult prison system. In a medium security institution with several gangs, Spenkelink grew afraid for his life. With the help of his girlfriend, he escaped and drove to Canada. After traveling in Canada, he returned to the United States.

Spenkelink drove aimlessly across the country. While driving through a Nebraska snowstorm he picked up a hitchhiker named Joseph Szymankiewicz, a man some years older than Spenkelink. An ex-convict whose life had been marked by violence, crime, and prison, Szymankiewicz had a revolver. Although Spenkelink also had a weapon, he was terrorized by the older man. He was threatened, sodomized, and forced to play Russian roulette. They drove on across the country. On the East Coast they picked up another hitchhiker.

Spenkelink and the third man were returning to the Tallahassee, Florida, motel room where the three were staying when Spenkelink told the other man he had decided to make his break, to escape from Szymankiewicz. He told the man to wait outside the room.

Szymankiewicz was asleep. Spenkelink slipped into the room and quietly gathered a few clothes to tuck into a suitcase.

"What are you doing?" demanded Szymankiewicz, suddenly awake.

"I'm leaving."

Szymankiewicz jumped out of the bed and tackled Spenkelink.

They fought. Spenkelink's gun was brought into the fray. As the two men fought over the gun, Spenkelink managed to turn the gun toward Szymankiewicz and pull the trigger.

(The prosecution rejected Spenkelink's account of the fight and argued that Spenkelink had shot Szymankiewicz while Szymankiewicz was lying in the bed.)

John Spenkelink, who had never physically harmed anyone in his prior lawbreaking, was charged with first-degree murder in the shooting death of Joseph Szymankiewicz.

— ▼ —

In 1972 the U.S. Supreme Court had ruled that the capital punishment laws of several states, including Florida, were unconstitutional. Now it was 1973, and the Florida legislature had just passed a new death penalty law, which they hoped would prove to be constitutional.

So John Spenkelink was on trial for his life in a state with a brand-new death penalty law and an eagerness to reinstate the electric chair as the ultimate punishment. He was an outsider with a criminal record, a funny-sounding name, and the unusual look of prematurely gray hair. His defense was handled by two court-appointed attorneys, neither of whom had ever tried a case in which a suspect was on trial for his life.

John Spenkelink rejected the prosecution's offer of a plea bargain which would have reduced the charge to second-degree murder. Spenkelink, whose naive faith in the judicial system had somehow survived in spite of several run-ins with the law, insisted on pleading self-defense. He was convinced the truth would triumph when his story was presented to the jury.

The Tallahassee jury convicted John Spenkelink of murder in the first degree.

In the sentencing phase of the trial—during which the court would decide between life imprisonment and the death penalty—Spenkelink insisted, against the advice of his attorneys, on taking the stand and telling the jury his side of the story. Spenkelink hadn't been well prepared for this by his legal counsel. The prosecutor confused him and caught him in contradictions. The jury recommended John Spenkelink be sentenced to death. The judge concurred. John Spenkelink was sentenced to die in the electric chair and was taken to Florida State Prison in Starke.

Over time I got to know John Spenkelink, became his friend, and worked with others to stop the state of Florida from killing him in the electric chair. I was struck time and again by a feeling that this should never have been a death penalty case. John had never before been convicted of a crime of violence. Many serious questions remained about his trial: the effectiveness of his legal counsel, for one.

It is estimated that across the United States more than 90 percent of the men and women now on Death Row were unable to afford a lawyer for their trial and were defended by court-appointed attorneys, many of whom had limited experience in such cases. Other condemned prisoners had been defended by inexperienced attorneys hired because they had once written a will or handled a lawsuit or other minor matters for the defendant's family. Many defendants on trial for their lives were represented by lawyers with little or no experience in trials for capital crimes: trials in which the defendant, if convicted, may be killed by the state.

Advocates of capital punishment often paint a frightening portrait of the kind of person for whom the death penalty is intended: the hardened career criminal whose crimes injure helpless and innocent victims, the unrepentant murderer, the sociopath undeterred and unrehabilitated by prison, the violent and irrepressible killer who will continue to prey on the public unless he is put to death by the state.

John Spenkelink had been convicted of a single violent act, which he (and many others involved with the case) perceived to be an act of self-defense. He struck me as an eminently decent person. He wrote letters for fellow prisoners who couldn't write. He helped research law cases for other prisoners and deciphered the legal process for the condemned men who didn't understand it. He did all he could to care for his family. None of us involved in trying to stop John's execution could begin to understand what would be gained by strapping this man into the electric chair and killing him in the name of justice.

In 1978 my fiancée, Becca Joffrion, and I were planning to spend Thanksgiving Day with her parents in Huntsville, Alabama. The whole

Joffrion clan would be there for the celebration, and we were really excited about it.

The inmates on Death Row in Florida State Prison had little enough to be thankful for—just brief holiday visits from families and friends—and that little was suddenly and cruelly taken from them.

Bobby Lewis, a Death Row inmate, had just escaped by donning a guard's uniform and simply walking out the front gate. The embarrassment of the prison officials was exceeded only by their fury. They couldn't lay hands on Bobby Lewis to vent their anger on him, so they punished anyone who was handy.

The day before Thanksgiving, prison authorities announced that all holiday visits for Death Row inmates were cancelled. It was too late for the men to get in touch with those coming to visit them. Their families and friends would travel to the prison, many of them from great distances, only to be turned away at the prison gate.

John Spenkelink knew the hardship and frustration this brought to all the men on Death Row. He also knew that this might be the last Thanksgiving he could share with his mother. He asked prison officials for permission to speak with his lawyer. His request and those of others who asked to contact people outside the prison were denied.

Death Row prisoners at FSP eat their meals in their cells. Prison trusties—convicts deemed trustworthy who are given special duties and privileges—bring the meal trays to each man's cell, shove the tray in through a slot in the door, and return later to pick them up. John Spenkelink told the trusty and the guards that he would not give back his tray until he received word that he would be allowed to telephone either his mother or his lawyer.

In his five years on Death Row, Spenkelink had earned the respect of his fellow inmates and had emerged as an unofficial leader of "the Row." Other inmates withheld their trays, joining Spenkelink in his protest.

The guards told the prison administrators, who sent a counselor to meet with John. John quietly explained that he would be happy to return the tray if his lawyer could be notified of the cancellation of Thanksgiving Day visiting privileges. The counselor promised to notify the lawyer, and the men withholding their trays in support of John relinquished them. But John held onto his tray and waited for the counselor to return as he had promised. He didn't return, but a second counselor met with

John and assured him that either permission would be obtained for John to make his call or the counselor would make the call for him. John turned over his tray. John did not see or hear from either counselor again.

It was suppertime and still no word. The tension on *R* wing was high. The other Death Row prisoners had steeled their support for John Spenkelink's request.

When the trusties came to pick up supper trays, John once again refused to return his tray. This time all the men on his tier of cells held onto their trays and said they would continue to do so until somebody called John Spenkelink's mother or his lawyer.

John Spenkelink had challenged prison authorities by his "refusal to obey a direct order." A squad of six guards walked into *R* wing and to the door of John's cell. Spenkelink urged his fellow prisoners to give up their trays, which they did. Then John repeated his request to the guards.

"You're going to kill me. Why not let my mother visit me?"

Guards unlocked his cell door. They stormed in, thrusting a five-foot high fiber glass shield ahead of them like a battering ram. They slammed John against the sink, knocking him unconscious, and beat him as he fell to the floor. They dragged him unconscious from his cell to *Q* wing, the notorious punishment wing of the prison.

We heard about the attack on Monday, November 26. The Florida office of SCJP, the Florida Clearinghouse on Criminal Justice, immediately began an investigation.

When I saw John later that week I was shaken. Knowing how prison "justice" is often administered, I was shocked but not surprised to see the knot on his neck where he had been struck by a guard's club, to see the lacerations and bruises on his head and neck, and to hear about the broken rib and the wounds on his chest, back, and shoulders. These things were bad enough, but what shook me was seeing what they had done to John's spirit. For the first time in the two years I'd known him he seemed . . . vulnerable.

John still had a fundamental belief in the goodness of people and a faith that right would triumph. He couldn't understand why six guards used such force and violence to stop a peaceful protest by one unarmed man locked in a cell. He couldn't understand why those men wanted to hurt him, any more than he could understand why the people the guards worked for wanted to kill him in the electric chair.

In response to SCJP's investigation of John's beating and the protests that grew out of it, the guard leading the squad that attacked John was transferred out of the prison.

— ▼ —

By early 1979 the team working to save John Spenkelink's life believed it likely that the U.S. Supreme Court would deny the appeal filed on John's behalf. We told John we believed his only hope was an appeal to the governor of Florida for clemency to commute John's sentence to life, or grant him a new trial. We tried to get an appointment with the newly elected Governor Bob Graham as soon as possible after his January inauguration.

David Kendall, the lawyer handling John's appeals, had taken on John's case while working for the NAACP Legal Defense Fund (LDF), a nonprofit organization in New York. Since then David had joined a prestigious Washington, D.C., law firm, but he continued to represent John without fee. The legal term for that is *pro bono publico*: for the good of the public.

We prepared for a March hearing before Governor Graham and his cabinet—who composed the clemency board—by urging people to write letters to the clemency board on John's behalf. It was vital that the board see John not merely as a criminal record or a faceless killer, but as a human being who, after making grave mistakes, had evolved and been transformed into a caring, thoughtful man. We hoped the letters would help the board to see John was not just a pawn in the debate over the effectiveness of the death penalty to deter criminal activity. It was crucial that the board see this case not as an abstract juridical argument about the ethics and efficacy of capital punishment but as a concrete and specific decision as to whether a man named John Spenkelink would be electrocuted or be allowed to live the next twenty years of his life in prison.

Since we believed the cabinet would follow the lead of the governor—the man with the power to sign the death warrant or the papers commuting John's death sentence to life imprisonment—we arranged to meet with the governor prior to the clemency board's meeting.

In early March of 1979 Governor Bob Graham met with four members of the religious community: a professor of Christian Ethics at Union Theological Seminary in New York, a Tallahassee resident and prominent Southern Presbyterian, a local preacher and revered leader of civil-rights movements in Florida, and me. I was present as a friend of John Spenkelink, a minister of the gospel, and the director of the SCJP.

Governor Graham, like the ethics professor and me, was a member of the United Church of Christ. Our delegation hoped the meeting would be a group of Christians working together to help one another face a moral and spiritual dilemma.

We met in a semi-circle of chairs in the governor's office at the capitol. The governor and his two aides, all in business suits, seemed pleasant and interested in what we had to say.

We shared our concerns about the death penalty with the governor and his aides. The governor stated his conviction that the death penalty served as "a deterrent" to crime.

I was stunned. Here sat an obviously intelligent man who held the lives of 200 condemned men in his hands. With a stroke of a pen on a death warrant he could send any of these men to the electric chair. He was justifying state-sanctioned killing by parroting one of the flimsiest and most easily refuted arguments for the death penalty.

I pointed out to him that not one study of scientific significance had found capital punishment to be an effective deterrent to criminal actions. In 1976 the U.S. Supreme Court had not found convincing evidence that the death penalty deterred anyone from the act of murder. In fact, a recent study had shown that murder rates *increased* in states after they reinstated the death penalty.[1]

Governor Graham looked thoughtful but seemed unpersuaded by the discussion. The efficacy of deterrence seemed to him to be a matter of "common sense" that wasn't open to new evidence, rational argument, or dialogue. It seemed to me that his personal opinion and a keen awareness of the political forces in favor of the death penalty had combined to set his position in stone. He had already made up his mind;

he wouldn't accept any evidence, appeals, or arguments that didn't jibe with the decision he had made before we arrived.

The ethics professor asked the governor a question.

"Governor, do you find retribution to be an adequate moral category for implementing the death penalty?"

"I do not. I certainly wouldn't sign a death warrant for somebody simply to exercise vengeance."

I realized we were asking a lot of this newly elected governor. Florida's prison system had more inmates on Death Row than any other state. It would be political suicide to abolish the death penalty by commuting to life imprisonment the death sentences of 200 condemned men. Though that's what we wanted, I knew it was too much to ask of this man on this day.

So I asked Governor Graham to appoint a blue-ribbon commission to study the racial discrimination that researchers had found permeated the application of the death penalty in Florida. Studies of discrimination in the application of the death penalty usually focus on the race of the convicted criminal who is sentenced to death. A recent study had looked deeper and discovered that defendants convicted in Florida of killing a white person were much more likely to be sentenced to death than those convicted of killing a black or Hispanic person.[2] This discrimination based on the race of the victim suggested a racially prejudiced judicial system in which murdering a white person was considered a more serious crime than murdering a person of color. This evidence of unequal treatment under the law had not been known at the time the U.S. Supreme Court upheld the Florida death penalty law. I urged Governor Graham to appoint a commission to look into this question and, more important, *to halt all executions pending the outcome of the commission's investigations.*

Governor Graham listened carefully to the presentation, interrupting occasionally with questions for clarification. He asked me to call his office the next day to dictate a letter to his secretary with details of the commission proposal along with recommendations for commission members. I agreed to do so.

Our meeting, scheduled for twenty minutes, had lasted more than an hour. Though Graham hadn't moved from his deterrence position, he seemed amenable to the idea of a commission's studying discrimination in the application of the Florida death penalty law.

Later, I called and dictated the memo to the govenor's secretary as I had promised. I awaited his response, which never came except in the form of John's death warrant.

Winter turned to spring as we continued the struggle to keep John Spenkelink out of the electric chair. In late March, David Kendall presented John's case to the Governor and his cabinet. With his rare combination of legal acumen and compassion, David offered persuasive arguments for commuting the death sentence of John Spenkelink, a troubled juvenile who had survived the evils of crime and prison to become a compassionate and mature human being with a strong faith in God.

I continued criss-crossing the South visiting Death Row inmates in various states. I worked with SCJP groups to organize the March Against Death to be held in Atlanta. On a hot and sunny May afternoon Becca Joffrion and I found ourselves marching from the Martin Luther King, Jr. Center to the Georgia Capitol. The lively and spirited crowd cheered speeches by Tom Wicker (the *New York Times* journalist whose book about the Attica riot had brought national attention to the conditions in American prisons) and Will Campbell and applauded songs by Joan Baez and Peter Yarrow of Peter, Paul, and Mary.

After the march Becca and I said so long to our friends and left for a week's vacation at our favorite North Carolina beach. With the hectic pace of the last few months behind us, we relaxed into a lazy week of sunbathing, swimming in the ocean, and reading books instead of legal briefs.

On Friday morning we headed for the beach for a final swim in the ocean. Then we would head back to Nashville, stopping along the way to visit my mother in Raleigh and some friends in Parkton, North Carolina.

As we walked toward the beach the assistant manager of the motel hailed me and said I had a phone call. I strolled from the sun-soaked morning with the sound of surf in the distance into the dark coolness of the motel office. I picked up the phone.

"Hello."

"Joe, this is Harmon. Dick is here with me." It was Harmon Wray and Dick Burr, two SCJP colleagues from Nashville. *"We have some bad news. Governor Graham signed John's death warrant this morning."*

Harmon's voice seemed to echo in my ear. I couldn't believe it. *"When's the execution set for?"*

"Seven A.M. next Wednesday."

"How in hell does he expect us to have a fair hearing before Wednesday? The judges won't do anything over the weekend. That leaves us just Monday and Tuesday to get a stay of execution somewhere."

We talked a while longer, going over the details of the situation. Then I went to tell Becca what had happened.

Though Becca had never met John Spenkelink, she felt as though she knew him. I had shared John's letters with her and talked with her about my friendship with him. Becca carried a picture of John in her wallet. The news upset her almost as much as it did me. We decided to drive the twelve hours back to Nashville in time for me to get a Sunday afternoon flight to Florida. We would stop for abbreviated visits with my mother and our friends along the way.

I landed in Jacksonville on Sunday afternoon. I rented a car and drove to Starke. I remembered the many times I had driven this route before and wondered if this would be my last time to see John Spenkelink. I checked into the Best Western Motel in Starke and telephoned the prison superintendent, David Brierton. I wanted to see John as soon as possible, and the superintendent was the man who could arrange the visit.

I remembered the superintendent from my previous meetings with him at Starke, all of which had been friendly. He was a big man, who looked as though he worked out with weights. He sat behind a glass-topped desk attached to a hunk of painted farm machinery. He liked to lean forward on that desk, his muscles bulging, and talk earnestly. Though I had participated in a press conference the previous December protesting John's beating by guards, I didn't expect any aftershock of that occasion to interfere with the business at hand.

It was after office hours, so I called the superintendent at his home. His daughter answered the phone and said he was out. I gave her a message asking him to call me at the Best Western when he returned. Scharlette Holdman, Florida director of SCJP, had told the superintendent I would call as soon as I arrived. Later that evening I called twice more, but the daughter said he hadn't returned. Twice more I left messages with her asking him to call me. I wondered if he was meeting with his subordinates deciding how best to kill John Spenkelink.

At 10:00 P.M. the motel room phone rang. I answered, and it was the prison superintendent returning my call. It was too late to visit John, so we arranged to meet the next morning to discuss visits with John.

On Monday, May 21, David Kendall, John's lawyer, was appealing to the Florida Supreme Court to stop John's execution. Nobody on our team was hopeful that we would get a stay of execution, or even a fair hearing, from that court. The Florida Supreme Court's justices are appointed by the governor and weren't likely to stay an execution when the death warrant already bore the governor's signature. Besides, experience had taught us that in death penalty cases, relief seldom comes from state courts. Our hope was that if the Florida Supreme Court would turn down the appeal quickly enough, we might have time to get a stay from the federal courts.

As David argued before the Florida Supreme Court in Tallahassee, I was meeting with the prison superintendent trying to get permission to visit John. The superintendent, like so many other prison officials we had dealt with in the past, said he was limiting visits "for security reasons." He said he was afraid that somebody might smuggle something into the prison to John that would enable him to commit suicide. I tried to be tactful as I explained that this idea was absurd for at least three reasons.

The Florida State Prison superintendent was facing the first execution in the United States since Gary Gilmore in 1977. The circus atmosphere around Gilmore's execution in Utah, including two suicide attempts by Gilmore, greatly concerned the superintendent. I sought to reassure him that none of us wanted John to die, much less help him kill himself. We also had negotiations about the visiting schedule, who could visit John, whether or not there would be a contact visit with his family so his mother could give him a final hug and kiss, clergy and legal visits, and the gamut of other details involved in meeting the needs of John and his family.

56

It seemed to me that the prison officials' overriding fear was that John Spenkelink might kill himself before they could. They didn't want John to cheat the electric chair and the will of the state of Florida.

After an hour of haggling, I set up a visitation schedule for John's family and friends. For some reason, which to this day has never been explained, the superintendent refused to allow John's sister, Carol Myers, to visit him. I also arranged to meet with the superintendent again the next morning.

I went straight into the prison to meet with John. Now that John was on a death warrant, we would be limited to a "no-contact" visit. We had to visit through a glass wall and speak through a small window. The condemned man was denied the privilege of shaking hands with a friend, denied the simple pleasure of human contact.

John and I talked about the work under way in the courts, about his family, and about the visiting schedule we had set up. He joked about his new situation on death watch in Q wing. When I told him about the superintendent's concern that John might try to kill himself, he smiled.

"If he knew me, he would know I wouldn't do anything to take myself out," John said. "If I have to die I'm going to show these people for what they really are: killers."

After about an hour I said good-bye to John and went to visit his family.

Lois Spenkelink, John's mother, was a heavy-set woman with white hair and a kindly disposition. She had moved to Starke from California to be near her son. I really liked her and enjoyed being with her. I was anxious to talk with her and see how she was doing.

Lois was staying with a kind-hearted couple who had opened their home to her. Their support of Lois and John cost them quite a few friends in the small community of Starke. As I drove up to the house I saw a sign in a neighbor's yard urging the state to "Fry Spenkelink."

I walked in the house and gave Lois a big hug. Lois had returned from Tallahassee where she had gone to seek an audience with Governor Graham. Denied an opportunity to see the governor, she had participated in a religious protest on the steps of the capitol. Along with the PAX (People Against Execution) protesters who had chained themselves to the fence surrounding the governor's mansion, matronly Lois Spenkelink was the big news item that Sunday. Dealing with the press and everyone else who wanted some of her time had worn her out.

I sat down to talk with Lois, Carol Myers, John's sister, and Carol's husband. We reviewed the visitation schedule. Carol was justly angry about being arbitrarily excluded. We talked over the legal situation and the day's plans. We had a long visit over a delicious lunch.

I spent most of the afternoon at the prison talking to the press, who had assembled in droves. Prison officials had erected a shelter where reporters and television crews could meet with us, a tin-roofed shelter in a cow pasture across from the prison.

I wanted to be with John and his family, but I also wanted to talk with reporters to make sure the message about the death penalty was being delivered throughout the country. I was convinced that most Americans knew as little about capital punishment as they did about the moon, and a part of our work in SCJP was to educate the public about their complicity in this horror. Alan McGregor, former director of North Carolina's SCJP project, proved invaluable in coordinating our media activities.

After supper that night, I went to visit with the Spenkelink family again. Lois looked rested. She joked with me. I finally persuaded her to go to bed because the next day promised to be a long one.

After Lois went to bed, Carol, her husband, and I talked over what we could do next. Carol's husband was trying to call California Governor Jerry Brown in the hope that he would ask for clemency for John, who was a California resident. Lois had been trying to reach Ted Kennedy, the U.S. Senator from Massachusetts who was opposed to the death penalty, hoping that he would intercede. They were also trying to reach President Jimmy Carter in the hope that as a professing Christian he would ask Governor Graham to stop the state from committing an act that seemed to us to be contrary to the life and teachings of Jesus Christ.

I left and returned to the motel where I met with David Kendall, John's lawyer, and a lawyer from the Legal Defense Fund. It was nearly 2:00 A.M., and they were both exhausted from their long day in court. David briefed me on our losing effort in the Florida Supreme Court. I reminded him of our meeting with superintendent Brierton in just a few hours. We went to our rooms to grab a few hours of sleep.

Early Tuesday morning David, Alan McGregor, and I met with an Episcopal priest who was close to John. We discussed the upcoming meeting with the FSP superintendent. Then David, the priest, and I left for the prison.

The meeting with the superintendent went more smoothly than our last encounter. He said that John now seemed to be in what the superintendent called "the angry stage."

"I'd be angry too," I thought to myself, "if I saw you standing outside my cell, pretending to be there to help me but at the same time making plans to kill me."

We talked over the plans for the execution and also discussed the case of Willie Darden, another man on Florida's Death Row. Darden was scheduled to be killed on Wednesday, the same day as John, but David Kendall assured me that Darden had many appeals left. I hoped he was right.

As we talked I got the feeling that the superintendent and other Florida officials knew as little as we did about the procedure of legally killing a man. The absurdity of talking about how a man would be electrocuted swept over me, and I was overcome with despair. I tried to clear my mind, to focus on the nightmare playing itself out in front of my eyes, but I could only listen as John's Episcopal priest and David Kendall made their forceful and articulate arguments. I could do nothing but offer to handle John's funeral arrangements.

Later that day I visited John. Once again I found a glass wall between us. God, I hated visiting like this!

John and I knew this might be the last time we would meet. We both choked back the emotion that lumped in our throats. We talked about little things. We joked about the superintendent's security mania. John asked how his family was taking all this, and I said they were holding up well.

He looked me straight in the eye, and his voice came through the small grill opening in the glass barrier.

"What are my chances, Joe? No bullshit. What are my chances?"

"It's going down to the wire, John. It's going down to the wire."

"I appreciate all everyone has done for me. Please tell them all that. I love you for who you are and what you've done for my family and me. Stay strong and don't give up the struggle no matter what happens to me."

"I love you, John."

"I love you too, Joe."

Later that day Lois and I drove to the prison and up to the shelter where we met with the press. Alan McGregor had done his usual superb job of coordinating media activities for the mid-afternoon press conference. The shelter was surrounded by cars, vans, and television remote-broadcast trucks topped with dish-shaped antennae. Print reporters and television and radio crews waited for the press conference to begin.

Lois read her statement and answered questions from reporters. Once again she appealed to Governor Graham to meet with her and to spare her son's life.

The prison administration had refused to allow John to meet with members of the press even though Department of Corrections regulations specifically allowed condemned prisoners this privilege. John had made a final statement and given it to David Kendall. The statement was read to the reporters.

On Tuesday night—the night before John was to be strapped into the electric chair—John's family were allowed brief "contact visits." Prison officials laid down strict guidelines for the visits. Each visitor was told that:

1. One embrace and one kiss would be allowed at the beginning of each visit.
2. John could hold hands with the visitor so long as hands remained on the table in open view of the guards. John's wrists would remain handcuffed throughout all visits.
3. One embrace and one kiss would be allowed at the end of each visit.

The Episcopal priest and I were informed that the state of Florida had denied John the right to meet with the clergy of his choice, thus barring us from sharing final communion with John. We were surprised by the callousness of this decision and asked for an explanation. None was given. Prison officials said that John could meet with one of the prison chaplains. We knew that John, like most Death Row inmates, had little use for the chaplains who, like the guards, the wardens, and the rest of the staff, were paid by the state. Their first responsibility was not to the prisoners but to the state.

John had told me that after his death warrant was signed one of the prison's staff chaplains came to his cell and said he wanted to pray with him.

John looked at him and asked, "Chaplain, are you for the death penalty?"

The chaplain admitted that he was.

"Well, how can I pray with someone who wants to see me killed?"

When I saw David Kendall that evening, he was furious over the arbitrary denial of John's choice of clergy. He called an aide to the governor to protest. He said if he didn't hear that very evening that John would have his choice of clergy, he, David, would release a statement to the press protesting this denial of a basic human right. As I listened to David's impassioned statement I couldn't help but believe that the governor would allow the priest or me to visit John. Not because of compassion for John, but because I didn't believe the politician Bob Graham would want to unnecessarily antagonize one of the leading law firms in the country, Williams and Connolly, with whom David now worked.

Night came as we waited anxiously for news. We had filed appeals with the federal courts—the Fifth Circuit Court of Appeals and the U.S. Supreme Court—and there was still a chance one of them might come through at the last minute. Failing that, we could at least hope that the priest or I could meet with John and share the Lord's Supper with him before Florida killed him.

A demonstration organized by SCJP was forming in the cow pasture across from the prison. Several hundred protesters chanted "Death-

Row-must-go! Death-Row-must-go!" Their voices carried across the field and through the wire fences to the prison cells where the men inside had organized a protest of their own. The harsh clanging of metal against metal pierced the night air. Inside the prison lights blinked on and off in rhythm. Burning towels and sheets were tossed from windows, and the flames flickered eerily, silhouetting the wire fences, the patrolling guard dogs, and the guard towers. Then from within the prison's cells the chant began all at once, as if on cue:

"Save-John-Spenkelink! Save-John-Spenkelink! Save-John-Spenkelink!"

Chill bumps crawled up and down my body as I witnessed the prisoners' love for John—and as I worried about the price the inmates would have to pay for their demonstration of concern. I thought of John in his cell in Q wing, near the electric chair. He had befriended these men, helped them in every way he could, become their natural leader, brought a sense of unity to the men on Death Row. I hoped he could hear the chants of his friends and see the flaming towels and sheets. I knew this determined display of resistance and affection would mean a lot to him.

As I watched the demonstration inside the prison, I recalled a statement John had made: "I don't hate Governor Graham. I don't understand why he wants to kill me or why he won't see me personally. But I don't hate him. In a way, I feel sorry for him because he is committing murder by killing me. It's kind of sad, isn't it?"

In the crowd at the shelter I saw two friends who had come to bear witness with us, Tony Dunbar and Will Campbell, who had been my first contacts with the SCJP. I told them about the situation at the prison. They told me that People Against Execution had occupied the governor's office in Tallahassee. We talked for a while longer and then I left the prison.

I stopped by to check in on Lois and then drove to the Best Western to see David Kendall. I wanted to learn if any progress had been made in getting permission for John's priest or me to share the Eucharist with John. I parked the car, went to David's room, and walked in.

David was talking intently on the telephone. The lawyer from the Legal Defense Fund jumped up and ran toward me as I entered the room.

"We got a stay! We got a stay!" she cried as she hugged me.

I was dumbfounded. We had actually gotten *two* stays of execution: one from Judge Elbert Tuttle of the Fifth Circuit Court of Appeals, the other from Associate Justice Thurgood Marshall of the U.S. Supreme Court. It seemed as though we'd have weeks, perhaps months, to prepare a new legal appeal.

I was still in a daze as David motioned to me to come to the phone. He was talking with John Spenkelink. He gave me the phone. John and I shared our relief and elation. I told him I'd go right over and tell Lois, Carol, and Carol's husband the wonderful news. John said he was glad he'd be able to see us all again and thankful for what we were doing to try to save his life.

As I put down the phone the vital importance of these new developments finally sank in. The fatigue and anxiety fell like a leaden cloak from my shoulders. Renewed strength and joyous energy surged through me. With a whoop of joy I circled my right arm around the lawyer's waist, picked her up, and ran out the door and down the flight of steps, carrying her under one arm as though she were made of air. I put her down at the bottom of the steps, both of us laughing joyously, and I jumped in the car to go tell John's family the news.

The living room of the home where Lois was staying was full of hugs and laughter as we shared the good news. Lois cried tears of happiness and relief. David and my friend Doug Magee joined us later and we talked and ate and celebrated until the early hours of the morning. As our celebration broke up we agreed to meet again later in the morning before we scattered for our separate destinations.

Alan McGregor and I met for an early breakfast at the Holiday Inn across from the Best Western on Highway 301. As we ate I saw the prison superintendent and some of his staff eating at a table across the restaurant. After Alan and I finished eating, I went over to superintendent Brierton's table to inform him of John's legal situation as I understood it. I ended by saying, "There's no emergency now." He nodded, thanked me, and said that John could now receive routine visits without the glass wall. I thanked him, and Alan and I left.

After breakfast we met briefly with religious leaders and other death penalty opponents at the Holiday Inn to plan strategy. Then Alan and I went to see Lois and the rest of John's family. At 11:00 A.M., after a round of hugs and good-byes with the Spenkelinks, I set out on the three-hour drive to Tallahassee and the office of the Florida Clearinghouse on Criminal Justice.

We arrived in Tallahassee in mid-afternoon. Scharlette Holdman and the host of volunteers were exhausted after their work on John Spenkelink's behalf, but were excited by the possibilities raised by the two stays of execution. A volunteer ordered buckets of fried chicken for us and we sat on the floor of the office eating chicken, talking, and making silly jokes. The fellowship, relaxation, laughter, and food helped to drain away the anxiety and fears of the last few feverish days.

The evening news on the office television brought word that Florida Attorney General Jim Smith vowed to have John Spenkelink killed by Friday, May 25. I began to worry that the state of Florida might have its way in spite of two stays of execution from the federal courts. My friends urged me to forget about it and relax for a while. Surely John was safe for the time being.

I spent the next day at the Florida Clearinghouse. About noon we learned that what we expected had happened. The U.S. Supreme Court had dissolved Justice Marshall's stay but had upheld the constitutionality and propriety of Judge Tuttle's stay.

I walked outside and sat on the front steps of the building. It was a beautiful evening. I prayed prayers of thanksgiving for the gorgeous weather and for the fact that John Spenkelink was still alive. It was a good day.

I climbed the stairs and walked back to the office. As I walked in the door I saw the anxious look on the face of Scharlette Holdman. Scharlette had just learned that the Fifth Circuit Court of Appeals was considering lifting Judge Tuttle's stay of execution. Our lawyers told us the court had no right to do so, but they were going ahead anyway. Apparently the judges were in a big hurry to decide the case. Instead of meeting in a courtroom to deliberate, they would decide John Spenkelink's fate by a telephone conference call. They wouldn't even have received the papers John's lawyers had filed in reply to recent events in the case. Still, they were going ahead with their exercise in jurisprudence by telephone.

I told Alan that I didn't like the way this was shaping up, and I was driving back to Starke. He volunteered to go with me.

Neither of us talked much as we drove through the clear, starry night. We took turns jiggling the car radio tuning knob, trying to get news of John's situation from the series of radio stations that faded in and out as we drove. At midnight, about halfway to Starke, we heard the news bulletin through the hissing and crackling static.

"The Fifth Circuit Court of Appeals has dissolved John Spenkelink's stay of execution, and he is scheduled to die in the electric chair at ten o'clock tomorrow morning."

I leaned out the car window and screamed into the rushing wind, "Is there no justice? Is there no justice? My God, is there no justice?"

Alan and I drove on to Starke, neither of us speaking, each deep in his own thoughts. Several times I saw in the headlight beams armadillos that had been run over by cars and crushed. I couldn't help but think that in a few hours John Spenkelink's body would also be a mutilated and lifeless shell, crushed and killed by overwhelming forces beyond his ability to control or even to understand.

As I pulled up to the prison all I could do was repeat the Jesus Prayer: "Oh Jesus, oh, sweet Jesus, have mercy upon us. God have mercy upon us. Christ have mercy upon us."

I stopped at the press shelter, and John's priest told us that visits had been arranged for family and friends but that the visits would end at 6:00 A.M. David's work had paid off: The priest would be allowed to give John communion after the visitors left and would stay with John until 8:00 A.M.

I decided not to visit John again. Better to leave the limited visiting time for the family. Besides, I had already said my good-bye to John. I simply could not bear the prospect of saying it again. Alan and I went to a motel to grab a few hours' sleep.

Friday, May 25, 1979, dawned breezy and clear. A few demonstrators had gathered outside the prison, but inside, behind the barred windows, all was quiet. Ominously quiet. I spoke with the reporters in the press shelter. Then Carol, her husband, and I talked over our plans. They would remain with the protesters while I took Lois to a motel where she could avoid the press, who would surely want to see her as John's execution grew closer.

Carol told me that our lawyers were appealing to the U.S. Supreme Court, protesting the midnight telephone deliberations that railroaded

John's case through in time to make the Florida Attorney General's deadline for killing John. We knew our lawyers would do their best, but given the current make-up of the Court we had little hope.

One of the ironies of this whole scenario was that if John had taken the district attorney's offer of a second-degree murder plea, he would be approaching parole now. Instead, he was hours from electrocution. "Good God," I thought, "what lunacy."

I arrived at the home where Lois was staying about 9:00 A.M. Lois was half-dressed and moving slowly, as though in a daze. I tried to hurry her along, afraid that if we didn't get away soon the press would find her, stick microphones and cameras in her face, and ask her how it felt to have her son killed. She needed to go somewhere where she could deal with John's death in privacy.

By 9:30 A.M. Lois was ready, and we left. I drove her to a rundown motel in Starke at which, so far as we knew, no reporters were staying. I checked her into a room and told the manager that I would answer the phone and screen all calls to keep reporters and cranks from getting through to Lois. She and I went into the room. I closed the blinds. We settled down to wait.

Lois sat on the edge of the bed, her face pallid and puffy. She asked about the calls we had made to Senator Ted Kennedy, to Governor Jerry Brown, to President Jimmy Carter. Why hadn't they called back? she wondered. Her sentences trailed off in exhaustion. I wondered how she would survive the next hour.

The telephone rang and Lois answered it before I could grab it. She nodded at me to let me know it was okay. She talked for a few moments and then, with a pleading expression, thrust the phone toward me.

"This is Richard Carzini calling for President Carter. Please tell Mrs. Spenkelink the president sympathizes with her deeply. But as you probably know, this is a matter of state law, and he doesn't think it would be proper for him to intervene and call Governor Graham."

The anger deep within me boiled over.

"Don't you understand? Don't you folks understand why we called? We aren't appealing to President Carter on the basis of law. We called for help because he claims to be a Christian. We are pleading with him in the name of Jesus Christ, to our Christian brother, to call Governor

Graham and stop this execution. Would you please give him that message?"

There was a long pause.

"I'll be sure the president gets the message."

When I hung up I saw that Lois had stretched out on the bed, exhausted. She was mumbling something about Senator Kennedy when, to my amazement, her voice faded, she began breathing deeply, and she fell asleep.

I whispered a silent prayer of thanks for the gift of sleep that would protect Lois from the agonies of waiting to hear whether her son would this day be saved or slain.

I paced the carpeted floor of the small room, my head swirling with the frenzied events of the last few days. Looking into John's eyes during our last visit . . . the impromptu party celebrating the stays of execution . . . straining to hear news of John on the car radio as Alan and I sped through the Florida night . . . the tension in the hearts of all of us who were trying so hard to keep Florida from killing John Spenkelink in just a few minutes. . . . It was all so cruel and senseless. Why, God, oh why does such injustice reign in your creation?

Though neither Lois nor I wore a watch, I knew the time must be drawing near. I turned the television on but left the volume turned all the way down so as not to wake Lois. I assumed a bulletin would flash across the screen when there was news of a stay or an execution.

A rerun of "All in the Family" was just beginning. "It must be ten o'clock," I thought.

I paced nervously, walking to the window occasionally to peek out through the blinds to make sure no reporters were on our trail. I wanted Lois to hear the news from a friend, not a stranger. I couldn't understand why we hadn't heard any news. David and John's priest were there to witness the execution and had said they would call us as soon as it was over. I was glad John had not asked me to be there. I didn't think I could bear to see him killed. Why hadn't anybody called? Had the Supreme Court intervened at the last minute? Had we somehow gotten another stay?

I paced and paced, keeping one eye on the television screen on which Archie Bunker yelled silently at Edith. Then below the silent screams, the news bulletin snaked its way across the bottom of the screen.

AT 10:12 A.M. JOHN SPENKELINK WAS ELECTROCUTED AT THE FLORIDA STATE PRISON. . . . THE U.S. SUPREME COURT DENIED SPENKELINK'S FINAL APPEAL.

I turned the television off and looked at Lois. She was still in a deep and peaceful sleep. I didn't want to wake her and give her the news that would change her world and her life forever. I didn't want to tell this mother that they had killed her son.

I peeked through the blinds again and saw the motel manager walking toward our room. I slipped silently out the door and met her in the parking lot.

"That's Mrs. Spenkelink in there, isn't it?"

"Yes."

"I just wanted to say that if there's anything I can do to help, just let me know."

"Thank you. Just screen all calls for us to be sure no crank gets through."

She nodded. "I'll be glad to."

I slipped back into the room and sat down on the edge of the bed. I looked down at Lois's eyelids, swollen from crying, and listened to the restful breathing of her deep sleep. I gently took hold of her shoulder and shook her. She didn't stir. I shook her again, more firmly. Still she slept. I shook her again and her eyelids fluttered open. Her eyes—blue like John's eyes had been—gazed up at me.

"Lois, I'm afraid I have some bad news."

"They've killed my Johnny." It was a statement, not a question.

"Yes, Lois, they've killed John."

She sat up. She looked at me without blinking as a tear formed in each eye. The tears rolled slowly down her face and she began to sob.

Lois began to ask again about the unreturned telephone calls, asked herself what she might have done to stop the execution, asked herself where she failed. I grabbed her hands and looked straight into her eyes.

"Lois! Lois, listen to me. You did all you could. We did all we could. All of us did what we could for John. We all loved him. There is simply nothing else that anybody could have done. Please don't second-guess yourself. Please don't punish yourself."

We sat quietly for a moment, holding hands. I asked her if she'd like to pray. She nodded, and we prayed together. After our prayer she stopped sobbing, but the tears kept streaming down her cheeks. We held hands and talked softly for a while.

The telephone rang, and I answered. It was Lois's brother, John's uncle, from California. I handed her the phone.

As Lois talked with her brother I walked into the bathroom and closed the door behind me. I turned both the sink faucets on full blast and flushed the toilet. Then, with the sound of the running water filling the room, I slammed my fist against the bathroom wall again and again as I said, "God, why, Why, WHY? Is there no justice? Is there no justice? Is there no justice!" I leaned on outstretched arms against the bathroom wall. I felt as though my heart had burst. My tears flowed unchecked, and the echoes of my sobs were masked by the sheets of sound from the sink faucets.

I stood up, washed and toweled my face, and turned off the faucets. I had to pull myself together for Lois's sake. I opened the bathroom door.

Lois was still on the phone with her brother. She looked as though she was feeling a little better. After saying good-bye to her brother she talked with me about John. We shared stories and memories of John.

The door opened, and in came John's sister, Carol, her husband, and other friends. We hugged one another, trying to comfort each other. The room was full of sadness, but somehow there was no despair. Somehow God had given us all the measures of grace and peace we needed to survive this day.

The door opened again, and David Kendall walked in. I had wondered why David hadn't called Lois and me as he had said he would after he witnessed the execution. David looked drawn and stunned. He had just seen a good friend, a man he had loved like a brother, killed before his eyes. One look at David's face told me why he hadn't telephoned. David stood there quietly, listening to the conversations but not taking much part in them. He did not tell us what happened at the execution.

So far as I know, he has never told a living soul what he saw that day.

At noon we decided to all go to a nearby steak house for lunch. Somehow the process of grieving, already stretched through the weeks and months of John's ordeal, gave way to the beginnings of healing. As we ate together the food and fellowship buoyed our spirits. We had somehow become a community whose support and affirmation of each other enabled us to weather the evil we had experienced together. We ate heartily and began to tease each other and laugh together.

John's priest was supposed to join us. Carol glanced out the restaurant window looking for him. She suddenly sat up ramrod straight in her chair, grabbed her napkin, and bolted for the women's restroom. Her husband went after her.

I looked out the window and saw the priest, who had apparently just driven up, talking to somebody in the parking lot. My stomach churned when I saw it was the prison superintendent. Fortunately, the priest had arrived just as the superintedent pulled up to eat at this very steak house. John's priest was no doubt telling him that John's family was inside. The superintendent left, and the priest came in to join us. Carol's husband returned to the table to say that Carol was vomiting up her lunch in the restroom.

The superintendent's appearance had ripped open the wounds that had just begun to heal. Nobody wanted to stay at the restaurant, so we left.

We had to talk over the funeral arrangements. Carol was adamant that John not wear a single thread of clothing provided by the state.

"The state of Florida," she said, "took a humorous, good man from us five and half years ago, and today they're giving us back a corpse. I don't want anything from the people who killed my brother."

As we parked at the funeral home we were surrounded by photographers. As we hurried Carol and her husband inside, their every step and look were recorded by the click, whir, and flash of cameras. I knew that the press was important in letting people know about the evils of state-sanctioned killing, but it made me angry to see these photographers intruding on the grief of John's family.

As we were selecting the coffin I explained to the funeral director that the family wanted to transport John's body to California themselves. They believed John had been in the hands of Florida long enough. Carol's husband would drive the casket across the country in a station wagon.

"You can, of course, choose any coffin you wish," the funeral director said, "but I must warn you that since you're talking of burying some days hence and in California, you might desire a sealed coffin."

I must have looked puzzled, so he went on.

"The body has been severely burned. We've wrapped the head to hide some of the marks. Although we certainly are going to embalm the body, I can't vouch that an unsealed coffin would preserve the body over a prolonged period of time in this weather."

My stomach turned over as I thought of Carol's husband driving through the Midwest with a decaying corpse in the back of a station wagon. We told the funeral director to seal the coffin.

We had heard that somebody from *The National Enquirer* had offered a sizable reward to anybody who could get him an exclusive photograph of John's corpse. We asked the funeral director to make sure nobody was allowed to photograph the body.

The family wanted John to be buried next to his father in the beautiful military cemetery overlooking the Pacific at Point Loma, California. Though John was not a military veteran, Lois wanted John to rest in the plot reserved for her next to John's father.

I telephoned the Veterans Administration to make the arrangements. The succession of clerks and bureaucrats I appealed to flatly refused to allow John's remains to be buried alongside those of his father. To bury a "criminal" in Point Loma, they said, would "desecrate" a military cemetery. I called Ramsey Clark, U.S. Attorney General in the Johnson administration, to see if he could help. A long-time opponent of the death penalty, Clark had been instrumental in gaining the Tuesday night stay of John's execution. I hoped that he might be able to intervene in the federal bureaucracy and find a way for John to be buried next to his father. Clark agreed to try and said he'd call back as soon as he had something to tell us.

The memorial service would be held Sunday afternoon at First Presbyterian Church in Tallahassee. Bruce Robertson, the pastor and his wife were old friends of mine. I was grateful to them for helping to set up the service. I feared he would pay a price for allowing a memorial service for an executed man to be held in a prestigious downtown church.

Ramsey Clark called back on Saturday to tell us that he had taken our request to the top of the Veterans Administration and had been refused.

We thanked him for his help. The family selected a cemetery in Los Angeles, and I agreed to telephone to make the arrangements.

Sunday morning dawned bright and beautiful. Becca had flown in to join me. The telephone had been a poor instrument for sharing this ordeal. I needed to be with her on this day. We decided to attend the 11:00 A.M. worship service at the church. The memorial service wasn't until three, but Becca and I felt the need for a time of worship before John's service.

Alan McGregor joined us as we entered the old white church possessed of a simple but elegant beauty.

Bruce spoke that morning about the events of the last week of John Spenkelink's life and the impact those events had on John, his family, his friends, and on those who opposed the death penalty. The words of the pastor generated a powerful and consoling message rooted in grace and love. Becca and I both began to weep.

After the service Becca and I went to the Robertsons' home for some quiet time to prepare ourselves for the memorial service.

At three o'clock the church was filled with people. Bruce opened the service with a prayer, and everyone joined in singing "O God, Our Help in Ages Past." A rabbi from a local synagogue read from the Old Testament. A representative of the Southern Presbyterian Church read from the New Testament. We all stood to sing "Amazing Grace." The simplicity and poignancy of the service filled me with a deep sense of comfort and peace. I could only hope it was doing the same for John's family and his other friends.

We sat down in the pews and David Kendall walked to the pulpit to speak.

> I'm speaking today not as John Spenkelink's lawyer but as his friend, and I'm speaking on behalf of many of his lawyers who were unable to attend this memorial service. I'd like to take just a few minutes to describe those personal qualities of John Spenkelink which made us able to speak of him not as a client, but as our friend, and to mourn him as a friend. It isn't necessary to romanticize him—he wasn't a saint by any means—but he was a good and decent man to whom something indecent happened.
>
> First of all, he was a good man. I say this in full recognition of his juvenile record and of what happened in the state of Florida. He

was good in the sense that he evolved through internal struggle and made something better of himself in prison. He was a changed man. He ministered to other inmates on Death Row in many ways. He wrote letters for those inmates who couldn't write, he read for those who couldn't read. He was put next to one of the most despised inmates on Death Row and he protected this inmate against the abuse of other inmates. One of the most bitter ironies of his execution is that he was "rehabilitated" in all the senses in which that term is usually applied.

He was a religious man. He had a very private religious sense, and he refused to talk very much about his religious beliefs because he felt he would somehow be using that religion for his own benefit. John Spenkelink wouldn't do that.

He was a brave man. Throughout his long ordeal, he was strong, and his lawyers and friends drew strength from him. He was reticent, good-humored, and consistently refused to blame his childhood. He didn't deny his complicity in the killing for which he was condemned. He didn't alibi—he was a stand-up guy. He chose as his epitaph the words: "Man is what he chooses to become. He chooses that for himself," and that was the way he conducted his life. I was there when John Spenkelink was electrocuted, and I can tell you that he met his death with all the grace, dignity, and courage that he'd shown throughout this long ordeal, and the way he met his death shamed the process he was going through. For the last few days, a line has being going through my head and I just was able to locate it as being from the play *Julius Caesar* : "Cowards die many times before their death, the valiant never taste of death but once." John Spenkelink was a valiant man.

Most important, he was a loving man. He cared very deeply about his mother, his sister, his brother-in-law, his sister's children, about his girlfriend and her children, and I think that one of the most difficult things about those last few days for him was the ordeal which he knew they were inevitably being put through. He tried to spare them in every way he possibly could. He was thankful for his friends and grateful for their support. I'd like to mention just two, Scharlette Holdman and Joe Ingle. I couldn't possibly mention all of the people who support him and I'm afraid if I tried I would omit many. But I'd like to simply read what John said in his Tuesday statement to the press:

"I don't know if I'll get the chance to make another statement, so I guess there are things I better say now. I want the people who have worked so hard to stop this thing to know how much I appreciate them. Not only for their endless work, but for being good people—for sharing with me, and supporting me, and looking out for my family in these hard days. I want them to know their friendship has been important to me. They know who they are. It helps me to know they will keep on with the fight, no matter what."

John Spenkelink was not a hater. He was sometimes angry with people but he did not hate them, and he didn't direct his anger upon all those with whom he had to come in contact. I think the story that best exemplifies this trait is that once when one of his lawyers came to see him, John's hands were handcuffed very tightly and painfully. The lawyer asked the guard to remove the handcuffs and the guard said he could not because his instructions had been to keep him handcuffed. The lawyer then began to argue with him and berate the guard when John intervened and said, "Look, don't do that to him. He's a good man and he does his job as well as he can and doesn't hassle us. He's just had his orders." I think it was that ability not to hate, to see the good in other people, that was one of John's most extraordinary qualities.

In the struggle against capital punishment, which we will win in only a matter of painful, painful time, we can't afford to be bitter and to hate—I think that is an important statement that John would have wanted to make today. He cared very deeply about the struggle against capital punishment, not only simply because of his own status, but because of what he saw around him, and I think he would have said we have to keep struggling, but we cannot hate. We must realize that the people who favor capital punishment do so either out of an ignorance about what it can effect, or simply out of a perfectly justified fear of violent crime. We must keep talking; we must insofar as possible let people on the other side know that we share their concern with violent crime, and that we reject violence in all of its forms. We believe in just and fair punishment for crime, but we also believe that this [capital] punishment is a barbarity that no civilized society can tolerate because it demeans us. We must continue to talk; we must continue to pray; we must continue to reason; we must continue to reach out and we must continue trying to convert others.

John Spenkelink stood in solidarity with the other inmates in the struggle against the death penalty. He was not a pawn in this long ordeal, although he necessarily had to take a passive role in some respects. He came to see that the death penalty is founded on, and nourished by, racial and economic injustice. He had a true sense of identification with others in his plight, be they black or white. In his statement on Tuesday he said, "The things that were said in my legal papers were not just issues brought up by my lawyers—they had to do with facts about the death penalty and discrimination in this country, that I can see, that I know about." John was neither a pawn nor, willingly, a symbol; he was somebody who studied, who read, who tried to learn. He told his lawyers time and time again that he did not want his case litigated in such a way that other inmates' cases would be unfavorably affected.

We will prevail in the end, because history is on our side. The death penalty even now, is a thing of the past, despite what happened Friday. We will ultimately win through love and concern, and I think that was the human lesson John Spenkelink taught: the importance of loving and not hating.

When I left the execution chamber on Friday . . . I was struck by a sense of wonder at all the military force that had been arrayed to snuff out John Spenkelink's life. Combined with that sense of wonder was a certitude that the death penalty was a thing of the past, and that ultimately we would prevail. And then I thought, "What will we tell our children when we try and explain this senseless, futile barbarism to them? How can we not be ashamed?" The death penalty will seem to them as incomprehensible as racial segregation and the burning of witches seem to us now. We have to be able to tell our children that we have struggled; that we have done something. None of us can do everything, but each of us can do something. We must continue to bear witness against this senseless violence, in whatever way we can.

As I listened to David speak, memories of the last two years flooded my mind. I began to weep. I struggled to get control, knowing I was to speak after David. After David sat down we sang another hymn. As we sang I struggled to pull myself together. When the hymn ended I walked to the pulpit.

I pointed out two special wreaths among the flowers at the front of the altar. One had been sent by John's fellow inhabitants of Florida's Death

Row. The other had been sent by the men on Death Row in Alabama. I explained what a difficult and dangerous business it was for prisoners to smuggle out the money and arrange to have the flowers sent. Those wreaths were powerful testaments to John Spenkelink's leadership and life. I reminded the congregation of Governor Graham's public pledge to send more and more people to die in the electric chair until the day came when executions would be "routine" in Florida. I shared with the congregation something John told me the last time that I saw him:

> Joe, whatever comes down, don't give up. Whatever happens to me, we have to win this struggle. Give my love to all those people out there and tell them I appreciate all that they have done for me. Tell them that I am grateful for all that they have done, not only for me, but for my family, and tell them not to forget all the others on the Row.

I sat down. We joined in singing "In the Garden," and a religion professor from Florida State University prayed a quiet, eloquent prayer. We sang "We Shall Overcome" and then closed the service with "A Mighty Fortress Is Our God."

The service was ended. Becca and I went over to hug Lois, Carol, Carol's husband, and the many friends who had come. The service left me feeling spiritually cleansed but emotionally drained. I could hardly stand. Scharlette Holdman, who had had reservations about coming to the service, summed it up best. "Not even the governor himself could have had a memorial service with such dignity."

A group of us got into a car, drove to the governor's mansion, and laid on his lawn the wreath sent to the memorial service by the men on Florida's Death Row.

We all gathered—John's family and friends and some of the people who had worked so hard to save his life—at a restaurant for a farewell meal before each of us went our separate way. We pulled tables together and swapped stories over a shared meal. John's body had been destroyed, but his spirit was still among us. John's spirit bound us together in ways none of us could describe and somehow brought us a sense of grace and peace. We finished eating and lingered in the restaurant parking lot. Nobody wanted to say good-bye. Finally Becca and I, who had a plane to catch, said good-bye to the folks with whom we had shared John's struggle. We hugged the members of John's family and assured them we would hold them in our prayers.

As the airplane climbed away from the Tallahassee airport I thought about John Spenkelink. Our friendship had been a gift of grace from God. I was grateful to God for letting me share in John's life.

I remembered the day I gave John a gift from Will Campbell. It was a Committee of Southern Churchmen medallion just like the one I wore around my neck. I had handed Will's gift to John in "the Colonel's room," the visitation room at Florida State Prison. John seemed on the verge of tears as he looked at the symbol.

John and I talked about the symbolic meaning of the medallion: the Cross over the world and an equal sign on the earth symbolizing the equality of all persons within God's creation. John's voice cracked as he told me that this symbol expressed his own personal religious convictions.

As the plane climbed higher I saw in my mind's eye John's gentle face and pale blue eyes brimming with tears as he looked at Will's gift. The deep and private Christian faith of John Spenkelink had sustained him in prison and propelled him into a ministry of service and friendship to his fellow prisoners on Death Row.

Doug McCray, John's friend and mine, had been on Death Row as long as John. I remembered what Doug had once told me:

"I don't know how John stood writing all those letters and answering all those legal questions from some of these guys. He was so patient, even with the crazies. I don't think I could bear my own situation, as he has done, and be so caring of others."

Doug McCray's words bespoke many people's feelings for John Spenkelink. John had given us all a lot to be grateful for, and my memories of him comforted me as the plane took me back to Nashville.

NOTES

1. Bowers and Pierce, "Deterrence and Brutalization: What Is the Effect of Executions?" *Crime and Delinquency,* vol. 26 (1980): pp. 453-84.
2. Bowers and Pierce, "Arbitrariness and Discrimination Under Post-Furman Capital statutes," *Crime and Delinquency,* vol. 26 (1980): pp. 563-635. (Bowers and Pierce were affiliated with Northeastern University.)

CHAPTER FOUR

FRANK COPPOLA
Virginia
August 10, 1982

On August 10, 1982, at approximately 11:25 P.M. eastern daylight time, Frank Coppola was executed in the Virginia electric chair. Coppola became the fifth person executed in the United States after the 1976 U.S. Supreme Court decisions that reinstated the death penalty. The following words of Caryl Chessman could very well have been the words of Frank Coppola.

> It seemed to me, just as it usually seems to my kind, that society was simply trying to strip or rip off my shield, that it was willing to do so ruthlessly, that it didn't care about me personally, or the amount of humiliation or degradation it might inflict in the process. I stubbornly balked at being manipulated, regulated, or being compelled to conform blindly through fear or threat or punishment, however severe. Indeed, I came to question the validity of a society that appeared more concerned with imposing its will than in inspiring respect. There seemed to me something grossly wrong with this. "We'll make you be good!" I was told, and I told myself nobody should, would, or could make me anything. And I proved it.

> **Caryl Chessman**
> Death Row, San Quentin Prison
> (Chessman was executed by the
> state of California on May 2, 1960.)

I entered Frank Coppola's life on July 29, 1982, when I spent a day with him in the holding cells near the electric chair in the Virginia State Penitentiary in Richmond.

Frank's thirty-seven-year-old body rippled with the muscles of someone who prided himself on staying in good shape. He worked out with weights in the prison recreation yard. Frank, a former cop, had always been athletic. He played basketball for a couple of years at Old

Dominion University while he was a student there. One of his real joys in life was a pick-up game of basketball. With his formidable build, his shaved head, and his Fu Manchu moustache, he was an imposing sight on a basketball court.

I visited Frank to convince him to resume the appeals that had been filed to block his August 10 execution date. The date had been set by the trial judge after Frank was convicted of murder. Frank had dismissed those appeal efforts so that the execution could proceed. I hoped that Frank's lawyer, his ex-wife, or I could persuade Frank to resume his appeals. But Frank was determined to let his execution proceed, not out of any death wish or desire to commit suicide, but because life on Death Row had become unbearable.

"I'm losing control, Joe," Frank told me. "I've always liked myself—I know this may sound egotistical—and I've always been proud of the fact that I have been able to like myself and care for my family. But five years on Death Row has found me now losing control, and I don't like it. I would just as soon go out liking myself and loving my family rather than doing something to someone I would later regret."

Frank's ex-wife and their two sons stayed in touch with Frank. The boys visited their father regularly. Each time an execution date was set, the children had to relive the sordid and painful experience of knowing that their father was on Death Row and scheduled to die in the electric chair. Frank believed it was unfair to them to prolong their ordeal by resuming his appeals. Though his killing by the state would be painful for them, it would also be final. Frank felt that by removing himself he would enable his family to go on with their lives without the shadow of his impending execution hanging over them.

Frank and I talked all day long in his cell and in a small room near Death Row. We got to know each other and became friends. Frank Coppola was a bright man, a caring man, a sensitive man, a decent man who had thought this whole matter through and had made his decision. I found myself, as I usually do in a Death Row visit, caring a great deal for this person before me. I did not want Frank Coppola to be killed.

I flew home to Nashville. As the days sped by, bringing August 10 closer, I tried to understand Frank's refusal to resume his appeals. I talked with SCJP colleagues who had worked with Death Row prisoners in other states who had given up their appeals. I talked with a psychiatrist in hope of gleaning some crucial insight into Frank that might help me touch him. As I reviewed my conversations with Frank I became convinced that the only way to get to him was to confront him.

I decided that when I had the chance, I would confront Frank with the one issue that seemed to be at the heart of his decision: the effect on his sons of experiencing their father's death. I knew firsthand what a traumatic experience this was. I was seven years old the night my father and I were driving home from a basketball game when he began to feel ill. As we pulled into the driveway he slumped over the steering wheel, gasping. Heart attack. The ambulance came, the attendants put my father on a gurney, and put the gurney into the ambulance. They closed the ambulance doors and roared off. I never saw my father alive again.

I flew to Richmond on August 8. Frank's ex-wife met me at the airport. Over supper we talked about her filing a "next friend" petition for a writ of habeas corpus on Frank's behalf. A habeas corpus is a writ ordering an imprisoned person to be brought before a court to decide the legality of the imprisonment. A "next friend" is someone who is admitted to court or to litigation to act on behalf of a person unable to act on his own behalf. In Frank's case we would assert that years of living under the dehumanizing and unconstitutional conditions on Death Row rendered Frank incompetent to make this decision.

Frank's ex-wife told me she had decided not to file a next friend habeas. She said that Frank, the boys, Frank's mother, and she were under tremendous strain. If the next friend petition were granted, the dreadful waiting would be stretched over months, perhaps even years, and then once again they would have to endure the torture of watching another execution date loom before them. She told me she didn't think they had the strength to endure this ordeal more than once. She ruled herself out of any legal action to stop the execution. My heart was heavy as I left her. Neither Frank nor she would act to block the execution. We could only try to get Frank's trial lawyer to file a next friend petition.

Monday, August 9, dawned as one of those clear, almost-fall days that you seldom see during August in the South. The glorious Richmond weather stood in stark contrast to the grim determination in the faces of those who worked to prevent Frank Coppola's execution. The executive director of the Virginia Civil Liberties Union and the director of the Southern Prisoners' Defense Committee were working with Bob

Brewbaker, an old college friend of mine who served as local counsel, and one of Frank's trial lawyers who had agreed to file a next friend petition for a writ of habeas corpus on Frank's behalf.

My conflicting duties were tearing me apart. I saw that Frank and his ex-wife wanted no part of efforts to block the execution, and I saw how much suffering this ordeal was putting him and his family through. But I had to remember that deciding whether to try to stop Frank's execution wasn't the same as not intervening with a terminally ill patient, not a matter of letting someone die of a disease without seeking medical treatment. It wasn't even like letting someone commit suicide. Frank wasn't going to die by natural causes or by accident or by his own hand. He was going to be the victim of a public murder to be committed by the state of Virginia. Since I opposed that act with every fiber of my being, I was determined to do all I could to stop it.

As I met with Frank on the evening of the ninth, my mind was clouded by the conflicting purposes of being a supporter and friend to Frank and his family while at the same time acting against their wishes by trying to stop the execution. Frank had been taken to Federal District Court earlier that day to meet with the judge who would determine whether Frank was competent to make the decision about dropping his appeals or whether a next friend should be allowed to speak for him. As Frank and I talked in the visiting area that Monday night, a guard told Frank that the Federal District Court judge had ruled Frank competent to make his decision and had denied the stay. The execution would proceed as scheduled. When Frank heard the news, he smiled.

At this time I pushed Frank with the only question I thought might reach him: What would his execution do to his children? Frank kept dancing away from the point or dismissing it by saying his children were strong. I shared with him what I went through after my father's death. I countered his arguments by saying there is no such thing as a strong fourteen- or fifteen-year-old who is left with a legacy not only of his father's death, but also his execution by the state. We talked back and forth on this question. Frank had told me he had read a lot of Freud since he had been in prison and was impressed by Freud's ideas, so I raised some questions rooted in Freud's work. Frank mulled them over. Finally he said that although he appreciated what I was trying to do, he would stand by his decision. He said he felt my frustration and wanted to reach out to me, but he also wanted me to understand his position. He said he simply would not change his mind. We made plans to meet again the next day, Tuesday the tenth. Then we said goodnight.

On Tuesday, the day Frank was scheduled to be killed, I visited with him in the morning between his visits with his ex-wife and his best childhood friend. When Frank's ex-wife and I left the prison for lunch, we were spotted by a group of reporters already at the prison to cover the impending execution. We had to jump into a car and speed off to keep them from cornering her.

We drove to a Mexican restaurant. Over lunch we talked about her visit with Frank. She was going back after lunch to visit from 2:00 till 7:00 P.M. It would be her last visit with Frank. Frank was scheduled to be killed at 11:00 P.M. I told her about the legal situation. The next friend habeas corpus petition was being appealed in the Fourth Circuit Court of Appeals even as we spoke. I told her I didn't know what the court would decide, but I was preparing myself for the worst.

She looked at me and nodded. She didn't know what "the worst" was—Frank's being killed that very day or having to go through the whole ordeal again in a matter of weeks or months.

I dropped Frank's ex-wife off for her visit and went to see Kathi Neblett. Associate warden at the Virginia State Penitentiary, she was a rarity in Southern prison administration: a competent, reasonable, and caring professional. She was unfailing in her help to Frank's family and to me in arranging visits and support for Frank. I had joked with her about cloning her and placing duplicates of her in some of the other Southern prisons. Kathi's thoughtful concern for the prisoners in her charge stood in stark contrast to the obtuse and narrow-minded bureaucracy we ran into from prison authorities in Florida in the days before John Spenkelink's execution.

Kathi told me she was concerned that a successful appeal resulting in a stay of execution might upset Coppola. I told her that even if the appeal now in the Fourth Circuit Court resulted in a stay, that appeal would then go to the U.S. Supreme Court and directly to Chief Justice Warren Burger. (Each of the nine justices dealt with appeals from a particular geographic region of the country, and Virginia lay within Burger's region.) My experience in the Spenkelink execution led me to expect that a last-minute petition to Chief Justice Burger would result in

Burger's promptly lifting the stay so the execution could proceed. I had little faith in a sheet of paper proclaiming a fragile stay from a lower court. One U.S. Supreme Court justice could overrule that with a stroke of a pen.

I left Kathi Neblett and went to visit Frank and his ex-wife. While I was there we learned that we had gotten a stay of execution.

"S——t!" said Frank.

We talked about the stay and what it meant. Frank believed the execution would take place in spite of the stay. I explained that the death warrant was only valid for the day of execution—August 10—and that it would be very difficult for the Supreme Court to act on the papers before the deadline at midnight.

"It's going to happen," Frank kept repeating over and over. "I know it's going to happen and I have to be ready for it."

Frank, his ex-wife, and I agreed that in spite of the stay we'd assume the execution would take place as scheduled. We felt the danger of facing an execution without being psychologically prepared was something we had to avoid at all costs.

We agreed that I would pick up Frank's personal effects from the prison and take them to the hotel where we were staying and that I would deal with the funeral home people that night. From 5:00 until 6:00 that afternoon Frank and I worked in his cell packing his belongings into cardboard boxes. Several guards helped me carry the boxes down to my car.

I dropped Frank's belongings at the hotel and went back to the prison at 7:00 P.M. to pick up Frank's ex-wife at the end of her visit with Frank. Back at the hotel again, I met with a number of friends from Norfolk who had come for a worship service to be held in a local church to oppose the execution.

I was headed back for the prison when I heard that the state of Virginia had flown the legal papers to Washington to ask the Supreme Court to overturn the Fourth Circuit judge's stay. I got to the prison about 8:00 P.M. and stopped by Kathi Neblett's office. I told her I'd be with Frank and that if anyone needed me I could be reached at the phone outside his cell.

I went down to the prison basement to Frank's cell. With all his possessions removed, Frank's cell was now bare except for a mattress and a chair. He sat on the bare metal bunk in his cell, and I sat on the floor outside his cell. Frank said he was sure Chief Justice Burger would overturn the stay. As Frank joked with the prison guards I could see from their rapport that they had come to respect and admire him. I could see there was even a certain affection between the guards and Frank.

At 10:00 P.M. the guards began removing their nametags—one of the preliminary steps in an execution. Why were they proceeding when, so far as we knew, we were still under a stay of execution? Alarmed, I hurried upstairs to find out what was going on.

While I was gone, some guards who had been assigned to the death squad came to Frank's cell and said they would escort him to the death chamber. Frank asked just what they meant when they said "escort." They said that one of them would grab each arm and lead him to the electric chair. Frank bridled at this suggestion and told the guards he'd coldcock the first person who laid a hand on him. It was important to Frank to die with dignity. He said he wanted to walk to the electric chair on his own, not be manhandled by guards.

Word of Frank's statement got to the warden's office. The warden, the corrections commissioner, and Kathi Neblett talked it over and decided that Frank could walk to the chair without being restrained by guards.

I made a quick call to Frank's lawyer and learned that there was no news from the Supreme Court.

I went back to Frank's cell and told him he could walk to the death chamber without being escorted by guards. He looked relieved.

Frank had been moved to a cell at the end of the walk nearest the electric chair. The cell contained a rolled-up mattress and a single chair. Frank sat on the concrete floor near the bars, and I sat on the other side of the bars in a plastic chair. While we sat and talked—mostly about his sons—the telephone near the cell rang. A guard answered it. I half-expected it to be for me, but the guard stretched the curled cord out and stuck the receiver through the bars into Frank's cell. Frank took the phone and listened. As he listened he looked up at me. He held up his right hand at shoulder level and let the hand drop at the wrist. Then with two fingers he made a walking motion. He was telling me that he would soon be taking that walk down the hall to the death chamber.

He handed the phone back to the guard.

"Is it for sure?" I asked Frank.

"It's for sure," Frank said.

Frank's lawyer had called him to tell him the Supreme Court had lifted the stay of execution. It was 10:34 P.M.

For the next forty minutes Frank and I sat and talked through the cell bars. We talked about many things. Much of what he had to say he summed up in one sentence:

"Just tell my family that the last thing I was thinking about was them."

I nodded and said I'd tell them.

Even as death approached, Frank couldn't resist teasing the guards. He borrowed my ballpoint pen, drew a serrated line on his left forearm, and wrote "DO NOT OPEN UNTIL CHRISTMAS" above the line. He showed that to the guards and everyone had a good laugh over it.

Shortly after 11:15 the death squad—nine guards and the warden—assembled outside Frank's cell. The warden read the death decree.

As the warden read the decree, Frank put on his long-sleeved shirt, rolled up the sleeves, and nodded that he understood the decree. A guard opened the cell door and Frank walked out. I stepped toward him and we embraced. It was a long, tender embrace—a moment I will always cherish.

"You're my friend," Frank said.

"You're my friend," I said.

"I love you."

"I love you too."

"Take care of my family," he said.

"Take care of yourself," I said.

We embraced for a while longer and then we parted. Frank Coppola walked down the hall toward death.

Somebody stopped Frank shortly before he entered the death chamber and asked if he had any final words. Frank shook his head, and then someone called out, "Fire it up!" Filled with revulsion, I asked the guards to let me out. I had no desire to witness Frank Coppola's killing even though the authorities had invited me to do so.

I walked up from the basement and into the main yard of the penitentiary. I was headed for the main gate. I tried to compose my thoughts to talk to the reporters who would be there. I couldn't do it. All

I could think about was my final exchange of words with Frank and our last embrace. As I reached the door and the guard began to open it, I heard him say something about Frank's boy. I stopped and turned to him.

"Would you repeat that?"

He said one of Frank's boys was in the prison. I was stunned. This was one of the fears Frank's ex-wife and I had discussed. We were worried about the effect the execution would have on the younger son who had expressed his desire to be there. He was probably the least able of all of us to deal with this crazy situation.

I looked into the office where the guard had motioned, and there sat Frank's younger son in a room with a man I hadn't seen before. I couldn't believe it. I went inside and asked Frank's son what he was doing there. He said a minister friend of the family—he motioned to the man waiting with him—had brought him.

I asked the minister to promise to bring the boy back to the hotel where his mother was staying as soon as the execution was completed. The minister said he would do so.

I left the prison and made a brief statement to the press. All the while I was thinking about getting back to the hotel, seeing Frank's ex-wife and sharing his last few hours with her.

They killed Frank Coppola at 11:25 P.M.

I went back to the hotel to see Frank's ex-wife. Her son returned a while later. Frank's ex-wife and I talked quietly in the darkened room so as not to disturb her son as he slept. We talked about the craziness of what we had endured, about what it all meant, about Frank, about the boys. As 3:00 A.M. approached, exhaustion overcame us. I said goodnight and left.

CHAPTER FIVE

JOHN EVANS
Alabama
April 22, 1983

The azaleas were in full flower. The pinks, reds, and an occasional azure seemed to burst forth to me. The dogwoods graced the countryside with their gentle blossoms, and the air was full of the scent of lilac and wisteria in bloom. Once again spring had come to Alabama.

Yet amid all the beauty I could not help but reflect that perhaps T. S. Eliot was correct when he said, "April is the cruellest month. . . ." For even as I retained the fragrance, the smell of Mobile in spring, I found myself hurtling down the highway at 100 MPH or better. The project director of the Alabama SCJP was rushing me to Atmore, Alabama, so we would be on time for a press conference being held by John Evans. Evans wanted to make his last statement publicly before being strapped into the Alabama electric chair.

John Evans had shot and killed a Mobile pawnbroker. It was an act of which he was not proud. Rather than appeal his case, he had chosen to drop his appeals after the Alabama Supreme Court ruled against him. A date was set for April 6, 1979, at midnight. I was trying to overcome the tardiness of my flight and arrive at the prison on time.

We arrived at the media center, which was improvised in an old building at the prison. We jumped out of the car, hustled into the center, and were promptly put aboard a vehicle bound for Holman Unit. As the prison van maneuvered past police blockades, I marveled that I was alive despite the reckless adventure of the eighty-five-mile journey from Mobile.

The Alabama SCJP director; Alan McGregor, former project director of the North Carolina SCJP; and I leaped from the van as soon as it halted and pushed our way through the press until we were leaning against the chain-link fence outside of Holman, the maximum security unit at Atmore. A door opened. John Evans appeared with guards and a priest. Evans read a brief statement, underscoring his regret for the killing, yet reiterating his desire not to live for endless years in a 6' x 8' cell on

Death Row while his appeals wound down. He then disappeared with the guards and the priest back through the door, not answering any questions from the press.

Although John Evans had chosen a course of action he thought best, I was opposed to it. I had discussed his situation with his lawyer, and we agreed that a next friend habeas corpus petition should be filed. John's lawyer asked Evans's mother, Betty Dickson, to file the habeas corpus petition. After discussing it with her son, she agreed. John Evans told his mother she was welcome to do what she thought was right but he was resolute in his decision. The petition was filed by Betty Dickson on behalf of her son, maintaining his lack of competency to make a decision to drop the appeals. As it proceeded through the various courts, the Alabama SCJP project director, Alan McGregor, John's priest, and I began to orchestrate calls to Governor Fob James to ask him to commute the sentence to life imprisonment.

Alan coordinated the activities with the press, while the project director, John's priest, and I drew up a list of whom we should call. Religious leaders had been previously contacted, but out of desperation we began a series of calls to locate the papal delegate in hopes of persuading him to have the pope intervene. As we sat on the floor of the priest's small house in the town of Atmore, we waited for the return call from the papal delegate and continued to brainstorm about whom to contact. It was then, in the context of discussing who was close to the governor, that the priest mentioned he had taught the Dooley brothers in parochial school.

"Father, are we talking about the same Dooley brothers? The football coaches?" I asked. The priest smiled and said in his Irish brogue: "I think they are football coaches." I was stunned by this piece of good news. I urged him to call Vince Dooley, the football coach at the University of Georgia. The Alabama SCJP director knew Vince Dooley and Governor Fob James had roomed together at Auburn. The priest dialed Athens, Georgia, directory assistance.

Of course, Coach Dooley had an unlisted number. The priest pleaded with the operator, told her it was a life and death matter, and she reluctantly agreed to call Vince Dooley and inform him that his Catholic priest from childhood was seeking to contact him. She promised to give Coach Dooley the number where the priest could be reached.

As we awaited the hoped-for call, the telephone rang. It was the papal delegate informing us he had passed our request on to the pope. The delegate did not know whether or not there would be any papal intervention but he had conveyed the message. The priest thanked him, and we resumed our wait, hoping that Vince Dooley would call. Eight hours remained before the scheduled execution.

The legal posture of Betty Dickson's appeal was not hopeful. It had proceeded through all the courts and was now on appeal to the U.S. Supreme Court. When informed that Justice White was unavailable for the appeal and it had gone to Justice Rehnquist, what little hope I had in the legal avenues died. It was inconceivable to me that the Court's most vociferous proponent of the death penalty would grant a stay of execution.

If we could persuade Governor James to grant a stay of execution . . . John Evans had said repeatedly that he would take a stopping of the execution as a sign from God. As I sat considering the rather grim situation, I couldn't help but think that if a stay was forthcoming, John Evans would be right. It would take a miracle to prevent his execution.

The phone rang and the priest answered. He nodded his head, smiled and said: "Thank you for returning my call, Vince." Vince Dooley had returned the call! The priest talked with Coach Dooley for more than fifteen minutes, and Dooley agreed to call Governor James. When the priest hung up, we hugged him and were joyful. Our long shot had paid off! We felt that if Vince Dooley made the request for the governor to talk to John Evans's priest, he would surely call.

The next phone call was from Governor James. The priest urged the governor to grant a stay of execution. The governor was noncommittal and left us dangling with a promise to get back to us. No one was feeling hopeful. For the governor, it was clearly a political decision and the life of John Evans was not important.

We had taken extraordinary steps to stop this execution. At that very moment Betty Dickson, John Evans's mother, was in transit from the airport by car. The renting of a private airplane to fly her in from Texas for a last chance visit with her son was an undertaking none of us could afford, but one that we all agreed had to be done. Perhaps a last, unexpected visit to John Evans by his mother would persuade him to change his mind. Although we did not know whether the attempt would succeed, it was worth the effort.

By now the execution was only six hours away. I resigned myself to the inevitability of this killing. I prayed with the priest. Then we all remained by the telephone. It was long past the time Governor James had promised to inform us of his decision, and we all smelled death in the air.

The phone rang once again and it was Harmon Wray, director of the Southern Coalition on Jails and Prisons Tennessee office. "Have you heard the news of the stay?"

I was incredulous. "What stay? From where?"

Harmon told us he had just heard ABC News report a stay of execution from Justice Rehnquist. I was stunned. But before we became too excited, I knew we had to verify this bit of news.

I drove down to the media center at the prison, and Alan McGregor greeted me. He confirmed there was a stay of execution indeed. The press wanted a statement and I could only say what I felt: "This is a miracle. For Justice Rehnquist to grant Evans a stay of execution, given his views on the death penalty, is nothing less than a miracle." John Evans had received his sign from God.

I arrived in Montgomery with a distinct feeling of déjà vu. Springtime of 1983 was as fulsome, although a bit further along, as it had been in 1979. The warmth of April in Alabama was a welcome respite from my Tennessee home, which was still chilly. I proceeded to the Southern Poverty Law Center, where I was to pick up a car and discuss John Evans's situation with his former lawyer.

The lawyer and I reviewed John Evans's legal situation and agreed it was grim. Evans had dropped his appeals in order to force a clemency hearing on his case. He was convinced he had a fair chance at a life sentence with parole from Governor Wallace, based on the governor's self-professed religious experience. I did not agree and told John Evans in several letters I thought he was being foolish.

Despite our disagreement on strategy, John Evans and I had become good friends in the four years that had passed since his near execution. We had corresponded and occasionally visited. I had no doubts that John was a stubborn, willful man, but also a man who had changed tremendously since our initial encounter. He had experienced a genuine Christian conversion through his near execution in 1979, and he thought Governor Wallace would realize the sincerity of his beliefs and commute his sentence to life.

The one aspect of John Evans's case that struck me repeatedly was that it had merit. In the *Beck* case the U.S. Supreme Court ruled that the Alabama Supreme Court should reconsider the Alabama death penalty law because it seemed to be mandatory, which the U.S. Supreme Court had struck down in its 1976 decisions. Under the Alabama law, if the members of the jury found someone guilty of murder, they were forced to give the defendant death. There was no flexibility to return a lesser charge if the jury determined there was cause for such. Presentation of this issue to the Eleventh Circuit Court of Appeals was John Evans's best hope of having his sentence overturned. Unfortunately, Evans had fired his lawyer and withdrawn his appeal from the Eleventh Circuit Court of Appeals in order to force newly elected Governor Wallace to consider his case for clemency.

I drove to Atmore and checked into the Best Western Motel. John Evans's family was waiting for me. Amid hugs and smiles, I settled in to be briefed by Evans's new lawyer, Russ Canan, about where the case stood legally.

When the Alabama Supreme Court set Evans's execution date, I called the Southern Prisoners' Defense Committee. Now that John had an execution date, legally it became a question of how to proceed.

Russ Canan, an SPDC lawyer, took the case and had done yeoman's work. Technically, there was no case to take since John Evans had dismissed his lawyers. However, Evans agreed to see Russ Canan. He then reached an understanding with the new lawyer that if the governor denied clemency, they would file the legal petition to the U.S. Supreme Court. On Monday Governor Wallace indicated he would not stop the execution, and Russ Canan, who had prepared all the papers with his colleagues, filed a timely petition for *cert.* to the U.S. Supreme Court. Given any other case in the country, this would mean an automatic stay of execution while the case was considered by the court. Given the reality of this case, however, we feared the Court would reject the petition out of hand. As one former clerk put it, "Some of the justices hate John Evans." It seemed that a number of the justices felt John Evans was jerking the courts around with his on again/off again legal posture.

The following day, I went for an early breakfast with Russ Canan. We discussed the possible events of the day, and I supported his decision to go to Mobile, to the Federal District Court, on the chance that the U.S. Supreme Court might turn down the case. The habeas corpus papers were already drafted to be filed before Judge Cox in Mobile, and we would stay in touch by phone. We also discussed my access problem. The Department of Corrections was keeping me out of the prison despite the fact that I was a Christian minister, a friend of John Evans, and despite Evans's repeated requests to see me. Russ thought a phone call from him might help, and I suggested he call the Department of Corrections if he had a chance.

John Evans had a full day of visits, and I spent the morning with the Evans family. It was good to see Betty Dickson and meet John's sister and brother. In the late morning we learned from the governor's office that the family's request for another meeting with Governor Wallace would be granted. Betty and Russ Canan had gone with John's priest the previous Friday, and Betty had no desire to go again. John's sister consented to go on the understanding she would be back in time for her late afternoon visit with John. Once again, it was clear we needed a private plane.

We made a few calls and were able to obtain one. I then called Russ Canan and informed him we needed him back in Atmore to fly up with Susan to see the governor. Since there was no word from the Supreme Court and another volunteer lawyer, George Kendall, was available to argue the case in Mobile if need be, Russ agreed to make the trip.

Evans's lawyer and sister flew off to see the governor. I drove out to the airport around 5:00 P.M. to pick them up. I didn't want John's sister to miss her final visit with her brother. The plane was late, and I simply hung around the small brick building that served as a terminal. Then a phone call came informing me that the U.S. Supreme Court had turned John Evans down by a 7-2 vote. My heart sank because I knew that was our best hope for a stay. I had no confidence in Governor Wallace, whom

I viewed as a politician and a creature of the public whim. Because everyone seemed tired of this case, despite its merits, the appellate courts seemed fruitless as well. I met the plane and told John's sister and Russ the bad news.

We drove back to the motel, making our plans during the fifteen-minute drive it took to get there. Evans's lawyer and sister also talked about their visit with Governor Wallace. Although the governor listened to their remarks about John, the medication he was taking made it hard to discern how much he could understand. Neither of them felt very hopeful after the visit. We mused over the fact that one very sick man, who probably couldn't even comprehend the issues of this case, held John Evans's life in his hands.

Upon arriving at the motel, Russ Canan and I went to the phone to call George Kendall in Mobile. John's sister made ready for her late visit to her brother, and Betty had just returned from the prison. We talked briefly and decided to have a private family service after the execution was carried out that night. John's priest and I would lead the service, immediately following the news of John's killing.

The Alabama SCJP director was back on the phone to the governor's aides, trying to obtain some final word about the governor's response to the afternoon meeting. In the course of her discussion, she once again mentioned John's requests to see me and officials of the Department of Corrections keeping me out. The aides promised to get back with her on both matters.

Betty was showing remarkable composure through the ordeal of the state of Alabama's preparing to kill her son. She quilted as she spoke in a quiet voice about her feelings. As the sun set and dark descended, we knew midnight would come all too soon. Her husband, a big, softspoken, and gentle man, was a source of strength for Betty. We had club sandwiches and talked about John, reminisced about experiences with him, and discussed the remarkable change his religious experience had made within him. John Evans imparted a peace to Betty in their final visit, which was his last gift to her. He was ready to die, at peace with himself and his God, and able to share his calm with his family and friends.

Russ Canan informed me that after talking with colleagues in Atlanta, they had decided John's lawyer should remain in Atmore since George

Kendall could handle the arguments before Judge Cox. Lawyers had the papers for the Eleventh Circuit Court of Appeals ready to file in Atlanta, as well as the final petition to the U.S. Supreme Court. The legal team had done a superhuman job in preparing for all the legal avenues. I knew that they were teetering on the brink of exhaustion. All that remained for us to do was wait.

The governor's aide called back to say I could go into the prison to visit Evans. He also made it clear the governor would not intervene to halt the execution. I quickly made arrangements to see Evans at 9:00 P.M. I was allowed a thirty-minute visit, immediately following the last rites by the priest.

Before going to see Evans I had a long conversation with Russ Canan about his witnessing the execution. John Evans had mentioned that he would be grateful if Russ would be there, but he understood if Russ chose otherwise. I sought to convey to Russ my deep ambiguity about his seeing a client killed in the electric chair. I relayed David Kendall's experience as John Spenkelink's lawyer in 1979. Kendall witnessed Spenkelink's execution, and to my knowledge had not discussed it with anyone. John Spenkelink was simply the last death penalty case for which he assumed responsibility. I told Russ that from my own selfish point of view, we couldn't afford to lose lawyers of his caliber and still succeed in the fight against the death penalty. Russ and I discussed the issue thoroughly. We left it with his feeling that he had a duty to attend so that John Evans would see at least one friend in the execution chamber. I understood his position and reluctantly agreed.

I drove out to the prison. Along the way I passed the group of protesters, assembled with candles to hold a vigil against the state sanctioned killing. Each individual candle stood out under the starry night and I muttered a little prayer of thanksgiving for this hardy band, and others across the South, whom I knew were doing the same. Although it may not be possible to stop this barbarity, it was possible to bear witness against it.

I arrived at the police blockade, climbed into the prison car, and was driven to Holman Unit along the back road. We arrived at the front gate, checked in with the tower guard, and went through the sliding chain-link gate into the building. I remained in the foyer while someone fetched the warden.

I had met the warden at breakfast in the Best Western restaurant. I liked the man. He was personable and had been as cooperative as possible in honoring John Evans's wishes. The warden represented the best of the good ol' boy syndrome.

The warden came out, and we shook hands. He led me to an office and asked the personnel to leave while I was searched. It was clear I was to be strip-searched. I complied with the officer's instructions to remove my shirt and pants. I removed my shoes first and then disrobed. Upon request, I pulled my jockey shorts down to my knees. The officer determined I was safe, and I put my clothes back on, listening to the warden's instructions concerning visitation as I dressed.

As I piled into the car with my four-guard escort, I realized that I had just endured my first strip-search. Although I had been going into prisons for ten years and had been closely involved with two men who had been executed, I had not been strip-searched previously. As we drove down the well-lighted prison to the rear gate, I couldn't help but consider the quirkiness of security procedures around each execution. I grimaced at the paramilitary connotations.

We arrived at the back gate and I walked across a well-lit area toward the back door into Death Row. The escort now consisted of five guards, and we were greeted at the door by another set of security personnel. I stepped inside, was patted down, and was then requested to give up my wallet. The search had revealed my wallet contained some "green money [$12.00]." "What," I wondered, "did they think John Evans would do with such a paltry sum three hours before his execution?" We then walked past the death chamber housing the bright yellow electric chair, and approached a nearby cell holding John Evans.

Evans was sitting on his bunk watching the police drama "Hill Street Blues" through the bars. He stood and we smiled and shook hands. John was clothed in long johns, and I was surprised at how thin he was. We fell into conversation naturally, as one would with any old friend.

I soon realized John Evans was anxious for me. He wanted to be sure I was okay and ready to handle whatever came down. I assured him I was, although I wasn't so sure, and we talked about his family. In addition to his concern for his family, John wanted to be sure I understood how grateful he was to me and everyone else who had befriended and helped him over the years. He still had his self-deprecating sense of humor, which he displayed several times during our conversation, and our meager half hour was soon gone. I shook hands good-bye, smiled, and thought how slight and frail my friend, whom the attorney general labeled "mad dog" and "crazed killer," was. We said so long and I left.

As I stood beyond the prison gate waiting for the prison car to take me and the four-guard escort back to the roadblock, I shuffled my feet and thought. It seemed incomprehensible to me that the people of Alabama would want to put to death the man I had just visited. The attorney general, and other law and order proponents, had painted John Evans to be a mythical "cold-blooded killer," without regard to the changes he had undergone in the last four years. The humanity of John Evans was lost amid the rhetoric, and I despaired that anyone in authority would be able to discern it. The reality was that in a little over two hours John Evans would be strapped into the yellow electric chair and killed.

At the checkpoint, I met the Alabama SCJP project director. I had no sooner entered her car than she told me the news. We had a stay of execution!

Federal District Court Judge Cox had granted a temporary stay of execution until Monday. On Monday arguments for John's case would be heard. The state was appealing to the Eleventh Circuit Court of Appeals, and it was unknown who the three-judge panel would be or when they would rule. George Kendall was returning from Mobile with a copy of the order from Judge Cox, so more would be known shortly.

The members of John's family were relieved, though dubious. We discussed the situation with John's lawyer.

After the lawyer left the room, John's sister and Betty spoke: "I know this sounds awful, Joe, but if they're going to kill him I wish they would go ahead and do it. John is at peace now. More at peace than anytime in his life. He is ready to die."

I agreed with them: "I know what you mean. I just came from him and he was calm, composed and peaceful. It would be better if they went ahead as scheduled if they're just going to restart this entire process in another week or so."

As I sat on the edge of the bed considering my emotions, I realized I was in the same position of conflict that I found myself in regarding Frank Coppola's execution the previous August. There was simply no doubt that on the personal level as far as John Evans's family, John himself, and his friends were concerned, the execution should proceed as quickly as possible if it could not be stopped. On the other hand, there was a real need to explore all legal options in hopes that the stay of execution would give time to present the serious legal issues involved. John Evans, under the *Beck* case, should receive a life sentence. As I looked into the faces of John's family and into my own heart, the internal conflict I felt was deeply saddening. Again I asked myself a question: "Why do we have a system that places human beings in a situation where the state kills them, and in the process, overwhelms the people who love them with suffering and grief?"

Around 10:00 P.M. we discovered who the panel would be in the Eleventh Circuit Court of Appeals: Judges Vance, Roney, and Anderson. John Evans's fate was now in their hands.

George Kendall dragged in from Mobile. He was euphoric. He recounted the arguments before the judge, and we expressed our gratitude to all the lawyers concerned for their tireless efforts against overwhelming odds. Still, we waited to hear from the Eleventh Circuit Court of Appeals. The prison announced that no matter what the courts did, there would be no execution during the night. We were clearly going past the one minute after midnight execution time, and since twenty-four hours remained for the state to kill John Evans before the affixed death date expired, the prison people decided to wait and see.

After midnight we heard from the Eleventh Circuit Court of Appeals. By a unanimous vote of 3-0, the court had ruled to uphold the stay given by Judge Cox. Even Judge Roney, a renowned death penalty proponent, had voted for Evans. The state of Alabama had given notice of appeal to the U.S. Supreme Court, and it became clear that for the second time in twenty-four hours, the highest court in the land would decide whether John Evans lived or died.

The stay of execution placed me in a personal dilemma. I had a speaking engagement at St. Andrews Presbyterian College, my alma mater, at 2:00 P.M. the following day. I could either cancel and stay with the family or go. I didn't know what to do. I felt that the Supreme Court would not act on this within the next twenty-four hours, but I wasn't sure. John's family expressed their support if I felt I had to go. It was also clear that I would be very welcome if I remained. I decided to go and try to get back as soon as we heard from the Court, if it was an adverse decision.

Cathy Ansheles, who now directed the Southern Coalition on Jails and Prisons Alabama Project, stayed up all night with me. Cathy agreed to drive me to Mobile, where I would catch a plane to North Carolina.

I flew to Raleigh-Durham and rented a car to drive to Laurinburg, home of St. Andrews. I arrived shortly after 1:00 P.M., slightly frazzled but still coherent. I had called the lawyer's office during the journey and everyone still awaited word from the Supreme Court.

I spoke for an hour at St. Andrews College about the death penalty. One hundred and fifty students attended, and I was surprised by the liveliness of the ensuing discussion. We finally finished up a little after four. There was still no word from the Court.

I was beginning to feel more optimistic as the day wore on and stayed for an alumni reception at the president's house. It was the fifteenth reunion of my class. It was good seeing some old friends, but I couldn't relax because I had yet to hear from the Court. As I was leaving the president's house around 9:00 P.M., I was summoned back for an emergency phone call from my wife in Nashville.

"Joe, they've lifted the stay, and they're going to kill John."

I wanted to weep. Becca continued: "His family called and wants you to call them at the Best Western. Here is the number."

I called the Best Western in Atmore. John's sister answered.

"This is Joe."

"Where are you, Joe? Are you on your way back?"

"No. I'm two hours from any airport. How are you doing?"

She told me that she was okay; they were all bearing up well. I asked her to put Betty on.

"Betty, I'm so sorry. I just heard. I want to be there so badly, but there is no way I can make it."

The softspoken reply warmed my chilled heart: "It's okay, Joe. We are all fine. The Lord is with us and with John. We will be okay."

We then talked for several minutes, and I hung up. I went to my motel to turn on the television so I would know when John Evans was killed.

Cable News Network informed me of John Evans's execution at 11:00 P.M. It sounded sickening. The electric chair malfunctioned, a strap burned off his leg, and it took fifteen minutes to kill him. All I could think about was Russ Canan, watching the horror of John's death. I prayed. Prayed for him, prayed for John's family, prayed for Cathy, prayed for the warden, and I prayed for myself. Finally, I prayed for John's soul.

The following is an account by UPI reporter Mark Harris on the execution of John Evans. Harris wrote the account after witnessing the execution.

Ten hours before being led into a small room to witness the execution of John Louis Evans III, I learned my wife was pregnant with our first child and my notions of life and death became something abruptly personal—beautifully and horribly.

More than a week later, there is a nagging regret that my joy over the impending birth was blurred by the chilling sight of Evans's chest rhythmically rising and falling after what was supposed to be an instantaneously lethal dose of electricity.

And there are lingering questions whether Evans still felt anything after the first lightning bolt ripped into his shaven skull.

Three reporters and two witnesses Evans asked to attend his execution were searched at Holman Prison, then ushered through a raging thunderstorm to a back door. After a short walk along a hall lined by prison guards, we were in the observation room.

Beyond the window was Evans, strapped around his legs, chest, arms, and trunk to the yellow electric chair. The leather straps pulled his shoulders back into an awkward and uncomfortable final position.

"Eaglelike"—that's how he looked with shaven head and sharp, handsome nose and chin.

But Evans's face was pure calm. His pale blue eyes stared straight ahead, blinking occasionally. He had said he was prepared to die. If that wasn't true, his face didn't betray him.

Inside the red brick death chamber with Evans—attired in a white button-up prison smock and white socks—were Holman Warden J. D. White and two uniformed guards.

White, standing directly in front of Evans, read the death warrant. That was supposed to take three minutes, but it seemed much shorter—perhaps because I was intent on committing the scene to memory. No paper or pen was allowed the media witnesses.

Evans, 33, a drifter from Beaumont, Texas, convicted of killing a Mobile, Alabama, pawnbroker, had asked that his final statement remain private.

But when the warrant was read and it was Evans's turn to speak, prison chaplain Martin Weber, one of nine men in the small observation room, began to quote the condemned man's last words.

"He's saying, I have no malice for anyone, no hatred for anyone," Weber, apparently knowing what Evans intended to say, whispered to the witnesses. Prison Commissioner Fred Smith turned and shook a finger as if scolding a child, and Weber fell silent.

One of Evans's final wishes had been violated. Evans's words weren't audible to the spectators, but he delivered them in unrushed sentences and even smiled once before the guards attached the electrode-filled skullcap to his shaven head.

Evans's head was snuggled to the chair with a chin strap and a black belt across the forehead. His expression disappeared behind a black veil.

Smith opened a telephone line to Governor George Wallace in Montgomery.

I folded my arms across my chest and said to myself I was ready.

A man I love and respect had witnessed an electrocution as a young reporter. He had given me a novelist's description of an electric chair execution, along with the warning, "It'll be loud and it will stink."

At the instant White pulled the switch and sent 1,900 volts burning into Evans, who clenched his fists and arched his body rigidly into the restraining straps, the folly of being prepared was gone.

A moment later, as spark and flame crackled around Evan's head and shaven, razor-nicked left leg, white smoke seeped from beneath the veil and curled from his head and leg.

Midway through the surge of electricity his body quivered, then fell back into the chair as the current ended.

We thought that was it—bad enough, but expected and bearable.

Two doctors filed out of the witness room to examine the body and pronounce Evans dead.

The prison doctor placed a red stethoscope to the smock, turned and nodded, the natural signal for "yes, he's dead."

But the nod meant he had found a heartbeat. The other doctor confirmed the gruesome discovery.

They left the chamber and a guard reattached the power lines to the chair and the electrode that fell away when a leg strap burned through.

Evans's chest rose against the straps the first time. It rose evenly once, twice, maybe again.

A stream of saliva ran down the front of the white prison smock.

"God, he's trying to signal them," I thought. I strained to figure out if this was convulsive movement in Evans's strap-crossed chest, and concluded absolutely not. This was slow deep breathing.

Turning to another witness, I said: "He survived." He nodded.

Behind us, Russell Canan, the lawyer who ninety minutes earlier lost a battle to win Evans a reprieve, stared resolutely ahead.

Spark and flame again accompanied the onset of the second charge, but this time, for a grim second, the veil slipped a fraction of an inch on the left side, giving the impression it was burning through and would fall away—exposing the face I'd noted was handsome earlier.

Almost in unison a kind of shuttering grunt came from the witnesses, but the mask stayed in place.

When the second charge subsided the doctors reexamined Evans and again it was clear they found a pulsating heart. Smith knocked on the viewing room window for a clue to Evans's state. Deputy Warden Ron Jones turned and shook his head.

From the back of the room, Canan suddenly, urgently blurted: "Commissioner, I ask for clemency. This is cruel and unusual punishment."

Smith, his back to Canan, did not respond or even indicate he had heard the plea, which Canan repeated, begging that the request be relayed to Wallace.

The commissioner then conveyed the appeal for clemency but before a reply came from the governor's office in Montgomery, the third charge was administered.

The doctors went back for the third time and Canan begged for clemency "in case they have to do it again."

Smith, eyes welling, communicated the message. His voice broke.

I thought Canan had snapped. Surely he didn't want Evans unstrapped at this point. I was convinced things were out of hand and was not sure the chair, for whatever reason, was capable of killing Evans. But surely the only thing worse than proceeding was stopping.

I seriously thought they would have to bring in a gun and shoot Evans in the chair.

Smith signaled White out of the death chamber as the doctors again listened for a heartbeat. The warden cracked the door to the witness room and heard Smith order: "Hold everything. They're asking for clemency."

Moments later, with things spiraling faster out of control, word came back from Wallace.

"The governor will not interfere. Proceed," Smith said.

Almost simultaneously a witness to my right said, "He's dead."

Cold as it sounds, it was welcome news. Evans's ordeal was over. And for the time being, so was the ordeal, however great or small, of those picked to watch him die.

The following is John Evans's last letter to me written exactly one month before his execution. It is printed with the permission of his family.

Dear Joe,

Please forgive the temporary delay in answering your letters and I hope that you know it was not intentional. I've got to tell you that I really was glad to hear from you—it's been a long time, huh? I meant to respond to the letter you wrote regarding the proceedings in the Barefoot case; if I was inclined to go back into the Federal system, the basics on that case would certainly have been one of the ways for me to proceed.

Yes, I realize that you have reservations about my decision to pursue the clemency route—to be perfectly honest, I have a few reservations myself. However, that is my decision and I am absolutely firm on it. This situation has dragged on far too long and it is time to bring it to its conclusion one way or the other. Even with the risks being what they are, Joe, I feel a lot better about my chances at getting my sentence commuted than you'd imagine.

For one thing, I have prepared more extensively for constructive public support than anyone realizes. Charles Graddick will be using the news media and I will be battling public opinion. Therefore, I have had to take that into account and arrange for heavy support in favor of clemency. My hope is that if Wallace is hit with enough support on my behalf, it will at least get him to think that he should talk to me.

However, the most important thing in my favor is that this whole situation is God's "show"—not mine. My faith in His love and wisdom is absolute and nothing is ever going to be able to shake that. No matter how this deal turns out, I will know that He has done what He deems best and I will be able to handle it just fine. You have to remember that it is *what He wants* that is important and what we want or desire is totally irrelevant. I'll tell you something else that I believe with my whole heart—no matter whether I am commuted or executed, God is going to make sure that something constructive comes out of the conclusion of this thing. If I did not really believe that, there is no way that I could handle the coming weeks.

I do want you to know that I am extremely grateful for your pledge to help in this situation; Lord knows, I'm going to need all the help that I can possibly get. I realize the apprehension everyone feels and I will be praying for God to grant all of us the strength and faith we are surely going to need. Well, my friend, hi to all the gang there and I hope that you will all remember that you will be in my heart and my prayers. Sorry that I must close so soon after such a short letter but I hope you'll understand that there is still a lot of work I have to get done in preparation. Take care of yourself and put an occasional grin on that mug for me. May Christ's love shower your every moment.

Respectfully—
John

CHAPTER SIX

JIMMY LEE GRAY
Mississippi
September 2, 1983

I confess to being captured by the beauty of the Mississippi Delta. Whether it be the bare fields in the gray of winter, the shining green of the winter wheat blowing in the spring breeze, the endless rows of cotton springing from the earth straight and true in summer, or the autumn cotton fields covered with snow-white cotton bolls, the land captivates me. Aside from the mountains and shore of my native North Carolina, no terrain cultivates my spirit the way the Mississippi Delta does.

In the northern part of this natural beauty sits one of the most godforsaken places on earth: Parchman, Mississippi. Parchman is a plantation-like prison that for generations has served as Mississippi's only prison. As I drive toward Parchman I can feel the wails of the old blues singers emanating from the fields. The five thousand convicts at Parchman work the fields just like in the old days. Guards on horseback cradle shotguns in their arms as they watch the prisoners, bent of back, toiling and sweating over the cotton or the soybeans. Four out of five of the prisoners' faces I see are black. I feel as though I'm frozen in time one hundred years ago. Freedom has yet to come to this part of Mississippi.

Within the prison at Parchman lies the Maximum Security Unit. The M.S.U., which houses Mississippi's rapidly growing Death Row population, squats behind two chain-link fences. As I walk toward the M.S.U. I see some men playing basketball on a court in the exercise area. They all wear the easily identifiable bright red jumpsuits, the uniform for condemned men.

I walk over to the fenced recreation yard to speak to some of the men through the fence. The guards unlock the doors so I can go into the M.S.U. and then into cellblock three. I speak with each man locked in his cell.

Standing behind the bars of the last cell in cellblock three is a slender

105

man with brown hair and a smiling face. He extends his hand through the bar, we shake hands, and I say hello to my friend Jimmy Lee Gray. I try to push out of my mind the fact that this man I know and love as a brother will probably be the first man since 1961 to be killed in Mississippi's gas chamber.

Jimmy Lee Gray committed a horrible crime. He molested and killed a three-year-old girl. He did this while on parole from an Arizona prison for killing his sixteen-year-old girlfriend. A lot of people believe the death penalty is designed especially for the person who commits such terrible crimes.

One problem with the abstract notion of eye-for-an-eye vengeance against child molesters and killers is that this notion doesn't consider the fact that the condemned man or woman is still a human being, is still capable of change and growth. However, I feared the image of Jimmy Lee Gray the child molester was frozen in the minds of the public and the politicians. In my visits with Jimmy Lee Gray over the years I found him to be a man of considerable sensitivity and depth. He was deeply troubled by his crimes and freely admitted he needed help. Indeed, he made it clear to his pastor and me that he did not ever want to be released unless he received the psychological help he needed. This soft-spoken man, a writer of poetry and prose, wrestled with the responsibility for his past actions from the perspective of genuine Christian faith. Jimmy Lee was a devout Christian who had committed crimes, who was intensely aware of his responsibility for those actions and the problems that contributed to his actions, and who sought help in getting the treatment he needed to keep himself from ever committing such acts again. This was the man the state of Mississippi wanted to kill.

It was the spring of 1983. Jimmy Lee Gray's case was now before the U.S. Supreme Court. If he was denied there, the only hope was an appeal for clemency to Governor William Winter. Many Mississippians thought Bill Winter would not allow an execution while he was governor. Though I didn't know Governor Winter, I knew the crime and the power of the politics of death. I was fearful for Jimmy Lee Gray.

The Supreme Court denied Jimmy's appeal. Jimmy's appeal lawyer, the former director of the Southern Prisoners' Defense Committee, filed for rehearing, which was also denied. The Mississippi Supreme Court set an execution date of July 6, 1983. The people concerned about Jimmy Lee Gray and about the death penalty began to appeal to Governor Winter for clemency. The hearing was set for June 16.

It had been twenty-two years since Mississippi had executed anybody, and no one was really sure how to proceed with the matter of a clemency hearing.

Jimmy's lawyer was told that John Henegan, the governor's legal counsel, was to handle the clemency hearing. It was implied that Governor Winter himself might attend, not so much to review the legal situation or to decide whether to intervene, but just to learn more about Jimmy Lee Gray, to get a picture of the man condemned to die in Mississippi's gas chamber if the governor refused clemency.

To give the governor a full and clear picture, we arranged to have a complete psychiatric evaluation of Jimmy Lee Gray. Amazingly, Jimmy had never had such an evaluation before—not before his trial for killing his girlfriend, not during his prison term in Arizona, not before he was released from Arizona's prison, not before his second trial, not during his prison time in Mississippi. Here was a man who had twice been convicted of serious, violent crimes but who had never been given a psychiatric evaluation that might have helped to unravel the problems that contributed to his acts of violence.

The psychiatric evaluation was scheduled for June 15, the day before the clemency hearing. L. C. Dorsey, director of the SCJP Mississippi project, arranged to meet with John Henegan, the governor's legal counsel, on June 15. Henry Hudson (Jimmy's pastor) and I set up an appointment with Henegan on June 21 to share our pastoral perspectives about Jimmy.

We put the word out through the SCJP network and to sister organizations such as the National Coalition Against the Death Penalty and Amnesty International. We urged people to appeal to Governor Winter in whatever way they could—letter, petition, telegram, telephone call, or personal visit—to ask for clemency for Jimmy Lee Gray.

The so-called security measures directed at Jimmy Lee Gray

increased after his execution date was set. He was manacled and shackled whenever he left his cell. Handcuffs were locked around his wrists and attached by a chain to his waist. His ankles were chained together with leg-irons so that he was forced to hobble rather than walk. He was chained up this way whenever he left his cell for any reason: to receive a visitor, to exercise, even to take a shower.

Despite his treatment, Jimmy's spirits remained high. In a letter he told me that he wanted simply to be judged on the basis of justice, not anger. As I read these and other outpourings of an unbound spirit in a bound body, I wanted to bow my head and weep at the thought that in a few weeks he would likely be killed.

On Wednesday, June 15, the day before the clemency hearing, John Henegan telephoned me in Nashville to say the governor wanted to act quickly on the clemency issue. Henegan wanted to set up a conference call between the governor, Henegan, Henry Hudson, and me to discuss Jimmy's case. This request filled me with foreboding. I repeated my request that Henry Hudson and I—or at least Henry—be allowed to meet with Governor Winter personally. I told Henegan we couldn't discuss the execution of a human being over the telephone. Henegan and I set up a meeting for the morning of Friday the seventeenth. I called Henry.

The Reverend Henry Hudson, an old friend of mine who had carried on his prison ministry for years, was Episcopal priest at the Church of the Advent in the nearby town of Sumner, Mississippi. Every Wednesday Henry brought communion to M.S.U. for those who wished to receive it. Over the last three years Henry had grown quite close to Jimmy Lee Gray, who was one of his communicants.

Henry, a lean, angular man, was fond of describing himself as "a simple parish priest." The kindness, understanding, and love that endeared Henry to his parishioners also shone for the men in Parchman prison. Henry personified German theologian Dietrich Bonhoeffer's description of a Christian: a man for others.

I flew from Nashville to Memphis on Thursday night. Henry picked me up at the Memphis airport and drove us the two hours back to Sumner to spend the night. Though it was after midnight when we arrived at Henry's house, we stayed up until 1 A.M. going over Jimmy's psychiatric evaluation, which I had received by overnight express before I left Nashville. I also filled Henry in on my conversation with Jimmy's lawyer, who had called me before I left Nashville to tell me about Thursday's clemency hearing.

Jimmy's lawyer had told me that Governor Winter hadn't attended the hearing, but the lawyer had met with him for about five minutes at the governor's mansion after the hearing. Winter had said he was troubled by two elements of Jimmy Lee Gray's appeal for clemency. First was the fact that this was the second murder Gray had committed. Second was the possibility that if he commuted Jimmy's death sentence to life in prison without parole—which is what Gray and his lawyer had asked for—there was the possibility that a future governor might commute the sentence to life in prison *with* the possibility of parole. The governor said he was concerned that at some point Gray might be eligible to be released from prison on parole. Jimmy's lawyer said he had tried to address each of the governor's concerns but that he left the five-minute meeting feeling pessimistic about Jimmy's chances.

Henry Hudson and I got up at 6:00 A.M. to begin the two-and-a-half-hour drive to Jackson, the state capital, to meet with John Henegan at 9:00 A.M. We hoped to see the governor after the meeting.

When we arrived at John Henegan's office he was meeting with the district attorneys who had prosecuted Jimmy Lee Gray and who were, presumably, arguing that he should be executed on schedule. Their meeting was running late. At 9:30 A.M. we were ushered into an office, and John Henegan introduced himself.

For the next two hours Henry Hudson and I pleaded for Jimmy Lee Gray's life. Henry was especially eloquent in describing Jimmy as a communicant. At different times in our conversation Henry and I broke down and wept. During the emotionally draining two hours we asked for mercy for a dear friend and a child of God.

Toward the end of our meeting Henegan said the governor had two concerns: He feared that if he commuted the death sentence to life without parole, a later governor might commute that sentence to life with possibility of parole and that Jimmy might someday be released from prison.

"John," I objected, "we both know that no gubernatorial candidate now running for office or any candidate we can possibly imagine would commute Jimmy's sentence to anything less than life without parole."

Henegan said, "But you don't know the history of paroles in Mississippi—"

"You're right," I interrupted, "I don't know the history. This history is not what's important. What is important is that we are discussing a human being's life. A man Henry and I love. A man who is trying to become, in his own words, 'a servant of others.' And you and the governor are discussing theoretical possibilities."

Henegan admitted that no one in Jimmy's family or among his friends was likely to seek to bribe officials to get a lesser sentence. It was my understanding that "buying" lighter sentences was a part of "the history of paroles in Mississippi" to which Henegan had alluded.

"What about the governor's second concern?" I asked.

Henegan said the governor was troubled because this was Gray's second murder. Winter was fearful that Gray might murder again.

I struggled to control the anger rising inside me.

"John, you can't hold Jimmy responsible for that second murder. It's not as if you, or I, or Henry, or the governor went out and killed someone. Jimmy's crime was not that of a responsible human being. It's as his maternal grandmother says: 'I hold Jimmy's mother and the state of Arizona to blame for that second murder just as much as I do Jimmy.' The Arizona parole people should have thoroughly evaluated him through a psychiatric work-up before they released him. They should have granted his request to stay in prison until he got the psychological help he needed. You've seen the psychiatric report. He suffered severe child abuse from his mother. He is full of anger and rage toward his mother. The only experience of love he has now is through the Christian faith. The love of Jesus means so much to Jimmy because it is the only love he has known in his life. If you or I had suffered the abuse Jimmy did as a child we might have committed a heinous crime as well. He hasn't forfeited his right to life. No one forfeits their life because of any action. Life is a gift from God, and we are begging you and the governor not to take this gift of life from Jimmy Lee Gray."

My voice had cracked, and I could feel tears welling in the corners of my eyes. I stopped and composed myself. Then Henry and I asked again to see Governor Winter. Henegan said he would call the governor and left the room.

Henry and I sat quietly, drained by our conversation with Henegan. Finally Henry spoke.

"Joe, there's a service at the cathedral at noon and I want to go to it."

"That sounds good to me, Henry."

Fifteen minutes later Henegan came back to tell us that Governor Winter had refused to see us. We told Henegan we were still anxious to see the governor any time he would see us. Then we left.

The Cathedral of St. Andrew is the Episcopal church in downtown Jackson. Henry and I walked into the chapel as the noon service was about to begin. After the regular Mass a special service of healing was held for those who wished to stay. I felt in deep need of healing and was heartened by the invitation to such a service.

As each member of the congregation knelt at the altar rail, the priest came to him or her and offered a blessing. The priest made the sign of the cross on my forehead with the healing oil, cradled my head in her hands, and said, "God, help Joe to do what he must do. Bless him and be with him."

As Henry and I drove back through the Delta, the priest's words of blessing echoed in my mind. "God, help Joe do what he must do. Bless him and be with him." I wondered why I had been singled out for this ministry to those on Death Row. God, surely there were others who could do this work. Why me? And why Henry? Such a beautiful soul to be racked with such suffering. How would he endure Jimmy's killing? So many questions, God. So much suffering. Please bless us and be with us, I prayed.

I returned to Nashville to await the decision about clemency. I believed we had answered the governor's stated concerns about Jimmy's clemency. But I was convinced that for Governor William Winter the issue would come down to weighing his political career against Jimmy's life. I had no doubt as to what his decision would be.

I was mowing my yard on the evening of June 29 when the mower sputtered and ran out of gas. As I was refilling the tank I heard the telephone ring. I ran inside the house and answered it.

It was Jimmy's lawyer calling to tell me that Governor Winter had released a public statement denying clemency to Jimmy Lee Gray. The lawyer told me that Winter's statement said that he didn't have the authority to intervene in the case except to correct a miscarriage of justice in the courts. But Winter *did* have the authority to grant clemency if he chose to do so, no matter what the courts might or might not have done in Jimmy's trial. And his public line on clemency was not what he had been telling us all along: that he was hesitant to grant clemency because of the two concerns Henegan had talked about with Henry and me. I felt there was another reason. If Winter had political ambitions beyond the governor's mansion, Jimmy Lee Gray and those who were trying to save him were mere stumbling blocks William Winter had to get over in his race for the U.S. Senate.

Jimmy's lawyer began second-guessing himself, wondering how he could have handled the situation better.

"We are not the governor," I told him. "We are not the judges. We don't have the power to stop this execution. We addressed every issue they raised. We gave them a true portrait of Jimmy. We spelled out his humanity and individual worth as a human being. The governor's statement dodges all that because the governor can't deal with it. We did all we could. We witnessed to the truth."

The Southern Poverty Law Center would file another appeal for Jimmy, but it was likely that the judges reviewing the case would see it the same way as Governor Winter: Political expediency would prevail, and they would kill Jimmy Lee Gray.

The phone rang again, and it was a reporter asking for my reaction to the denial of clemency. I told him that Governor Winter had seen the psychiatric evaluation and must have known that Jimmy Lee Gray had not been competent to stand trial for a capital crime and had probably been mentally incompetent when he committed the crime. I told him that Governor Winter was playing politics with Jimmy's life, that he was using this execution to further his own political ambitions, and that he wasn't dealing with the needs of Jimmy Lee Gray the human being.

Henry Hudson called. He was crying. He had been watching the television news announcement of the denial of clemency when John Henegan had telephoned him. Henry had hung up on Henegan. I told Henry about the status of Jimmy's legal appeal and tried to console him. He said he would visit Jimmy the next morning.

John Henegan called me, concerned that Henry had hung up on him in mid-conversation. I tried to explain to Henegan that he would have to face the fact that he was an accomplice in the killing of one of Henry's communicants. People react strongly to other people who are trying to kill their friends.

I asked Henegan to read the governor's statement to me, and he did. It was as bad as Jimmy's lawyer had characterized it. It ducked all the questions that the governor had raised and we had answered when we talked with Henegan about clemency.

The next day Henry called me to tell me what had happened at Parchman prison that morning. Henry said that associate warden Joe Cook and five prison officers entered Jimmy Lee Gray's cell and took away all his possessions. They took away his clothes and strip-searched him. Cook gave Jimmy a paper hospital gown to wear. Cook had said to Jimmy: "I'm not going to let you cheat me out of my chance to kill you."

Henry said Jimmy was upset, but that by the end of Henry's visit he was calming down somewhat. I called John Henegan. While Jimmy sat humiliated in a paper gown with Delta mosquitoes chewing his bare legs, Henegan requested that the Mississippi Department of Corrections investigate the overzealousness of one of their staff.

I talked almost daily with L. C. Dorsey, the SCJP Mississippi project director. L. C., a resilient woman, a grandmother at forty-three, was a child of the Delta. After meeting with Henegan she said she felt we were all just jumping through hoops and that the governor was going to kill Jimmy Lee Gray on July 6, 1983. We talked about how Jimmy had been stripped of all clothing and possessions. (His red Death Row jumpsuit and reading and writing materials were later returned.)

L. C. said, "I've struggled for three years over a remark Scharlette [Holdman, SCJP Florida director] made when we were discussing folks on Death Row. We were talking about how you cared for them, how you loved them, how you struggled to do so without being destroyed yourself when they are killed. I finally know what I want to say to that. You and Scharlette have not been lied to, deceived, cheated, or seen your most cherished ideas smashed all your lives. In short, you and Scharlette have not been treated as niggers. If you are treated as a nigger, you learn to distance yourself, even from those you love, so you can survive. That's the way I feel about Jimmy."

L. C. helped me realize that we couldn't save Jimmy Lee Gray from the gas chamber: That was beyond our power. But we could continue to love Jimmy. We could witness against this killing and survive to witness again. We could love all the others who sat in cells on Death Row waiting to be killed. We could tell their story to the nation and bear witness to a morality that places the sanctity of human life on a plane beyond the reach of political ambition. These things we could do.

On Tuesday, June 28, a week before the scheduled execution, Governor Winter communicated with several people who were trying to stop Mississippi from killing Jimmy Lee Gray. He agreed to listen to them even though he clearly indicated he wouldn't change his mind.

The Reverend Randy Taylor, moderator of the newly merged Presbyterian Church (U.S.A.), sent a telegram to Governor Winter— who was a Presbyterian layman—reminding him of his denomination's position against the death penalty and requesting that he abide by his faith community's stated position.

The Reverend Vernon S. Broyles III, Presbyterian Director of the Office of Corporate Witness and Public Affairs in Atlanta, talked with Governor Winter on the telephone. Broyles also discussed the pending execution with Governor Winter's pastor. The pastor spent the morning talking with the governor. Then the governor's pastor held an afternoon news conference in which he clearly stated his own opposition to the execution.

During his pastor's press conference, the governor met with a representative of the Episcopal Church. Bishop Duncan Gray (no relation to Jimmy Lee Gray), the Episcopal Bishop of Mississippi, was abroad and had telephoned asking the governor to meet with the priest whom the bishop had chosen to represent him in this request for clemency. The priest was Henry Hudson.

Henry took a message to the governor from Jimmy Lee Gray: "Tell him I am sorry I have caused him so much pain over this decision."

Jimmy's statement echoed his most recent letter to me in which he talked about trying to become a servant of Christ.

Henry recently recalled his meeting with the governor in a letter to me.

> Mrs. Winter had asked to be present with her husband. The four of us were together for two hours, far beyond the scheduled thirty minutes, because it turned out that she wanted to stop the execution, and like Pilate's wife, she tried with me to turn the governor's heart. It was an intense meeting. I cried; she cried, and he did, too. Caught in the bonds of the law, ambition, public opinion, tradition, and fear, he could not bring himself to act. It was horrible. I left completely spent, drenched with sweat, yet I had found him, I understood.

That night Henry and I talked over his meeting with Governor Winter. There was no doubt that William Winter was "a good man." Indeed, the fact that he seemed to be such a good man made this execution decision harder for us to bear. How could Governor Winter allow Jimmy Lee Gray to be killed? The answer I came to was theological as well as political.

My Old Testament professor at Union Theological Seminary in New York was fond of exploring the message of the creation story in Genesis. He said that in eating the forbidden fruit Adam and Eve were not pursuing knowledge. They ate the apple because they wanted to become like God and exercise power over all creation. They did this even though God had already placed them in paradise and given them dominion over all the earth. The real message of the creation story, he said, was the human quest for godlike power. William Winter sought such godlike power over the life of Jimmy Lee Gray. Winter, I believed, must be bearing a terrible sense of responsibility as governor; he must have felt that he had a responsibility to kill Jimmy Gray so that Jimmy could never kill again. As chief of state he saw it as his burden to end the life of Jimmy Gray. Those close to him had said that this stoic, noble, self-inflicted position Governor Winter had taken was a source of great anguish to him. Yet however noble his sense of political duty might be, William Winter, like Adam and Eve, was usurping the sovereignty of God by taking on God's power. Winter would be imposing his own will—not the Creator's will—by denying Jimmy Gray clemency. Power is a seductive force, an idol that draws many into its grasp, but in Mississippi, as in the Garden of Eden, the choice for idolatry leads invariably to death.

The state of Mississippi sent out invitations to the execution. It was as though the state saw this as just another government function like a reception or a formal dinner party.

I began to have dreams about Jimmy's coming execution, dreams in which I attended the gassing and watched the entire sickening scenario unfold. Night after night on our farm these dreams would return. My wife, Becca, helped to steady me as the day of Jimmy Gray's date with death grew nearer and nearer.

The Mississippi Supreme Court turned down the appeal, and the case moved on to Federal District Court, where the appeal was to be reviewed by Judge Cox—the judge who denied Jimmy's appeal the first time around. Judge Cox had begun his opinion by quoting the Old Testament on why society needed to have the death penalty. Arguments were to be made by Friday, July 1, and then the case would move on to the Fifth Circuit Court of Appeals. We hoped that by then the U.S. Supreme Court would have released a decision in *Barefoot* v. *Texas*, which would establish a uniform standard for granting stays of execution in all federal courts. A good decision in *Barefoot* could help bring consistency and justice to Death Row prisoners across the United States.

I was driving my pick-up truck from our farm to my office on Friday morning, July 1, when I saw what looked like a dead fawn lying by the road. I slowed as I passed it. The young deer raised its head slightly. I slammed on the brakes and jumped out of the truck and ran over to the deer. She was no more than three months old. She struggled to rise to her thin legs, but the back legs weren't working, and she collapsed. Blood seeped from her rectum. I feared she had suffered broken legs, maybe even a broken hip, and internal bleeding. I was sure she had been hit by a car. I stroked the young deer, trying to calm her, and tried to decide what to do.

As I knelt by the fawn and stroked her white-dappled brown coat I thought of how the young deer was like Jimmy Gray: helplessly waiting for unknown and unforeseen forces to act upon it and determine its fate.

The fawn lay suffering here on the side of the road while Jimmy Lee Gray lay on his bunk in his cell at Parchman wondering whether he would be killed in the gas chamber.

The young deer raised her head and bleated. I almost wept as I saw her struggle to hold on to her life. I slid my arms under her and picked her up. She was surprisingly light, much lighter than my eighty-five-pound Labrador retriever. Her long legs made walking awkward as I carried her out of the scorching July sun and into the shade of a nearby tree. I looked at her one last time—I realized she was probably dying—and decided to go telephone for help.

Just then another pick-up stopped. The driver said he'd call the game warden and report the injured deer. I got back into my truck, drove to my office in Nashville, and called Wildlife Resources. They assured me they would take care of the deer.

By late Friday afternoon Judge Cox had ruled against Jimmy Lee Gray. Only two appeals remained.

That evening I drove home past the spot where I'd found the wounded deer. When I got back to our farm and walked up to the house I looked up at the swallows' nest in the corner of the front porch. Each year swallows hatched their brood on our front porch in a marvelous nest of intertwined twigs and mud. I walked over to the nest and stood on a concrete block to peer into it. Two little balls of down peeked out at me. The rough-winged swallows had hatched! After dealing with death all day long, my spirits lightened as I witnessed this reaffirmation of life.

Late Saturday afternoon the Fifth Circuit Court of Appeals granted a stay for Jimmy Gray. The three-judge panel ruled that it had to stay the execution so long as *Barefoot*—the case dealing with the process of granting stays—was still pending before the U.S. Supreme Court. The panel was also concerned about the gas chamber's being a form of execution that might violate the constitutional ban against cruel and unusual punishment.

I tried to keep my jubilation in check when I heard the news, for I knew that the state of Mississippi was appealing the ruling to the U.S. Supreme Court. Supreme Court Associate Justice Byron White had denied the state's request to lift the stay of execution, and they had taken it to Justice Rehnquist. The stay was still on—for the moment—but the execution was still scheduled for one minute after midnight on Wednesday, July 6.

Adyn Schuyler picked me up at the Memphis Airport on the evening of July 4, and we drove through the Delta bound for Henry Hudson's house in Sumner. Schuyler, a friend of Henry Hudson, was a son of the Mississippi Delta. After leaving and spending years as far away from Mississippi as possible, one day Schuyler realized that he really loved the Delta. He came home to farm. He had planted hundreds of acres of soybeans on land he rented from his grandmother. He knew Mississippi and the people who lived there. As we drove through the night we talked about Jimmy Lee Gray.

"Joe," he said as he tooled his pick-up along the road, "they're going to kill that boy. Maybe not tomorrow, maybe not next week, but they will kill him. He doesn't have any money, no friends beyond you and Henry, no influence at all, and he just doesn't stack up too high on Bill Winter's list.

"I know what moves the William Winters of this world," he said. "I've grown up with them, dealt with them all my life. He may like to put forward a good image, but when you scratch the surface you find the desire which all these folks have: success. They will be as polite to you as can be, but in the end they are going to do you in because they don't care about the right as much as they care about who supports them. Winter is not going to go to the U.S. Senate or become the Chancellor of Ole Miss by commuting this sentence. Jimmy Lee Gray just isn't very high on his list."

I could find little to disagree with in what Schuyler said.

As we drove through the Delta night the conversation wandered to women, drinking, and other verities of Southern man-talk.

As we drew near Henry's house, Adyn Schuyler drove me along what he called "the back way." We rolled down the truck windows so we could smell the rich Delta earth as we drove the dirt roads that wound through fields of cotton and soybeans. The air was heavy with the rich smell of the earth, full of the splendor of creation.

We pulled into Henry Hudson's driveway about 10:30 P.M. I hugged Henry and his wife, Mary Beth. Their younger son, Willy, was nursing; T.J., the five-year-old, was already in bed. We visited a while and then pulled out the sofa-bed where I would sleep. We needed to turn in early since we were entering Parchman at 8:00 the next morning.

The morning newspaper said that Justice Rehnquist, deferring to Justice White's earlier decision, had denied the state's request to lift the stay of execution. Mississippi's attorney general was taking the appeal to Chief Justice Burger.

Henry and I stopped by the Church of the Advent for morning prayer and drove to Parchman.

We told the guards at the gate that we were supposed to pick up special passes that would allow us to enter the prison. The guards said they didn't have the passes, and they waved us on through. We drove to the Chaplain's Department, a rundown building that smelled of dried urine.

We had no sooner entered the office than Henry received a telephone call. He hung up the phone and smiled at me.

"The front gate wants us to pick up our passes," he said.

I laughed. We were back in the bizarre looking-glass craziness of prison "security." We now had to leave the interior of the prison to drive back to the entrance gate to pick up the passes that would authorize us to enter the prison.

My execution pass—a yellow piece of plastic with the number "80" printed on it—allowed me to enter the Maximum Security Unit. Henry's black pass with the number "3" authorized him to witness the execution. With the passes we got two prison memos. One described the prescribed method for shooting a fleeing convict. The other described rules for the press to follow during the time surrounding the execution.

As we walked over to visit Jimmy Lee Gray I noticed that the M.S.U. had been polished and painted in preparation for the execution and the visitors it would draw. A new chain-link fence topped with rolled razor wire had been installed inside the old fence. The barred gate leading into M.S.U. had been painted a shiny black, and the building had been spruced up. As we waited to see Jimmy a prisoner mopped the floor in the waiting room. There's nothing like an execution to improve the looks of a prison.

Parchman officials had declared a state of emergency within the prison to ward off disturbances they feared might result from the execution. Stay or no stay, the prison officials seemed to be proceeding with their plans to kill Jimmy Lee Gray shortly after midnight.

Henry and I met with Jimmy in the visiting room. An air conditioner hummed as we talked through the barred window screen. Jimmy was bleary-eyed and nervous when we first arrived, but as we talked he began to relax. He had been up most of the night writing letters. At the end of our hour-and-a-half visit we urged him to try to get some rest. We promised to return in the afternoon when we had more news from the courts.

I called Stephen J. Ellmann, Jimmy's lawyer. He said that since the *Barefoot* ruling wouldn't be announced until Wednesday, and since Chief Justice Burger had denied the state's request to lift the stay of execution, Jimmy would make it past the one-minute-after-midnight execution time. But the death warrant technically allowed the state to kill Jimmy anytime during Wednesday, July 6. Still, there was some reason to hope that if Jimmy survived the scheduled execution time he might live through the day and still have a chance. There was nothing more Henry and I could do but wait, so we went to the Lake Lodge for lunch.

The Lake Lodge, the dining hall for prison staff, overlooked a small lake on the prison farm. As Henry and I ate, joking and laughing to relieve the tension, we were joined by a prison employee who told us about her hectic day. A secretary at the prison, she had been drafted to be a member of the Prison Information Point Squad—P.I.P.S. The acronym sounded like the nickname for a paramilitary assault team. When the deputy warden had that morning issued the stern order "Activate P.I.P.S." the team swung into action. "Action" had consisted of photocopying and distributing memos, shuffling papers, and other frantic busywork.

Henry and I were amused by the secretary's description of the petty tasks she had to carry out with the utmost seriousness. She was astounded by our levity. Laughing, we explained that there would be no execution at midnight. We would have to let tomorrow bring what it might. For now we were rejoicing even as those around us in the prison proceeded with their plans to carry out their execution.

"I don't want this to happen," she said over and over as we talked. "I just want to return to my normal job and forget all about P.I.P.S."

As night shrouded Parchman, Henry and I returned to the prison for the Eucharist service with Jimmy. Jimmy, Henry, the prison chaplain, and John Johnson—another minister who was a friend of Jimmy's—and I gathered in a small cell around a wooden table. Henry led the service. Jimmy's handcuffs were removed so he could play the guitar. At the end of the service we stood behind Jimmy's chair and sang hymns as Jimmy accompanied on his guitar.

The door leading to the gas chamber stood behind us as we sang. We were in the bowels of death itself; yet we sang of the love and sovereignty of God. The guard joined in singing from outside the cell, and our slightly off-key but enthusiastic chorus lifted the roof of the Maximum Security Unit.

When the service was over, each of us hugged Jimmy Gray. Jimmy said it was the first time in his life he had ever been hugged by a man.

Wednesday morning the Supreme Court delivered its *Barefoot* ruling. By a 6-3 vote the Court ruled the Fifth Circuit Court of Appeals had acted properly in denying Andy Barefoot's stay of execution. The Court then laid down procedure for all federal courts to follow in the staying of executions. In effect the Court declared successor habeas corpus petitions (such as Jimmy Lee Gray's current appeal) to be of dubious value no matter what the merit of the legal issues or questions involved. The Court asked each circuit court of appeals to establish mechanisms for expediting death sentence appeals. The Court was in effect saying, "Tighten up your judicial procedures so we can speed the execution of these prisoners no matter what the legal merits of their cases."

Jimmy Lee Gray couldn't be killed until the Fifth Circuit Court of Appeals responded to the Mississippi attorney general's request to lift Jimmy's stay of execution.

Henry and I visited with Jimmy the next morning. The previous night's communion service had buoyed Jimmy's spirits. He seemed relaxed. He thanked Henry and me for all we had done. We promised to return as soon as we heard from the Fifth Circuit Court of Appeals.

After we left Jimmy I telephoned his attorney, Steve Ellmann, who told me the Fifth Circuit Court of Appeals judges had set up a telephone conference call for 4:00 that afternoon to decide whether to lift the stay. My heart sank. In each of the three executions I had been involved with, the stays had been lifted after conference calls. The pressure of the state on the judges must have been almost unbearable. The power and momentum of a state geared up to kill was a juggernaut compared to efforts to stop the execution. Perhaps the insulation of a telephone line, the distance, the disembodied voices over the phone made the judges' situation more abstract, less real, so that they could, without looking another person in the eye, speak the words that would send a man to be killed.

All we could do was wait.

Now that *Barefoot* was decided, the reason for the July 14 hearing was to deal with the question of Jimmy's sanity and to question the constitutionality of the gas chamber as a means of execution. The courts were faced with two questions. The first—should we execute a mentally ill man who has never received proper treatment, a man who may be mentally incompetent?—seemed not to interest the courts very much. They seemed more interested in the second question: What's the best method to kill this man?

We waited to hear what they would decide.

Just after 4:00 P.M. Steve Ellmann called me.

"Joe, they've upheld the stay. It seems the state of Mississippi failed to deliver the papers to one of the judges, and he refused to make a decision without them."

"Is the state going to appeal to the Supreme Court?"

Steve hesitated.

"It's hard to tell," he said, "but I don't think so. Let me know if you hear anything on that end."

Henry and I sped to the M.S.U. with the good news for Jimmy. As we stood outside Jimmy's cell explaining the situation, the execution watch around the cell ended. The card table and electric fan were removed from Jimmy's cell, as were the cassette tapes, the tape recorder, and the many books. These special amenities Jimmy had been allowed when he was about to be killed were now taken away. Jimmy was being returned to the status of other Death Row inmates: a sign that suggested the state was not appealing to the U.S. Supreme Court to have Jimmy's stay lifted.

"What are they going for next?" Jimmy asked us. He had steeled himself for being killed and was unable to think of the stay except in terms of how and when the state would seek to have it dissolved. We shared his concern and told him we'd just have to wait and see. Henry and I left Jimmy with the understanding that if he saw us again that night it would be because we were bringing bad news.

Despite the adverse ruling in *Barefoot*, Jimmy Lee Gray had made it into safe harbor for another day. July 6 had come and gone, and Jimmy was still alive.

— ▼ —

Thursday, July 7, was unusually cool, as if the Lord had sent the day as a gift to Jimmy Gray so he wouldn't swelter in his cell after the guards took away his fan.

I returned to Nashville. I hoped the baby rough-winged swallows in the nest on our front porch would still be there. I wanted to see the two little birds embark on their maiden flight. Those swallows served as a symbol of the good of creation amid the evil of state-sanctioned murder. Wait for me, little swallows, wait for me. Then you can stretch those wings and fly away from the madness and feel the freedom of creation and wind and sun. Feel the goodness of life. But wait for me, wait for me. I want to see you leave that nest and touch that Tennessee sky.

The two baby rough-winged swallows took flight on July 14. They joined their parents perching on the electrical wires leading from our house. The "swallow watch," Becca's and my watching the birds swoop and dart, would continue all summer.

On July 15 the Fifth Circuit Court of Appeals in a 3-0 decision denied Jimmy Lee Gray's appeal but did not lift the stay of execution. Their opinion showed they were deeply troubled by the means of execution: the gas chamber. Steve Ellmann had put into the record the excruciating death brought about by poisonous gas, noting that the first prisoner to be killed in Mississippi's gas chamber took twenty agonizing minutes to die because the drunk executioner botched the job.

The week of July 18 found us trying once again to move Governor William Winter. Though he had publicly stated that he wouldn't give in to the church on the death penalty, I believed he needed to continually face the fact that he was contradicting the teachings of his own Presbyterian denomination by allowing this execution. I asked the Reverend Randy

Taylor, moderator of the Presbyterian Church, to visit Winter again. Taylor agreed, and a visit to the governor's mansion was set up for late July.

I warned Randy Taylor that behind the genteel graciousness—the invitation to spend the night at the governor's mansion and breakfast with the governor—lay a determined and well-calculated ambition to kill Jimmy Lee Gray. I believed that by talking with the governor, Randy Taylor could witness to the truth of the Gospel of Jesus Christ. Then we would have to leave Jimmy's fate in God's hands. It seemed that witnessing to the governor, speaking out against capital punishment, and offering comfort and solace to Jimmy Lee Gray was all anyone could do.

I spoke with Randy on the phone after his visit with Governor Winter. He said Winter was acutely aware that he contradicted his denomination's position by opting to kill Jimmy Lee Gray but that he gave no indication of changing his mind. After talking with Taylor I wrote Governor Winter a personal letter, sharing my relationship with Jimmy Lee Gray as a Christian and asking him to commute the death sentence. There was nothing for me to do now but keep writing to Jimmy and stay in touch with Henry Hudson to keep track of Jimmy's condition.

The Fifth Circuit Court of Appeals denied the petition for rehearing on Friday, August 19. Steve Ellmann called on August 22 to tell me the attorney general of Mississippi had petitioned the Mississippi Supreme Court to set an execution date of August 31—a mere seventy-two hours after the Fifth Circuit Court would lift its stay of execution. There remained only the forlorn hope that the U.S. Supreme Court would grant a stay so an appeal could be considered.

I phoned Henry Hudson with the news. "Oh, my Lord," Henry said. Episcopal Bishop Duncan Gray had returned from sabbatical, and Henry and I agreed that we should ask him to try to change Governor Winter's mind. The Southern Poverty Law Center forwarded copies of the proposed commutation order to Bishop Gray. Steve Ellmann had secured Jimmy's signature on an affidavit waiving all future possibility of parole in an effort to meet Winter's stated worries about Jimmy's being paroled by a future governor.

Around the country the execution machine seemed to be gearing up. John Eldon Smith was scheduled to be executed in Georgia on August

25. Howard Mathison was to die in Louisiana on August 26. Florida's Governor Graham continued his relentless pace of vengeance by signing death warrants fifty-eight and fifty-nine. The end of the summer of 1983 gave a glimpse of the future of the death penalty, and it was a grim vision indeed.

Henry Hudson kept me posted on how Jimmy was bearing up. Jimmy had told Henry that he signed the affidavit waiving parole because he had no desire ever to be released from prison. He was comfortabl~ in the prison world because he knew he wouldn't hurt anyone while he was in prison.

Bishop Gray carried the clemency proposal and Jimmy's affidavit to Governor Winter on Friday, August 25. That same day U.S. Supreme Court Justice White denied the stay of execution application for Jimmy Gray. Whatever execution date the Mississippi Supreme Court set would be binding.

From my office I called every SCJP project office, Amnesty International, and the National Coalition Against the Death Penalty. I called Henry Hudson. We discussed the legal situation, and he went to the prison so Jimmy could hear the bad news from a friend who cared for him and could answer his questions. Reporters began calling me for statements, but no statements could be made until Jimmy had been told about the situation and until we knew the outcome of Bishop Gray's meeting with Governor Winter.

When I got home that night I found a letter from Governor Winter. He made it clear he would not stop the execution despite our efforts and my "eloquence." I knew then that barring a miracle, Jimmy Lee Gray was going to be killed.

Justice demands—and American law clearly states—that a mentally incompetent person cannot be held legally accountable for his or her actions. Such people may be institutionalized for treatment or for the protection of society, but they can't be punished—and certainly cannot be executed—for committing crimes if they had no awareness of their actions and their consequences, or if they were unable to control their own actions.

Jimmy Lee Gray was mentally disturbed. It was obvious in conversations with him, and his psychiatric evaluation had confirmed it. He had acknowledged his problems many times and had sought help—help that he never got. But instead of dealing with Jimmy as a sick man who might not have been legally responsible for his actions, Governor Winter chose to ignore Jimmy's illness and his pleas for help in order to kill him. Nobody—not the governor, not the courts, not the prison system—wanted to deal with Jimmy Lee Gray as a human being. They insisted on dealing with him only as a faceless child molester and murderer. I doubted that Governor Winter would kill Jimmy if he had once met him face to face. As in the case of John Spenkelink, the governor and the judges with the power over the condemned prisoner's life kept their calculated distance so they could insulate themselves from their action and not see the results of their bloody deed. Politicians and bureaucrats could kill a man from their comfortable offices with the mere stroke of a pen without having to watch him die before their eyes.

Saint Augustine's instruction to "Hate the sin but love the sinner" clearly was lost on Governor Winter and the judiciary.

The arbitrariness of the death penalty in the United States makes a mockery of justice. The week John Spenkelink was killed by Florida, former San Francisco Supervisor Dan White was convicted on only two counts of manslaughter and sentenced to seven years and eight months in prison for murdering Mayor George Moscone and Supervisor Harvey Milk. He would serve only five years.

On the day we knew Jimmy Lee Gray would die, the morning newspaper told of a man who had killed thirteen people in a Seattle nightclub. The victims were bound, gagged, and systematically shot. The jury returned a sentence of life in prison without parole.

Three men are convicted of murder. A prominent San Francisco politician gets less than eight years in prison. A man in Seattle gets life in prison. A man in Mississippi gets the gas chamber. This is equality under the law? This is justice for all?

Shortly after 4 P.M. on August 24, the Mississippi Supreme Court set Jimmy Lee Gray's execution date for September 2. The Fifth Circuit

Court of Appeals had lifted its stay of execution earlier in the day, leaving the Mississippi court free to act. This expediting of the process was due to the insistence of Mississippi's attorney general. He had ordered a state trooper to drive to New Orleans to pick up the Fifth Circuit Court's order and drive it back to Jackson, Mississippi, where it was hand-delivered to the State Supreme Court. Overnight express wasn't quick enough for the state of Mississippi to move the paperwork that would empower them to kill Jimmy Lee Gray.

Henry Hudson telephoned me Friday night, August 25, to tell me about Bishop Gray's visit that afternoon with Governor Winter. When Bishop Gray handed Winter the affidavit in which Jimmy waived any right to future parole, Winter said he would have to reevaluate his position. The handwritten copy the governor received from Bishop Gray was hard to read. I told Henry I'd have the original affidavit, along with a formal request for clemency, sent to the governor by overnight express.

We spent the next two days using the telephone and overnight express to mobilize the national network of organizations against the death penalty and to move the documents that might block Jimmy Lee Gray's execution.

On Wednesday, August 31, I boarded an early morning flight for Memphis. One of Henry Hudson's parishioners who happened to be in Memphis graciously agreed to let me ride back to the Delta with him. I was anxious to get to Parchman in time for the 12:15 communion service Henry Hudson would conduct in the prison. Mary Beth Hudson and her son T. J. met me at the parishioner's home to take me to the prison in time for the service.

After the service Henry and I drove to the Lake Lodge for lunch. Henry said the execution plans were less frantic than they had been in July. The newly minted gate pass was labeled "Security Pass" rather than "Execution Pass." This time there was no Press Information Point Squad, and no flurry of memos. Apparently Mississippi wanted to host a subdued, professional, sophisticated killing.

After lunch Henry and I went to the M.S.U. Jimmy was in the hall, shackled, making telephone calls to his family. I talked with Jimmy between phone calls while Henry visited the Death Row cellblocks.

"Jimmy, you look good. You have a new hair-do, don't you?"

Jimmy smiled and said in his soft-spoken way that he had just parted his hair down the middle. It made him look younger and taller.

He leaned over toward me.

"Do you see that guard with the two kids?" he asked softly.

I nodded as the trio passed behind me in the hallway.

"He hates me. He has brought those kids in so they can look at me and say 'that's the one. That's the one they're gonna kill.'"

I watched the guard—a major—pass through the sliding barred gate with the two boys. The major, the older boy (who looked to be about fifteen), and the younger boy had walked by twice as Jimmy and I visited.

I turned toward the guard at the desk.

"Doesn't the message on the chalkboard say no visitors in the M.S.U., including the gas chamber?"

"Yes," the guard said.

"How then can a major bring those boys back here to the gas chamber and let them gawk at Jimmy?"

The officer shrugged.

"He's not supposed to, but those are his relatives. Besides, Parchman is still Parchman."

No matter how professional this execution was supposed to be, the prison was still governed to a large extent by the good ol' boys, and they wanted to see Jimmy Lee Gray dead. This personal relish for killing turned my stomach.

After Jimmy finished his telephone calls, Henry and I met him in the visiting room. Barred windows separated us. Mosquitoes filled the air. A guard sat near us while we talked.

The Catholic chaplain at the prison joined us. She sprayed the area with an aerosol mosquito repellent and played some soft music on her tape recorder. Sister had a way of taking the edge off the barbarity of the situation.

Jimmy was in high spirits and thoughtful. We talked about a wide range of subjects. Henry and I shared communion with Jimmy. Each Wednesday for more than three years Jimmy had shared the bread and wine of the Lord's Last Supper with Henry, his priest. After tonight there would be no more Wednesdays for Jimmy Lee Gray.

We left a while later. We didn't want to tire Jimmy out, and he needed time to write a few final letters. Though Jimmy's lawyers were filing last-minute appeals to the U.S. Supreme Court, there was little hope.

"See you tomorrow," I said to Jimmy as we left. I knew this could well be the last time I could say those words to Jimmy Lee Gray.

Henry and I drove to his house where the "Joe Ingle Suite"—a fold-out sofa in the den—was waiting for me. My day had begun at 5 A.M., and I was eager to turn in.

The next day, Thursday, September 1, dawned clear and beautiful. A little after 11:30 A.M. Henry came to the door of the county courthouse, where I was visiting a friend. He looked anxious and wan. His voice cracked as he said, "A lawyer from the Southern Poverty Law Center just called you at the house. The Supreme Court turned Jimmy down. We need to go."

We drove straight to the prison. Henry went to give Jimmy the bad news. Jimmy had spent the morning visiting with a minister friend. He had also telephoned his mother and his father. Jimmy was saying his good-byes and making his peace with those he loved.

Jimmy's minister friend, the prison chaplain, and I waited for Henry to return. I was scheduled for a 2 P.M. visit with Jimmy. I would be accompanied by John Johnson, a minister who used to visit Jimmy and who had arrived too late for his scheduled morning visit. I knew that visiting Jimmy with Johnson rather than with Henry Hudson would change the dynamics of the visit, and I selfishly regretted it. But the pressures of the situation required all of us to adjust to changes. John Johnson arrived about 1:30, and we chatted until Henry returned from his visit.

Henry said Jimmy had taken the news hard. Jimmy knew there were no more appeals, no more chances, no more stays, no more hope. Nothing stood between him and the gas chamber except nine hours.

Jimmy invited Johnson and me to sit down as we entered the visiting room. I wasn't sure where to start this conversation, but John Johnson plunged in right away.

Johnson rambled on about how inadequate he felt in his ministry to Jimmy, how full of doubt and guilt he was over their relationship.

Jimmy handled this surprising outburst of remorse and contrition gracefully. He reassured Johnson and repeatedly told him there was nothing else Johnson could have done for him. It was like a confessional, only Johnson was the one seeking absolution and Jimmy was granting it. Jimmy, who was nine hours away from being killed in the gas chamber, ministered to John Johnson with grace and compassion. If only Governor Winter could have witnessed this expression of love and caring on Jimmy's part.

Jimmy told us about his telephone conversation with his mother. Jimmy's mother had abused him as a child, and I believe she bears much of the responsibility for Jimmy's mental illness and his crimes. Since Jimmy had been sentenced to die she had repeatedly and publicly called for him to be executed.

In spite of all this, Jimmy clearly loved his mother, and had told her so in that telephone call.

"She asked me if there was anything she could do for me," Jimmy said. "I said no, but then I thought, there is one thing. I told her she could love her mother. That could be her gift to me."

Jimmy's grandmother held her daughter, Jimmy's mother, responsible for Jimmy's traumatic childhood. There was a terrible rift between mother and daughter over Jimmy. Yet the last request of Jimmy Lee Gray, the abused child now a man, was to ask his mother to forgive, to overcome the barrier between daughter and mother, to reconcile as a last gift to him. Jimmy's account of the conversation moved me to tears.

Jimmy and I talked about the announcement the governor had made denying clemency to Jimmy.

"Joe," Jimmy said, "when I was in the jail in Pascagoula hating myself and hating what I had done, I hoped for the lightning bolt of justice to strike me. As I sat in my cell unable to accept myself, I prayed to be struck by the lightning bolt of justice. Instead, I was struck by the lightning bolt of mercy. Through the grace of God I found myself able to accept myself and the fact that I had done such an awful thing. You really have to need mercy to be able to grant it. Governor Winter has grown up prosperous, well-to-do, and is successful. He doesn't know what it is to really need mercy. So he can't give it. I understand why he isn't granting mercy, and without my experience in the Pascagoula jail of being struck by the lightning bolt of mercy, I probably wouldn't understand."

In his story of experiencing God's grace, Jimmy Lee Gray revealed a genuine feeling for his own worth in God's eyes and a forgiveness for the man whose failure to grant clemency would in a few hours bring about Jimmy's death. I leaned back on the wooden bench in the visiting room. I too had been struck by the grace of God—through the words of Jimmy Lee Gray.

John Johnson returned to the theme of his own self-doubts. Jimmy reassured Johnson and let him know he loved him. Then he looked Johnson straight in the eye and said, "It has been my experience that most of the time. . . . " Jimmy hesitated as though wanting to make sure of what he would say next. " . . . No, I guess all of the time it has been my experience that those who talk about God the most, love the least."

Jimmy quickly changed the subject so Johnson wouldn't take the statement as a direct rebuke. But his words summed up what was wrong with the institutional religion in this country, and especially in the fundamentalist brand I constantly encountered among many people involved in prison ministries. Jimmy Lee Gray would not wear his religion on his sleeve. It was enough to live out his belief in the Christian faith without advertising through verbiage. Jimmy's quiet faith reminded me of John Spenkelink.

Two hours had flown by. Jimmy needed some time alone to write his final letters and sort his possessions—which amounted to little more than a few books and a carton of letters—with Henry Hudson. Johnson and I left Jimmy about 4:30.

I left the M.S.U. and went to the prison press center where I talked with reporters, made a statement, and made one last public plea to Governor Winter to say the word that would stop the execution. I wandered back to the chaplain's office. The quiet of the deserted office gave me a welcome chance to sit and think and pray.

About 6:30 John Johnson, the prison chaplain, and Jimmy's friend returned to the office. Then Henry returned. Henry had shared Jimmy's last meal—a Mexican dinner—before Henry left. Henry and I left to take a walk to stretch our legs after a day of sitting.

Henry said Jimmy was doing as well as could be expected. I shared with Henry the remarkable visit with Jimmy that afternoon. We laughed, celebrating Jimmy's sense of humor and our shared companionship. God, it was a good time to be with a friend.

The other four ministers and I met at the chaplain's office about 8:30

and climbed into a van that the prison chaplain drove to the M.S.U. The execution was now only two and a half hours away. The Mississippi twilight had given way to darkness, and my soul matched the Delta's black summer night. I searched my soul for some twinkling stars to correspond to those lighting the sky above me. I found only darkness.

The van stopped at the first M.S.U. checkpoint. I stared through the chain-link fence at the squatty M.S.U. building awash with spotlights. Two hundred yards separated me from the bowels of the death chamber. I was transfixed by dread.

"Joe. Joe!" Henry said, rousing me from my trance. "The guard needs to see your security pass."

We moved on to checkpoint two, which was manned by a handful of guards, some of whom were on horseback. All these men and guns—did they think one unarmed man locked in maximum security was going to escape amid such a panoply of force?

After passing checkpoint two we got out of the van and walked up the drive to the M.S.U.

We walked past a man in camouflage fatigues standing at parade rest facing the M.S.U. An officer opened the heavy barred door and ushered us down the hallway to the back tier of the M.S.U., through the gates leading to Jimmy's tier, cellblock three. The guard walked ahead of us down the passageway, checking each cell door to see that it was locked. Then he took us to Jimmy's cell.

As we walked down the cellblock I wanted to stop and talk to the men in the cells. Some I knew; others I didn't. Yet I wanted to linger at each cell door and talk with each man. All I could do was simply nod or wave to each man as I walked by his cell.

We walked into the room where we would share communion. The Catholic nun joined us. Jimmy was brought into the room. He was handcuffed and shackled. The guard locked us in the room and remained outside.

Each of us embraced Jimmy and then we all sat down around the table. Jimmy Lee didn't have his guitar. Henry began with the opening prayer from the Episcopal liturgy.

After we had broken bread together and shared wine from the communion cup, we held hands and prayed. We each took a turn with the prayers. As I awaited my turn, my mind went blank. I didn't know what to utter to my God in the midst of this unmitigated evil. No words seemed sufficient to convey my anguish or to bring Jimmy peace. My head hung, and I sweated as I listened to the prayers of the others.

My parched soul wavered amid my brothers' and sister's words. With damp palms I held hands with John and with the prison chaplain. The words for a prayer would not come. Suddenly, like a freshet of water in a dry creek bed, I recalled the apostle Paul's words in Romans. When my turn came I opened a Bible and read them aloud.

> After saying this, what can we add? With God on our side who can be against us? Since God did not spare his own Son, but gave him up to benefit us all, we may be certain, after such a gift, that he will not refuse anything he can give. Could anyone accuse those that God has chosen? When God acquits, could anyone condemn? Could Christ Jesus? No! He not only died for us—he rose from the dead, and there at God's right hand he stands and pleads for us.
>
> Nothing therefore can come between us and the love of Christ, even if we are troubled or worried, or being persecuted, or lacking food or clothes, or being threatened or even attacked. As scripture promised: "For your sake we are being massacred daily and reckoned as sheep for the slaughter." These are the trials through which we triumph, by the power of him who loved us.
>
> For I am certain of this: neither death nor life, no angel, no prince, nothing that exists, nothing still to come, not any power or height or depth, nor any created thing, can ever come between us and the love of God made visible in Christ Jesus our Lord.
>
> (8:31–39, JB)

Henry concluded the service with a prayer. Then we talked with one another about whatever came to mind. The guards brought in a pizza we had brought into the holding area. We ate pizza and shared one another's company just twenty feet from the gas chamber.

At eleven o'clock it was time for us to go. Jimmy gave John, his friend, Sister, and me a final hug and thanked us. We left the cell, leaving Henry and the prison chaplain with Jimmy. It was one hour until the execution.

As we left the cellblock I stopped here and there to talk with some of the condemned men. As we emerged into the main hallway I saw Dennis Balske, one of Jimmy's lawyers. He wanted to see Jimmy, but I told him Jimmy had said he wanted to be alone with the prison chaplain and

Henry. I invited him to ride with me to Lonnie Herring's house on the prison grounds to wait until time for Balske to witness the execution. Lonnie, the director of training for the Department of Corrections, was a member of Henry's church. Lonnie's wife, Cindy, drove Balske and me back to the house. We mixed a drink, sat on the sofa, and talked about Jimmy Lee Gray.

"If only Bill Winter could have spent an hour with Jimmy Lee Gray he could not kill him!" I exclaimed.

The time ticked away. At 11:45 Balske rose to return to the M.S.U. The execution was set for shortly after midnight. Balske was driven back to the M.S.U. in a Department of Corrections van. Cindy and I kept an anxious vigil. When the digital clock on the radio flashed a blue 12:10 I felt a need to make a statement to the press and then return to be with Henry Hudson.

Cindy drove me to the media center. It was jammed with reporters assembled to hear the grisly story of Jimmy Lee Gray's killing. Suddenly Corrections Commissioner Morris Thigpen emerged from a door, sat down in a chair behind a table covered with microphones, and said:

"At twelve eighteen the warden called and informed me that Jimmy Lee Gray was pronounced dead by the doctor."

Appearing shaken, Thigpen rose suddenly and disappeared back through the door from which he had entered.

The press center was buzzing with protest over such a brief statement with no opportunity for reporters to ask questions. Then Dennis Balske sat down behind the microphones. He described Jimmy Lee Gray's last minutes on this earth: being strapped into the chair, breathing the noxious cyanide gas, going into spasms, convulsively banging his head against the chair back.

I thought of Henry Hudson, who had also witnessed this suffering—Henry Hudson, the priest who had ministered to Jimmy for three years, who had done all in his power to sway the governor, who had stood by helplessly as his communicant and friend breathed his last tortured breath, sucking the killing gas into his dying lungs. I resolved to make a quick statement and return to the Herrings's to see Henry.

After Balske was done, I spoke briefly to the press and answered their questions. Then I walked to the back of the room as a corrections department spokesman tried to refute Balske's claim that Jimmy's death constituted "cruel and unusual punishment." I listened half-heartedly to the debate, disconsolate and angry at the same time. Jimmy Lee Gray was dead. He had been killed by Governor William Winter acting in the name of the people of Mississippi. He was the victim of a public, state-sanctioned murder. *That* was the issue, not the method of execution.

Cindy Herring slipped up behind me and said, "Joe, Lonnie says you need to come back to the house. Henry is there." We left the press center and headed for the car.

As we drove back to the house, I thought of Mary Beth Hudson's question to me the previous spring.

"How do I help Henry if Jimmy ever gets killed? How do I love him if he watches such suffering? It will break his heart. How do I reach out to him?"

"The only thing I know, Mary Beth, is to make him talk. Make him share it with you. It is absolute madness he is caught up in, but he has to talk about it or it will burden him forever. This is what Becca has done for me, and it is one of the ways I bear up."

I hoped Henry would talk about it, no matter how painful it might be. I was there for him to share it with, and I prayed he would feel free to do so. I knew we could talk forever and still not make any sense out of the killing, but I also knew our souls could share this insanity and in so doing, survive.

I walked into the Herring house to find Henry Hudson sitting with loosened collar, a Scotch in hand, looking pale and drawn. We sat and talked aimlessly for a while, waiting for the media to leave the prison grounds. Neither of us wanted to talk to reporters any more. At about 1:30 A.M. we left to return to Henry's house. We made chit-chat on the way home, unable to talk about the killing. At the house we found wine and a note Mary Beth left for Henry. I had called Mary Beth earlier urging her to go on to bed. Willy and T. J. were early risers, and I knew neither Henry nor I would be in any shape to handle the children in the morning.

Henry and I sat down at the kitchen table. Henry began to talk.

"After you left," Henry said, "the guards moved us all into the holding room adjacent to the gas chamber. Jimmy sat on an examining table as we talked. As the execution time grew nigh, a doctor appeared with guards to examine Jimmy. At midnight the death squad came to strap him into the chair in the gas chamber. I walked with Jimmy to the door of the death chamber. We embraced and Jimmy whispered, 'I love you, my brother.' Then he was gone."

I listened as Henry recounted the hour preceding the execution, the killing itself, and how he anointed Jimmy Lee Gray's body when Jimmy was still strapped to the chair. I shuddered. No matter how many times I experienced this sickening event, I felt the same revulsion. My brother who told this tale to me, who wept with me, who was Jimmy Lee Gray's brother, was brokenhearted. The suffering was etched within him forever. I simply listened and shared the ordeal as best I could. Finally, after two hours of talking about the grief, the tragedy, weariness overcame bereavement. We went to bed with unanswered questions and with untold horror haunting us.

Willy and T. J. were up early the next morning. Children's laughter filled the house long before I could force myself to rise. Shortly after eight I finally staggered to the kitchen table for a cup of coffee. Mary Beth had been up since 5:30 with Willy. Henry had been up for half an hour and was preparing for morning prayer at his church. I wanted to join him, but lethargy kept me sitting and drinking coffee, listening to Mary Beth's pointed humor about the quality of writing in the newspaper stories describing the events leading up to the execution. Slowly I came fully awake.

The late summer sun shone brightly, the cotton in the fields was near the picking stage, T. J. and Willy Hudson were a joy, life was full and bountiful. Yet I couldn't shake the feeling that I had been fundamentally changed by the events of the previous night. When Henry returned home in mid-morning I told him I felt like the lad in Faulkner's *The Reivers*. The boy returns after adventures that transformed him and was startled by how little the town had changed in his absence. How could the town be just the same as it had always been when he had changed so much?

This late summer day in Sumner, Mississippi, was like any other summer day. The world seemed the same, but I had changed. The killing of Jimmy Lee Gray had changed me. No single event had done it—not the gawking guards, not the callousness of the governor and the courts, not the formal invitation to the execution, not even the execution itself. But my perspective on life had shifted subtly but fundamentally. The collage of events of that summer burned itself permanently into my soul.

The Mass for Jimmy Lee Gray was held at Parchman with Father Henry Hudson conducting the service. A dozen of us gathered to remember Jimmy Lee Gray and to celebrate his gifts to us. The communion we shared annealed our suffering. We embraced at the end of the service.

After a quick lunch at the Lake Lodge, the Hudson family and I climbed into their car to take me to the Memphis airport. The two-hour journey through the Delta rocked me to sleep. I was soon aboard the plane flying back to Nashville. Jimmy Lee Gray was buried in the Mississippi earth and in my memory. I recalled some words of William Faulkner. "The past is not forgotten. It is not even past."

Among the letters and papers of Jimmy Lee Gray's final effects was a 1978 telegram from a member of the family of the girl Jimmy was convicted of killing. It said, "MAY YOUR SOUL FOREVER BURN IN THE FIRES OF HELL."

CHAPTER SEVEN

BOB SULLIVAN
Florida
November 30, 1983

Robert Austin Sullivan was convicted of the 1973 robbery and murder of a restaurant assistant manager in Homestead, Florida. He was sentenced to die in Florida's electric chair.

Bob Sullivan was not a typical Death Row inmate. Bob came from a middle-class family in Massachusetts. His adoptive father was a surgeon. Bob attended the University of Miami for four years. He had lots of friends and an active social life. He was an avid Boston Red Sox fan.

Bob was a chunky man with blue eyes and a sparkling wit. When I first visited him I offered him postage stamps, as I often did when visiting prisoners. He said "No, thanks," and suggested other men who could use the stamps and who would also appreciate a visit.

Bob Sullivan was articulate (in spite of a severe stutter) and intelligent. His wry sense of humor livened his conversation. A devout Catholic, he wanted very much for the Catholic community to become involved in his case. Deeply involved in his own legal appeals, he knew as much about death penalty law as many lawyers. His letters were full of legal points and suggested courtroom strategies. Sometimes he even offered advice to his lawyers. A friend in Massachusetts had set up the Robert Austin Sullivan Legal Defense Fund to raise money for Bob's legal battles. With some of the money raised, Bob hired a private investigator to find evidence to support his claim that he was innocent of the murder of which he had been convicted.

By the spring of 1983 Bob Sullivan was in deep trouble. His legal appeals virtually exhausted, he had only a routine appeal remaining to the U.S. Supreme Court and a possible successor habeas corpus petition, if new legal issues were raised.

But in the meantime the private investigator had obtained sworn affidavits from two witnesses who said Sullivan was in a Miami bar at the time of the robbery/murder of which he was convicted. The crime took place in Homestead, forty miles away from the bar at which witnesses placed Sullivan at the time of crime.

Other evidence also strongly suggested Sullivan might be innocent of robbing and murdering the assistant manager of the restaurant. The restaurant manager disappeared during Sullivan's arraignment after stealing $5,000 from the restaurant. The victim's widow filed a federal suit charging that restaurant employees had carried out the crime. Two potential defense witnesses were murdered under circumstances similar to the murder of which Sullivan was accused. Evidence supporting Sullivan's claim of innocence continued to mount.

It had also been discovered that Sullivan's lawyer and the lawyer's investigator contradicted each other on an important aspect of the trial. The lawyer stated that before the trial he had given the investigator a list of potential witnesses who Sullivan had said would provide an alibi. The lawyer said he had asked the investigator to locate those people so they could testify that Sullivan wasn't anywhere near the crime scene. But the investigator stated in an affidavit filed five years after Sullivan's conviction that the lawyer only approached him *a year after the trial* and that he didn't give specific names of potential witnesses but just asked him to try to find somebody who could corroborate Sullivan's story. The investigator's statement raised serious questions about Sullivan's defense during the trial and during the initial appeal of his conviction.

Though mounting evidence pointed toward Sullivan's innocence, I didn't want to base his appeals on this alone. I asked Catholic Bishop Rene Gracida of the Diocese of Pensacola-Tallahassee to raise Bob Sullivan's case with the governor. He agreed to discuss it with the other Catholic bishops of Florida. The bishops breakfasted with Graham in March of 1983 and made a plea to Governor Graham to commute Sullivan's sentence. Graham heard them out but didn't say what he intended to do. In June the bishops followed up with a petition to Graham, requesting once again that he intervene in the Sullivan case. In a cold, formal letter of reply Graham said that the case was still in the courts and he had no intention of intervening.

I visited Bob Sullivan as often as I could. We talked about his case, of course, and sometimes we talked about our favorite topic: baseball. He bemoaned the lack of pitching his Red Sox endured, and we discussed our picks for the 1983 World Series. We were both rooting for the Orioles because of their team approach to the game.

Bob Sullivan's appeal was to have been presented at a hearing scheduled for June in the Eleventh Circuit Court of Appeals. The three-judge panel scheduled for that hearing was reputed to be open-minded and sympathetic to death-penalty cases. But Bob's lawyer at the time had been forced by another commitment to postpone the hearing. The luck of the judicial draw didn't turn out so well the next time. When the hearing took place Bob faced a panel of judges known to be conservative and less likely to listen to appeals from Death Row prisoners. When they rejected the appeal we could only speculate on what might have happened with the original panel of judges.

The judges had been unwilling to consider Bob's claim of innocence because the appeal and the technicalities involved hadn't been raised in a timely fashion. Sullivan had been on Death Row ten years, but it was only after five years had passed that he began to actively pursue his case by creating the defense fund with and by hiring a new attorney and an investigator. That five-year delay gave the judges the legal excuse to reject the appeal.

Perhaps the court would consider a claim of ineffective assistance of counsel. This claim serves well in death penalty appeals because it is so often true. Most lawyers defending clients facing the death penalty have no experience in capital trials. They do little if any investigation; they fail to prepare properly for the sentencing phase of the trial. Ninety percent of the people facing the death penalty can't afford a lawyer, so the court appoints an attorney to defend them. These lawyers seldom do an effective job. Since it is often the ability of the defense attorney that determines whether a defendant receives the death penalty or life imprisonment, an appeal based on ineffective assistance of counsel should be taken seriously by the courts.

To make this appeal work we needed time: time to do the legal research, time to investigate the alibi witnesses, time to pick up the cold trail of evidence that was now ten years old. If the governor would just give us a little time—if he would just hold off signing Bob's death warrant until 1984—we might be able to find the evidence we needed to get Bob's sentence commuted, perhaps even get him a new trial.

On November 8, Governor Bob Graham signed Bob Sullivan's death warrant. The execution was set for 7:00 A.M. on November 29.

Bob's new lawyer was already in the Florida courts with his successor habeas corpus petition. I asked Bishop Gracida, former Catholic bishop of Pensacola-Tallahassee and now bishop of Corpus Christi, and Bishop Snyder of St. Augustine to contact the Vatican's delegate to the United States and seek the intervention of Pope John Paul II on Bob Sullivan's behalf.

We needed time. We hoped that the Eleventh Circuit Court of Appeals, needing to examine the lengthy legal record of the case, might not want to work through the Thanksgiving weekend and might grant a stay of execution to continue their deliberations after the holiday.

We set up a meeting of PAX—People Against Executions—in Tallahassee on November 27. We would meet to organize acts of civil disobedience—coordinated nonviolent direct actions in Tallahassee, Gainesville, and Starke—to protest Sullivan's execution.

Father Daniel Berrigan came to take part in the nonviolent action. Berrigan, a Jesuit priest and long-time peace and social justice activist, had corresponded with Bob Sullivan.

At the meeting, which lasted until after midnight, we decided on our strategy. The PAX group would don black executioner's hoods and stand outside the door to the governor's office from 2:00 P.M. Monday until the governor left for the day. On Tuesday another group would stage a mock execution in front of Governor Graham and his cabinet at their regular meeting.

Graham had made a point of carrying on "business as usual" while he was having people put to death. Determined not to allow protesters to disrupt his daily routine—or to be arrested and draw public attention to Florida's state-sanctioned killings—he had put out the word to the police and security guards that protesters were not to be arrested unless they attempted to stop the government from carrying on its business.

Monday morning I got word that I could visit Bob Sullivan that evening at Florida State Prison in Starke. I wanted to take part in the protests, but my primary commitment was to Bob. I'd need to leave Tallahassee by 4:00 P.M. to get to the prison in time for the visit.

I had lunch with Bruce Robertson, who had done so much to help all those who mourned John Spenkelink just four years before. I needed to talk with him about a dilemma I faced.

Bob Sullivan had asked me to witness the execution if his lawyer was unable to do so. For me, watching a good friend be killed by the state would violate my cardinal rule of refusing to witness such a barbarity. Each person who works against the death penalty finds there are limits beyond which he or she shouldn't go. I knew in my heart that watching loved ones being put to death could be the one thing that would stop me from continuing my ministry to others on Death Row.

Yet as a person who sought to be a Christian, I was keenly aware that I might be called to set aside my revulsion of state-sanctioned murder so I could be present to minister to Bob. A person being killed by the state dies under the eyes of a host of official functionaries in the witness room. It was crucial that during his last moments he be able to see among those strangers the face of someone who supported him and who loved him.

As I shared this burden with Bruce, I was once again grateful for his support. He had a way of helping me see the issue in perspective. I decided to witness the execution, if Bob's lawyer could not.

Bruce also volunteered to drive with me to Starke. I rejoiced at his willingness to make the three-hour trip with me so I wouldn't have to travel that road alone.

I rented a car for the trip and then, just before we left, I called the SCJP Florida office to see if the Eleventh Circuit Court of Appeals had made a decision. In a tired voice, staffer Jimmy Lohman gave me the bad news: The judges ruled 2-1 against Bob Sullivan. Since there was no indication that any of the judges on the panel had asked for an appeal to the entire Eleventh Circuit Court, it appeared that the case was headed for the U.S. Supreme Court. I held out little hope for help there. As I listened I finally realized that Bob Sullivan was going to be killed.

As we left Tallahassee and drove due east toward Starke, we talked a little about the case, but I didn't feel like dwelling on what now seemed inevitable. We started swapping stories about our alma mater, Union Theological Seminary in New York, and about the teachers with whom we had studied.

As we entered Starke on U.S. Highway 301 we drove by the town water tower, which was topped by a blood-red neon cross glowing garishly in the Florida night. The prison near Starke held more than 200 men who were condemned to die in the electric chair. It seemed appropriate that the town should be marked by a blood-red replica of an ancient device for executing prisoners.

As we checked into the Best Western, the clerk gave me a message to call Scharlette Holdman at SCJP in Tallahassee as soon as possible. We went to our room, and I made the call.

"Clearinghouse."

"Scharlette, it's Joe. We just checked in and I'm—"

"Joe! Joe! We got the pope. The pope asked Graham to stop Bob's execution."

"What?!"

"Archbishop McCarthy conveyed a message directly from Pope John Paul II to Governor Graham asking him to stop Bob's execution. Of course, Graham turned him down."

For the first time in recent U.S. history, a pope had intervened to try to stop an execution. Unfortunately, the governor who had signed more death warrants than any other governor in recent U.S. history refused the request.

Shortly after 7 P.M. I went to the prison. Inside I met Bob's lawyer, who told me the legal prognosis looked bad. He said he had decided to witness the execution the next morning. I was greatly relieved that he, and not I, would have that task.

I was cleared by security and entered the visiting room where I found Margaret Vandiver, who is a paralegal, and three Catholic priests. I hugged Margaret and was introduced to the priests who had come from Boston to be with Bob. Then I turned to greet Bob.

Behind the glass partition of the visiting room—this was to be a no-contact visit—Bob's eyes were puffy and red, his face somber. Clearly he was suffering greatly. The calm, intelligent, witty Bob Sullivan I knew and loved was weeping at the prospect of his death the next morning.

Bob splayed his manacled hand flat against the glass partition in a sign of greeting. I pressed my hand against the partition where his hand was. The cold, hard glass kept us from touching.

The six of us spent the next two hours talking with one another. Bob's voice came through a tinny speaker in the partition. We shared soda pop and snacks. We cried with one another. I briefed Bob on the current legal situation and said I felt Graham had reached a new low in his refusal to honor the pope's request to commute Bob's death sentence.

"When you turn down the pope, that is cold!" I said.

Five heads snapped toward me.

"What did you say?" asked Bob through the speaker.

I had assumed they all knew about the pope's request and Graham's denial of it. They hadn't. I told them about it.

"Joe," said Bob, smiling, "that is an answer to my prayers. I had prayed that the Holy Father would intervene. It really doesn't matter that the governor turned him down. My church has done all it could for me. That is what matters, and I am grateful for it."

Toward the end of our three-hour visit we sang hymns and prayed together. Bob stopped us halfway through our informal service to say, "I don't want this to be a downer. It's getting too sad. It is a serious situation, but I want us to end on an uplifted note. There is a lot to be grateful for and happy about. Let's think of that and celebrate it."

Bob Sullivan had come full circle with his emotions in the course of our visit. Whether it was news of the pope's concern or the simple grace of the Holy Spirit, Bob had been transformed. He was composed and was leading us, shifting the tenor of our prayer and conversation.

The time had come for us to say good-bye. I pressed both my hands against the glass partition in farewell.

Margaret and one of the priests went to join Bob for a contact visit at 11:00 P.M. As their visit neared its completion at 11:55, they began to say their good-byes. Then the door opened and a prison officer said, "The warden wanted me to inform you that there was a stay."

Bob was stunned. His visitors began bombarding the officer with questions to which he had no answers. Bob was escorted back to his cell, and the visitors were ushered out. I received the news from them and was just as stunned as they were. I went directly to the administration building to call Scharlette and find out how the stay of execution came about. I was excited, but I tried not to get my hopes up. I remembered how hard the governor and the attorney general had worked to kill John Spenkelink. I was sure they'd work just as hard to kill Bob Sullivan.

"Scharlette, what's going on?"

She laughed and said, "We got a stay from Judge Godbold."

"Why? And for how long? Will they still try to kill him tomorrow?"

"For some reason—we don't know why—Anderson [the dissenting judge on the panel] wanted a poll of all the judges of the circuit, but this hadn't been communicated. Since he had made the request, the judges must be polled about the panel's decision. Our lawyers don't think there's any way this can be done overnight."

"I thought this was before the Supremes."

"That's what we all thought," she said. "But it's still in the jurisdiction of the Eleventh Circuit."

As we spoke I could see through the window that the extra shift of guards brought in for the execution was leaving the prison, so clearly the prison authorities had called off the execution for tomorrow morning.

I hurried back to tell Margaret and the priests what I had learned. Then I met with reporters outside the prison. I returned to my motel and found another message to call the Florida SCJP office. It was Doug Magee, an old seminary friend and a member of PAX.

"Joe, can you be here for the civil disobedience we've planned for the cabinet meeting tomorrow?"

I was emotionally drained and physically weary from the day's events.

"Doug, you know it's a three-hour drive back to Tallahassee. I wouldn't get in until almost four in the morning. Do you really need me?"

He said that over two hundred people had turned out for a worship service at First Presbyterian Church to hear Father Dan Berrigan speak and to protest the planned execution. Dan had read the pope's message to the gathering and called on the governor to reconsider Bob Sullivan's situation. The plan was to use nonviolent direct action to build on the momentum of Monday's events and make a strong statement of protest on Tuesday.

I asked him to hold while I talked with Bruce who had come with me from Tallahassee. He said he could drive us back to Tallahassee that night and I could sleep along the way.

"I'll be there. What time?" I said into the phone.

"We're meeting at the office at 8:30 in the morning."

The middle-of-the-night drive from Starke to Tallahassee reminded me of journeys we had made on that road trying to save John

Spenkelink. Those memories haunted me as the miles rolled by, but finally adrenalin and memories gave way to exhaustion and I dozed off.

After two hours of sleep at my friend's house I joined fellow protesters at the capitol. Dan Berrigan and two other PAX members would stage the mock execution in the cabinet meeting room. Bob Gross, Jimmy Lohman, and I would don black executioner's hoods and point fingers of responsibility at the governor as the mock execution took place. We would hold that pose until we were arrested or physically removed from the room.

We all entered the cabinet room under the watchful eye of security guards. We each found a seat in the part of the room where we had to be for our roles in the event to come. We waited for the governor and his cabinet.

Reporters and photographers swarmed around the entrance leading to the raised platform as members of the cabinet entered and sat behind a long curved table. Governor Graham walked in about 9:10 and stopped to answer questions from reporters about the postponed execution. He said he was concerned over the continuing delay and the effect it must be having on the men on Death Row, especially Bob Sullivan.

"Can you believe that?" I whispered to Dan Berrigan, who sat beside me. Dan just shook his head.

The governor walked to his chair in the middle of the table and asked everyone to stand for the invocation. With all heads bowed in prayer, a small-town Baptist minister indulged us in a display of civic religion, asking the Lord to "strengthen those in leadership, especially during these times of grave decisions."

"Bullshit!" Father Dan Berrigan whispered loudly.

Every time the minister called on God to bless these men who were engaged in ritual acts of murder, Berrigan loudly whispered, "Bullshit!" I admired his courage, but I hoped he wouldn't be removed before we did what we had come to do.

The prayer ended, mercifully, and everyone sat down. As the governor read the first item on the agenda, the protesters sprang into action. There would be no "business as usual" for the governor and his cabinet that day.

One of the PAX members covered her head with a black hood. Dan and the other PAX member grabbed her by the arms and dragged her down the aisle toward Graham and his cabinet. She screamed, "No! Please, no. No. NO!" Dan yelled, "We're going to execute you. It's the law! It's the law! It's the law!"

When they had dragged the hooded woman to the front row Bob Gross jumped out of his first-row-center seat. Dan shoved her into the seat and tied her down with imaginary straps. The other PAX member threw an imaginary switch and she convulsed in her chair. Three times he hit the switch. Three times she quivered and arched her body as the imaginary killing charge coursed through her body. She collapsed in the chair. Dan untied the straps and threw the limp body at the feet of Governor Bob Graham.

Bob Gross stepped forward, his head now covered by an executioner's hood, read the official decree of death, and threw the paper at the governor's feet, near where the apparently lifeless body lay crumpled on the floor. A profound silence hung in the room.

Governor Graham sat straight, immobile, rigid in his chair, his face betraying no emotion. He seemed determined not to let this get to him. Apparently the security guards had been ordered not to respond to acts of peaceful resistance. No one interfered with the mock execution.

Dan picked the limp body up and carried it out of the cabinet room. The other four protesters remained in our seats, placed black hoods over our heads, and extended our arms to point our index fingers at Governor Graham. We sat there silently as the cabinet meeting began, as the governor and his cabinet tried to carry on as though nothing had happened. After about fifteen minutes we all rose and left the room together.

We met back at the Florida SCJP office, jubilant that we had carried out our guerrilla theater and relieved that we weren't in the county jail where we had expected to be by this time. Gradually we came down from the emotional peak and began to focus once again on the immediate future and Bob Sullivan's legal situation.

We hoped the stay of execution would take us past the week during which the death warrant was in effect. Twenty-eight hours was all we needed.

I decided to head back to Starke. Chuck McVoy, an elder in Bruce's church offered to drive Bruce and me to Starke. I was grateful and relieved; we were both too weary to get behind the wheel of a car. We were getting ready to leave about 4:30 in the afternoon when I made one last call to the SCJP office. Jimmy Lohman answered the phone and told me that the entire Eleventh Circuit Court had declined to hear Bob's case. The stay of execution was dissolved. Bob's lawyers had been ready for this and had already filed legal papers with the U.S. Supreme Court, but no one held any hope for that appeal. We anticipated the worst.

We were on the way to Starke when the radio gave us the news: The execution was set for 10 A.M. the next day. I knew this was it; the day had come when they would kill Bob Sullivan.

We arrived at the prison, and I was cleared by security. I headed straight for the visiting room. I felt calm and desolate as I went in to visit Bob Sullivan for the last time.

Margaret Vandiver and the three priests were already in the visiting room. I greeted them and turned to Bob, pressing my open hand against the glass where he was pressing his hand. It was a cold and sterile substitute for a handshake or an embrace, but it was all we were allowed in a no-contact visit with a man who had only hours to live.

Bob was composed. He told us he had seen the mock execution on the television evening news and was pleased and grateful for that demonstration. Bob had read news accounts of the service Dan Berrigan had led at First Presbyterian Church in Tallahassee (Bruce Robertson's church). He was thankful for the people who had rallied about him in this hour of crisis.

As the six of us talked, our conversation moved to a plane that transcended talk of legal battles and executions. The conversation rose to a spiritual plane where, as Bob said it so well, "My death is a victory." Bob had made a transformation in the last twenty-four hours. He had integrated the reality of his coming execution with his genuine Christian faith so that he now saw his execution in that light. Bob kept us buoyed through the evening, joking, sharing stories, expressing his deep appreciation for what had been done for him, and for the friendships that had endured through the years.

Midway through our visit the news came that the U.S. Supreme Court had rejected Bob's appeal 7-2.

"It was expected," Bob said resignedly.

At that point one of the priests suggested that we read Psalm 62. I looked it up in the *Jerusalem Bible,* and we all followed as Father read:

> In God alone there is rest for my soul,
>   from him comes my safety;
> with him alone, for my rock, my safety,
>   my fortress, I can never fail.

> How many times will you come rushing at a man,
>   all of you, to bring him down,
> like a wall already leaning over,
>   like a rampart undermined?

> Deceit their sole intention,
>   their delight is to mislead,
> with lies on their lips they bless aloud,
>   while cursing inwardly.

> Rest in God alone, my soul!
>   He is the source of my hope;
> With him alone for my rock, my safety,
>   my fortress, I can never fail;
> rest in God, my safety, my glory,
>   the rock of my strength.

> In God I find shelter; rely on him
>   people, at all times;
> unburden your hearts to him,
>   God is a shelter for us.

> Ordinary men are only a puff of wind,
>   important men delusion;
> put both in the scales and up they go,
>   lighter than a puff of wind.
> Put no reliance on extortion,
>   no empty hopes in robbery;
> though riches may increase,
>   keep your heart detached.
> God has spoken once,
>   twice I have heard this;

it is for God to be strong,
  for you, Lord to be loving;
and you yourself repay
  man as his works deserve.

It seemed the Psalmist was talking about this situation! The only succor we had was with God. The politicians had decided to sacrifice Bob at the altar of the god of political expediency. Governor Graham was that man of "delusion" who believed that it was his choice to play God and decide who would live or die, to pretend omnipotence in the name of civic duty and political power. The Psalmist said God would "repay man as his works deserve."

As Bob Sullivan and I talked through the glass partition, I realized how much I would miss him. My eyes brimmed with tears as I fought to keep the upbeat mood he so clearly wanted to maintain.

"What do you think my epitaph should be?" he asked me.

I wasn't ready for that question.

"Bob, that is a personal decision. I wouldn't begin to advise you about it."

He nodded and we talked about other things.

A few minutes later he said, "I've got it. How does this sound? 'The cause is just.' "

I agreed it was an excellent epitaph.

The six of us huddled together as best we could against the glass partition and prayed for strength, for the grace of our Lord. Bob Sullivan prayed for those who sought his death, especially Governor Graham and Attorney General Jim Smith. We finished our prayer and sent for some food. In an informal communion we broke bread and drank soda pop and orange juice. Bob Sullivan ate with the relish of a man who enjoyed food—and who knew he would have no need of food the next day.

It was time for two of the priests and me to leave. Margaret and the other priest would remain for a contact visit with Bob. The priest would stay with Bob for the rest of the night. The others moved away so I could have a moment of private conversation with Bob before leaving.

"Bob, I haven't told anyone else this, but I regard it to be true of you. I think you are dying the death of a Christian martyr. I mean that in the sense that you have triumphed through the strength of the Spirit in circumstances designed to conquer you. You have provided a witness to all of us of the power of reconciliation. You are able to pray for Bob Graham, for Jim Smith. I know I should pray for them too, but I am too full of anger to do so. I pray for the anger to subside and the reconciling presence of the Spirit to reside with me as it does within you.

"Your witness has been a powerful one, not only to us but to many. The letters you have written to folks all over the world, the interviews you have given to newspapers and television, the presence you have shared with the other men on Death Row, it has been, and will continue to be a powerful beacon shining in this darkness surrounding us. I want to thank you for being my friend."

Bob responded, his eyes moist with tears, and as I heard his words through the speaker I wondered who was ministering to whom. His gratitude, his thanksgiving, his encouragement overwhelmed me. His final concern was that I make sure that a fellow Death Row prisoner with mental retardation, was taken care of and nurtured after Bob was killed. I agreed to see to it. We pressed our hands on the glass in a parting gesture, and I motioned for the others to rejoin us.

A guard was at the door waiting for us to leave. His grim face indicated he bore no message of glad tidings this night.

When I talked with Scharlette Holdman on the phone, she said that U.S. Supreme Court Chief Justice Burger, like Governor Graham, had chastised Bob Sullivan's lawyers for dragging out his stay on Death Row. (We saw this as trying to save Bob's life.) Burger said this caused emotional suffering for the prisoner. I was appalled. The people trying to kill Bob criticized those who fought to save his life, accused Bob's supporters of causing him unnecessary suffering.

I exploded in anger over this blatant hypocrisy. Bob had been actively involved in his own legal appeals, and he continually thanked his lawyers for their work and support. When Bob learned of these criticisms he said, "It's my ten years [on Death Row], and if anyone should be upset with the lawyers it should be me, not Graham or Burger."

At Scharlette's request Bruce and I went to Jacksonville to deliver some legal papers for a last-minute appeal to be filed in the morning. By the time we drove to Jacksonville and dropped the paper in the lawyer's mailbox it was 4 A.M. We looked for a restaurant to have breakfast.

We lingered over breakfast, watching the dawn light the sky. Our conversation meandered, exhaustion reducing us to talk that required little thought but kept us awake. After breakfast we drove back to Starke, arriving about 7 A.M.

After a shower and a short rest in the motel room we drove to the prison about 9 A.M. I made a statement to reporters and then joined the protesters for a worship service in the cow pasture across from the prison. When the service ended we all turned to face the prison and waited. It was 9:45 A.M. Bob Sullivan had about fifteen minutes to live.

A white hearse drove into the prison.

Memories of Bob swept over me. I thought of his friendship with James Hill, the prisoner Bob had asked me to look after. Hill was a twenty-five-year-old Death Row prisoner whose psychiatric evaluation showed him to have an emotional age of eleven years. His severe retardation made it difficult for him to understand his environment. Sometimes forgetting to take his medication, he had suffered several epileptic seizures, during one of which he had broken several ribs. Bob had taken Hill under his wing. He taught Hill to read and write, helped him adjust to prison life, arranged to have Hill put in the cell next to him. James looked to Bob daily for advice and help.

In our last visit the night before, Bob had told us that he had intentionally been caught with a handcuff key so that he would be sent to the punishment wing of the prison. Bob's absence forced Hill to learn to deal with life without Bob's guidance. Bob was weaning James Hill from his dependency so Hill could survive on Death Row after Bob was gone.

This was a typical action for this man the state of Florida was about to kill. Whatever happened ten years before, whether Bob Sullivan committed the crime or not, was not the central issue now. Sullivan had become a giving, caring, deeply spiritual human being with a lot to offer the world. It was cruel and insane to kill him.

Word passed quickly from the reporters that Bob Sullivan had been electrocuted. A short while later the hearse, gleaming white in the Florida sun, emerged from the prison gate. I was tired, spent. I felt numb inside.

We drove back to Tallahassee. By the time we arrived at the SCJP office everybody had gone home to collapse. I left a note on the door telling Scharlette when the memorial service would be held in Gainesville. Then I went to my friend's home.

I called my Nashville office to get messages. Several reporters had asked me to call. I returned those calls and then went to bed.

November 30, 1983, had come and gone. The state of Florida had killed Bob Sullivan. There was little to say or do but simply rest and endure.

— ▼ —

(After John Spenkelink's execution May 25, 1979, allegations of brutal treatment of him by guards were made. The resultant investigation commissioned by Governor Graham determined the importance of the presence of a "free world" person with the condemned in the last hours of life. Thus an official "independent observer" was present with Bob Sullivan from 7:02 A.M. until the witnesses viewed Sullivan strapped in the electric chair at 10:00 A.M. The following is the account of the final three hours of Bob Sullivan's life by the independent observer).

On November 30, 1983, at 7:02 A.M., I arrived at the Death Row cell containing Mr. Sullivan. His priest was present and the two were conversing quietly. They then embraced each other through the cell bars and the priest left in tears.

I sat down in a chair positioned directly in front of the cell with a clear view of Mr. Sullivan, and began taking notes.

Mr. Sullivan was wearing white sneakers, undershirt, and shorts. A television was set upon a chair just outside the cell bars and he began to watch morning news shows. Continuous stories were broadcast reporting the imminent execution. A discussion with the Bishop of St. Augustine was a reported story.

I spoke with Mr. Sullivan, informing him that my function was a "neutral, third-party observer who was here to make sure they don't do something before they do what they're going to do." It was further related to him that I would not witness the execution.

I asked Mr. Sullivan if he had prepared a statement, offering to help him draft one or if I could write or phone anyone for him. His reply: "No, thanks, everything's taken care of." My limited conversations and observations of him revealed a defined sophistication in voice, words, and relationship with others. He displayed strength and composure.

At 8:00 A.M., the guard sitting across the table prepared to leave, said good-bye to Mr. Sullivan and the two shook hands. Mr.

Sullivan began to cry at the guard's farewell. Another guard came over to the cell bars to talk and joke with Mr. Sullivan. The guard asked in a friendly manner whether Mr. Sullivan had given up hope for a reprieve. Mr. Sullivan, in response, said that he did not expect any stay, that "there was no other court to go to." The same guard asked me if I were the "neutral observer" to which I responded "absolutely." The guard turned again to Mr. Sullivan, apparently to joke with him, but Mr. Sullivan retorted, "Please, no jokes today." The guard said okay and departed.

Mr. Sullivan informed me that the sheets covering the windows had been installed around 4:30 A.M. on that day.

The time was 8:10 A.M and the NBC *Today Show* was airing. At 8:12 A.M., Mr. Sullivan turned the television to another channel.

At 8:30 A.M. a television story on Mr. Sullivan's execution was broadcast. The Clearinghouse had filed a Petition for Extraordinary Relief with the Florida Supreme Court alleging that the death penalty was "cruel and unusual punishment." The report stated that the filing of the petition appeared to be a gesture only, with no expectation of success.

Another television news story on the execution was broadcast, reporting Chief Justice Burger's opinion that ten years of appeals was "worse cruel and unusual punishment" than the death penalty itself.

Four prison guards in white shirts arrived. Guard Barton approached Mr. Sullivan's cell and told him what was going to happen. The television was turned off, unplugged, and removed. Mr. Sullivan was told that his hair would be cut, he would shower and dress, that he would be taken to the "chamber" four minutes before 10:00 A.M., he would be "strapped in" and then given a chance for a "statement."

Mr. Sullivan was then handcuffed with his hands in front of him. The cell door was unlocked and opened and he was led out and seated in a folding chair outside the cell.

A briefcase was opened revealing shaving material. Mr. Sullivan sat quietly while his head was shaved, appearing resigned, almost embarrassed by the proceeding. An electric barber's hair cutter is used.

Mr. Sullivan's head was then shaved with a Norelco electric shaver. He requested his bottle of Maalox from the cardboard box, took a drink of the medication, and said "thank you" as he handed the bottle back to the guard.

8:55 A.M.

He was asked by the guard shaving him if he wanted his "whiskers cut too." He hesitated for a second and replied, "Naw, that's not necessary." His head was then shaved a third time with shaving cream and a Bic razor.

Silence pervaded the area except for the sound of birds from outside.

The electric barber's hair cutter was then used to remove the hair from his right leg. His attitude was cooperative, offering neither resistance nor words. He moved his right leg to allow the guard to remove the hair from behind his leg. The right leg was then shaved with shaving cream and the Bic razor. The electric extension cord previously used for the television and then the electric razor was removed and the hair swept away.

Signs of vomit on the toilet of the second cell (next to the cell previously holding Mr. Sullivan) were observed.

9:08 A.M.

Mr. Sullivan removed his clothing and was locked in the cell containing a shower. The guards took out of a brown bag a new Hanes t-shirt and boxer shorts. A new white short-sleeved dress shirt was also removed from the bag. A new dark blue suit was brought in, along with a new striped tie and dark blue socks.

I noted a mimeographed document in the possession of the guard-in-charge entitled, "Execution Day." One of the guards put on a white hand glove.

Mr. Sullivan completed his shower and was handed the boxer shorts to put on—no t-shirt was used. He was returned to the original cell, locked in, and was handed the dress shirt to put on with the instructions to leave the top two buttons unbuttoned. The guard instructed him to put on the dark blue pants and roll up the right leg. Mr. Sullivan put on the dress shirt, socks, and pants, and rolled up the right pants leg.

Superintendent Duggar arrived on the cell block and asked the guards to leave—they proceeded past the shower area to the other end of the block. Two plastic glasses filled with ice were brought to the cell by the superintendent. He entered the cell, poured a shot of Scotch from a half-pint into each glass, added water, and handed one glass to Mr. Sullivan. The phone (located at the entrance to the cell block) rang and the superintendent left the cell and took the call.

He returned soon thereafter and he and Mr. Sullivan sat on the cell bed, drank, and talked. Mr. Sullivan expressed his thanks to the superintendent for the "courtesies over the last couple of days." The superintendent then told Mr. Sullivan that people from "all over" had called, even a call from England. The superintendent then left the cell to talk with the guards by the entrance area and retrieve some more ice for the glasses. He returned to the cell and resumed his conversation with Mr. Sullivan.

9:36 A.M.

Mr. Sullivan and the superintendent were still talking. The phone rang again and the superintendent talked briefly with guard Barton. I peered through the sheets hung over the windows and observed approximately fifty people outside the prison grounds. A larger cardboard box near the shower area was observed containing news magazines (*Time, U.S. News and World Report, National Geographic,* and *Esquire*) addressed to Mr. Sullivan. He was overheard talking with the superintendent and occasionally sobbing.

The phone rang again and the superintendent left the cell to take the call.

Mr. Sullivan asked a guard for a tissue, but then stood up from the cell bed and blew his nose on some toilet paper.

The superintendent returned to the cell and mixed another drink for Mr. Sullivan; more ice was brought in from a small igloo cooler. Mr. Sullivan asked for more water in his drink.

Mr. Sullivan and the superintendent sat talking quietly. The superintendent asked Mr. Sullivan if he wanted him to read his "statement." The response was inaudible except for Mr. Sullivan's words, "fair enough."

Mr. Sullivan: "They're making murderers out of you people. Please, tell them, for both sides."

Superintendent: "We're not political entities."

Mr. Sullivan: "No one benefits. The only one who benefits is Bob Graham and Jim Smith."

Then they agreed not to argue.

Superintendent: "I agree that you are way down on my list of who should be executed."

9:50 A.M.

The superintendent left. The guards entered the cell and the guard who had previously put on a white glove applied a gel (Electro-Creme) to Mr. Sullivan's head and right leg. Mr. Sullivan shook hands with guard Jewett.

9:53:42 A.M.

Mr. Sullivan asked me to come into the cell and take a statement from him. I entered the cell and sat down so close to him that he startled and then moved over a bit. He said he didn't remember my name and didn't know how neutral I was, whereupon, I assured him that I was. He began to dictate the following three-part statement:

"1. The whole thing is insanity on all involved—an insane situation.

"2. I steadfastly maintain my innocence.

"3. [notes not clear] of what I personally consider a barbaric ritual which dehumanizes the victim and correctional officers who must do it. That despite all I have said, I have not [emphasized *not*] been dehumanized beyond those limits. [The superintendent told him he had to go, but he continued.] The staff has been both respectful of me and those people who have come to see me [the superintendent told him again that it was time to go, to which he responded: 'I'm not trying to filibuster this thing, just let me finish my statement,' and continued] and I want that clearly noted on the record because I do not [emphasized *not*] want anything after the fact such as what happened after Spenkelink's execution."

As he was led out of the cell by the guards, he asked, "Is it possible without the [hand] cuffs?" He was led by the guards, one on each side of him, each with a single handcuff attached to each hand, through the door on the right, and back down a short hallway (twice the depth of his cell) through a door and into the room holding the electric chair. I was behind him as he was whisked down the hallway. As he entered the room, I heard him exclaim: "I'm sorry it has to be this way!"

I stood in the doorway to the room and saw Mr. Sullivan seated in the chair. I looked up and observed the witnesses to the execution with their eyes fastened on Mr. Sullivan. The door was closed and through a window, I observed Mr. Sullivan being strapped into the device.

10:01 A.M.

I left the door, walked back down the hallway and returned to the cell where Mr. Sullivan had been. I looked out a window in the guard area, onto the perpendicular wing of Death Row, and noted that the windows had been wrapped in black cloth strippings.

J. Thomas Wright

A statement made by Robert A. Sullivan on November 22, 1983:

I firmly believe that I have been selected as a sacrificial lamb by the officials of the state of Florida NOT for what I have been accused of doing, but instead because I am the antithesis of the type of person who has traditionally been the victim of capital punishment, especially in the South. Because I am white, attended college, and had considerable support including much by the Catholic Bishops of Florida and Massachusetts, [Governor] Graham and [Attorney General] Smith decided to come after me. If they succeed, Graham and Smith can say that we are not reserving the death penalty exclusively for the uneducated, or minorities, or the friendless.

Governor Bob Graham's words in announcing that the execution had taken place were, "God save us all."

Bob Sullivan's last words before being executed were, "May God bless us all."

DEATH WARRANT
STATE OF FLORIDA

WHEREAS, ROBERT A. SULLIVAN, did on the 9th day of April, 1973, in Dade County, Florida, murder Donald Schmidt; and

WHEREAS, ROBERT A. SULLIVAN was found guilty of murder in the first degree and was sentenced to death on the 12th day of November, 1973; and

WHEREAS, on the 27th day of November, 1974, the Florida Supreme Court upheld the sentence of death imposed upon ROBERT A. SULLIVAN and Certiorari to the United States Supreme Court was denied on the 6th day of July, 1976; and

WHEREAS, it has been determined that Executive Clemency, as authorized by Article IV, Section 8(a), Florida Constitution, is not appropriate; and

WHEREAS, attached hereto is a copy of the record pursuant to Section 922.09, Florida Statutes;

NOW, THEREFORE, I, BOB GRAHAM, as Governor of the State of Florida and pursuant to the authority and responsibility vested by the Constitution and Laws of Florida do hereby issue this warrant directing the Superintendent of the Florida State Prison to cause the sentence of death to be executed upon ROBERT A. SULLIVAN on some day of the week beginning noon, Wednesday, the 23rd day of November, 1983, and ending noon, Wednesday, the 30th day of November, 1983, in accord with the provisions of the laws of the State of Florida.

IN TESTIMONY WHEREOF, I have hereunto set my hand and caused the Great Seal of the State of Florida to be affixed at Tallahassee, the Capitol, this _2nd_ day of November, 1983.

GOVERNOR

ATTEST:

SECRETARY OF STATE

CERTIFICATE OF DEATH
FLORIDA

LOCAL FILE NO. 135   STATE FILE NO.

DECEDENT

DECEDENT—NAME FIRST	MIDDLE	LAST	SEX	DATE OF DEATH (Mo., Day, Yr.)
Robert	Austin	Sullivan	Male	Nov. 30, 1983

RACE	AGE—Last Birthday	UNDER 1 YEAR MOS DAYS	UNDER 1 DAY HOURS MINS	DATE OF BIRTH (Mo., Day, Yr.)	COUNTY OF DEATH
White	36			July 20, 1947	Bradford

CITY, TOWN OR LOCATION OF DEATH	HOSPITAL OR OTHER INSTITUTION—Name (If not in either, give street and number)	IF HOSP OR INST (Specify D OP/Emer Rm., Inpatient) Spec
Starke	Florida State Prison	Death House

STATE OF BIRTH	CITIZEN OF WHAT COUNTRY	MARRIED, NEVER MARRIED, WIDOWED, DIVORCED (Specify)	SURVIVING SPOUSE (If wife, give maiden name)
Massachusetts	U.S.A.	Never Married	None

SOCIAL SECURITY NUMBER	USUAL OCCUPATION (Give kind of work done during most of working life, even if retired)	KIND OF BUSINESS OR INDUSTRY
029-24-0977	Food Service	Restaurant

USUAL RESIDENCE WHERE DECEASED LIVED. IF DEATH OCCURRED IN INSTITUTION, GIVE RESIDENCE BEFORE ADMISSION

RESIDENCE—STATE	COUNTY	CITY, TOWN OR LOCATION	STREET AND NUMBER	INSIDE CITY LIMITS (Specify Yes or No)
Florida	Bradford	Starke	P.O. Box 747	No

PARENTS

FATHER—NAME FIRST	MIDDLE	LAST	MOTHER—MAIDEN NAME FIRST	MIDDLE	LAST
Daniel	J.	Sullivan	Flynn	Stella	Sullivan

INFORMANT—NAME (Type or Print)	MAILING ADDRESS	STATE
Paul C. Decker	P.O. Box 747, Starke, Fl. 32091	

DISPOSITION

BURIAL, CREMATION, REMOVAL, OTHER (Specify)	CEMETERY OR CREMATORY—NAME	LOCATION CITY OR TOWN STATE
Cremation	Colonial Crematory	Gainesville, Fl.

FUNERAL DIRECTOR (Signature)	FUNERAL HOME	ADDRESS
Phillip Steven Futch	Jones Funeral Home, Drawer H, Starke, Florida 32091

CERTIFIER

To the best of my knowledge, death occurred at the time, date and place and due to the cause(s) stated.

(Signature and Title)	(Signature and Title)
	Chas. F. Hamilton M.E.

DATE SIGNED (Mo., Day, Yr.)	HOUR OF DEATH	DATE SIGNED (Mo., Day, Yr.)	HOUR OF DEATH
	M	12-1-83	10:11 A. M

NAME OF ATTENDING PHYSICIAN IF OTHER THAN CERTIFIER (Type or print)	PRONOUNCED DEAD (Mo., Day, Yr.)	PRONOUNCED DEAD (Hour)
	11-30-83	AT 10:16 A. M

NAME AND ADDRESS OF CERTIFIER (PHYSICIAN, MEDICAL EXAMINER) (Type or print) 815 S.W. 4th Avenue, Suite #2 32601
William F. Hamilton, M.D. Office Of The Medical Examiner, Gainesville, Florida

REGISTRAR (Signature)	DATE RECEIVED BY REGISTRAR (Mo., Day, Yr.)
Ernest A. Hays	December 8, 1983

CAUSE OF DEATH

CONDITIONS IF ANY WHICH GAVE RISE TO IMMEDIATE CAUSE (a) STATING THE UNDERLYING CAUSE LAST

IMMEDIATE CAUSE PART (a)	Electrocution.	Immediate
DUE TO, OR AS A CONSEQUENCE OF: (b)		Interval between onset and death
DUE TO, OR AS A CONSEQUENCE OF: (c)		Interval between onset and death

PART II OTHER SIGNIFICANT CONDITIONS—Conditions contributing to death but not related to cause given in PART I (a)	AUTOPSY (Specify Yes or No)	WAS CASE REFERRED TO MEDICAL EXAMINER (Specify Yes or No)
	Yes	Yes

(Probably) ACCIDENT, SUICIDE or HOMICIDE or UNDETERMINED (Specify)	DATE OF INJURY (Mo., Day, Yr.)	HOUR OF INJURY	DESCRIBE HOW INJURY OCCURRED
Homicide	11-30-83	10:11 A.	Put to death in compliance with legal sentence.

INJURY AT WORK (Spec. Yes or No)	PLACE OF INJURY—At home, farm, street, factory, office building, etc. (Specify)	LOCATION STREET OR R.F.D. No.	CITY OR TOWN	STA
No	Prison Death House	Florida State Prison, Starke, Florida		

I CERTIFY THAT THIS IS A TRUE AND CORRECT COPY OF THE ORIGINAL RECORD ON FILE IN THIS HEALTH DEPARTMENT.

REGISTRAR

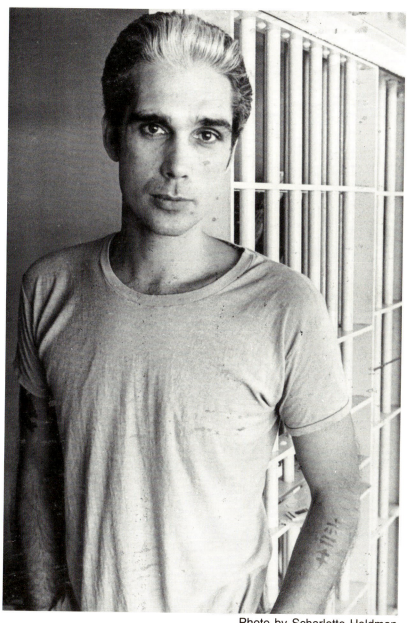

Photo by Scharlette Holdman

John Spenkelink

Photo by Doug Magee

Jimmy Lee Gray

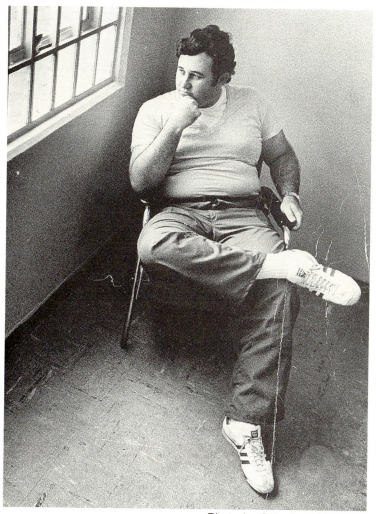

Photo by Scharlette Holdman

Robert Sullivan

David Washington

Photo by Doug Magee

Robert Wayne Williams

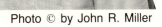

Photo © by John R. Miller

Tim Baldwin

Photo courtesy of Michelle McIntosh

Velma Barfield

Photo by Elin Schoen

James Adams

Photo by Joe Ingle

Photo © by Available Light Photography

Jimmy Lohman, Willie Lawrence Adams, and Rose Williams at a vigil for James Adams at the Florida State Capitol.

Willie Darden

Photo by Scharlette Holdman

Morris Mason

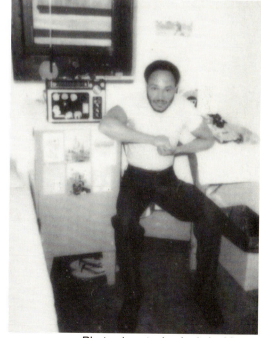

Photo given to Joe Ingle by Mason
on the day of his execution

Photo by Scharlette Holdman

The Florida Death Chamber

CHAPTER EIGHT

ROBERT WAYNE WILLIAMS
Louisiana
December 14, 1983

As I drove through a black neighborhood in Baton Rouge, Louisiana, in the spring of 1982, I was searching for the house of Rose Williams. When I found the house and knocked on the door, Rose Williams opened it. I introduced myself. Rose's clear eyes and unlined ebony face gave her the appearance of a woman considerably younger than her fifty-three years. She smiled, extended her hand in greeting, and invited me in.

Rose Williams insisted I partake of some tea cakes her mother had prepared in expectation of my visit. She disappeared into the kitchen. In her absence I surveyed the room.

I saw a beautiful photograph above the couch. The expression in the picture was serious, and the brown eyes had a searching quality. The face was clean-shaven and tranquil. I recognized Robert Wayne Williams, the son of the woman I was visiting.

Directly across from me was another, smaller picture of Robert Wayne Williams. A smile lighted his face; this photograph included the moustache and goatee, the familiar look I knew well. The picture was inserted into a burnt-tip wooden-match folder, which I assumed Robert Wayne had handcrafted and given to his mother. Adjoining the picture was a small mirror framed by the match-stick picture foldout. The carefully constructed folder was a familiar sight since many prisoners used the wooden matches for various hobby crafts. I noted that the picture folder must be several years old since matches were no longer allowed by the warden of the Louisiana State Prison to the men on Death Row for their hobbies.

In my ten years of work throughout the South for criminal justice reform, I had met with countless families of prisoners. Almost every family was poor and hardworking, as was Rose Williams. She worked the night shift as a nurse's aide in a local hospital, and often went a week or more without a day off. Yet as she entered the living room with the tea cakes and coffee, I felt serenity exuding from her. My colleagues in the Louisiana office of the Southern Coalition on Jails and Prisons had spoken of her admiringly—in almost reverential tones. As we conversed about her son, Robert Wayne, I was immediately impressed by her concern for all of his fellow prisoners on Death Row at Angola, home of the Louisiana State Prison. She was a caring and humble person with a deep sense of God calling her. She was an ordained lay minister in the Church of God. I had the distinct notion that this woman was going to do all in her power for her son and everyone else on Death Row in Louisiana.

We talked into mid-morning and I knew Rose must be exhausted from the previous night's work at the hospital. I got ready to leave for the prison to visit her son, as well as others on Death Row at Angola. She asked if we could close our meeting with a prayer. I nodded affirmatively.

The prayer Rose Williams uttered was not for herself or her son. Rather, it was for me and my ministry to Death Row inmates in Louisiana and throughout the South. I felt a sense of genuine grace, and my soul was comforted by her. As we held hands during the prayer, I knew the power of a woman who had been touched by God. As we neared the completion of the prayer, I offered a prayer for Robert Wayne and his mother, as well as others on Death Row at Angola. We uttered an "Amen" and I left to drive the back roads to the Louisiana State Penitentiary.

I came to know Robert Wayne Williams through his friend Tim Baldwin, whom I befriended during his near execution in the spring of 1982. Tim spoke warmly of Robert Wayne, and I began to include him on my visiting list. Robert Wayne Williams was in many ways a counterpoint to Tim Baldwin. Baldwin was white and Robert Wayne black. Baldwin was an older convict, almost forty-two, and Williams was only twenty-seven when he came to the "Row." Yet they shared a fierce independence and a concern for everyone on Death Row.

One of Tim's, Robert Wayne's, and my joint projects was putting together a lawsuit over the barbaric conditions on Death Row. Such basic amenities as electric lights in the cells were denied Death Row prisoners. We chose this course after my overtures to the warden were flatly rejected and conditions remained intolerable.

After Baldwin and Williams prepared their legal complaint, I shared it with various lawyers. Unfortunately, I could find no one to pursue the case.

Robert Wayne Williams had been involved in a robbery of a drug store in Baton Rouge. He had a gun. The security guard, Willie Kelly, was killed. Williams was on drugs at the time and was not in command of himself. Williams's was one of the common crimes that result in someone receiving the death penalty: a robbery-murder while under the influence of a drug.

"Slim," as Williams was nicknamed by prisoners on the Row, delighted in the visits of his family on the weekends. His face creased into a big smile whenever he discussed his three daughters and son who visited him often. The children scampered about the visiting room while Robert Wayne visited with other members of his family through the wire-mesh screen separating them.

As the summer of 1983 progressed, Robert Wayne Williams was an example of the difference a good lawyer could make. He was defended by the director of Southern Prisoners' Defense Committee with a New Orleans lawyer assisting on his appeal.

Although Williams's petition was denied by the U.S. Supreme Court in July 1983, quick work by his lawyer prevented a new execution date from being set until the Court decided on the rehearing petition and the mandate was issued. Even with able representation, I feared for Williams. I believed the Supreme Court's decisions in July 1983 hastened the time when he would be killed. I had no illusions for Robert Wayne Williams through clemency since the incumbent Republican governor, David Treen, was running for reelection. I knew Robert Wayne would be a pawn in a political game and that his life would be forfeited when placed against political ambition.

After the U.S. Supreme Court denied a rehearing, the trial court judge set Williams's execution date for October 26. This was three days after the gubernatorial election and before the inauguration, so no matter who won, Governor Treen would make any clemency decision. Although Robert Wayne had lost by a 4-3 vote in the Louisiana Supreme Court and 6-5 in the Fifth Circuit Court of Appeals, the substantial dissents indicated the strength of his case. Yet I was worried that after the Supreme Court's *Barefoot* decision over the summer, successor habeas corpus petitions such as Robert Wayne's might not be well received.

I stayed in touch with Robert Wayne and his mother, Rose, throughout the month, then journeyed to Baton Rouge on Saturday, October 22, to be with them. After settling in with friends in Baton Rouge, I arranged to visit Rose Williams the next evening.

On Sunday Rose had an extended visit at the prison, so by the time she made the forty-five-minute trek back to Baton Rouge it was evening. I arranged to see her after she had eaten supper.

Rose and I conversed about the impending execution and determined that she needed to go see Governor Treen. We decided to simply drive over to the governor's mansion and ring his doorbell. As we bundled up for protection against the chilly night, I gazed about the small house at the family who had come together at this hour. Before we left, Sister Mary, an ordained minister in the Church of God with Rose, asked if she could pray. We consented and soon a small circle gathered about Sister Mary as we bowed our heads.

As a North Carolinian, I had heard some prayers in my time. Yet the fervent, eloquent focus of Sister Mary overpowered me. All my worries disappeared as her words caressed my soul. When Sister Mary finished, I was calm and prepared for any eventuality. As I glanced at each face in our prayer circle, I could see everyone had been moved by the prayer. I thanked God for the blessing of being with such good people.

Rose, two of her children and their spouses, and I set off to meet Reverend Pitcher. He had volunteered to accompany us to the governor's mansion, and we drove to the New Prospect Missionary Baptist Church to meet him at the conclusion of his Sunday evening services. Rose went in to get him but returned in a few minutes. "They're still going on. They are getting ready to have communion, and I think I'll join them."

I wanted to go with her. We walked into the church together and took a seat in a pew.

I must have seemed out of place to the members of the congregation. I was the only white person in the building, but I was clearly welcomed as a brother in the faith. We sang a hymn, witnessed a baptism, and partook of communion. As I listened to the joyful singing, observed the warmhearted fellowship, and shook hands with members of the church at the conclusion of the service, I was grateful that I had joined Rose rather than waiting in the car with the others. The Spirit was moving on this night in Baton Rouge, and I felt greatly comforted despite the impending reality of Robert Wayne's killing.

Reverend Pitcher joined us and we drove to the governor's mansion. It was a beautiful, white-columned building. A camera peeked down at us from the porch roof as we rang the bell.

A young man with a holstered .38 caliber handgun opened the door. I introduced the group. "I'm the Reverend Joe Ingle, and this is Robert Wayne Williams's family along with Reverend Pitcher. This is Rose Williams, Robert Wayne's mother. We would like to see Governor Treen to talk about Robert Wayne's situation."

The young man replied, "You have a stay of execution. It came at 7:23 tonight."

I was too surprised to be anything but matter of fact. "Do you have any details?" I inquired.

"No. The Fifth Circuit Court of Appeals gave the stay."

I thanked him, and we walked back to the car.

I cautioned the family about becoming too excited until we had a chance to talk to the lawyers. We drove back to the house amid building excitement.

Robert Wayne's grandmother met us at the door.

"It's hallelujah time! It's hallelujah time!" She clapped her hands together, rocking back and forth in her chair. A big smile creased her lined face and happiness radiated from within her. As the children, teenagers, adults, all mingled, hugged, smiled, and gave thanks, it truly was hallelujah time.

Robert Wayne received the news of the stay of execution about one hour after he had been moved to the death house. He called us, and for the next forty-five minutes one family member after another went to the phone to speak with him.

I caught the bus to New Orleans the next morning. A colleague who worked in the Southern Coalition on Jails and Prisons New Orleans office met me at the station, and we drove to the Fifth Circuit Court of Appeals to pick up a copy of the *Williams* decision. Reading it, I saw clearly the stay of execution was a temporary situation. The Fifth

Circuit had denied all the legal issues but concluded in a final paragraph that since the appeals did have a substantial basis, and the U.S. Supreme Court had not clearly delineated the parameters of some of the issues, a stay of execution was granted. Robert Wayne's counsel could appeal the decision to the entire Fifth Circuit, which would carry the legal process well into the next year. When I returned to Nashville, I wrote Robert Wayne a note expressing my relief, although the long range picture did not look promising.

On November 7 the U.S. Supreme Court vacated the stay of execution and took the highly unusual step of reaching into the Fifth Circuit, where the *Williams* case was under consideration, and denying all the claims. This meant the trial court could move immediately to set a new execution date for Robert Wayne. Clearly, a majority of the Supreme Court wanted to get on with executions and Robert Wayne Williams was the first person they could use to send that message to the federal judges throughout the land.

I discussed the situation with Robert Wayne's lawyer over the phone. Our only hope remained in mounting another clemency effort. I decided to call a friend from Prison Fellowship, who was also an acquaintance of Governor Treen. There was also a prominent New Orleans lawyer I knew who might have some connection to Governor Treen. Both were long shots, and I was not optimistic about Robert Wayne's future.

The morning of November 9 brought the announcement that Governor Graham of Florida had signed Bob Sullivan's death warrant for execution on November 29. Governor Graham had taken the U.S. Supreme Court's actions in *Williams* as a sign to move forward. I wrote a long letter to Bob Sullivan, and began calling people in the Catholic community to discuss how we might make the best possible witness against what now seemed imminent.

A week later I learned that Robert Wayne was scheduled to die on December 14. Events were picking up speed; if Bob Sullivan and Robert Wayne Williams were killed by the state, it would bring the total to four for the year. It would be the highest number of people executed in one year since 1976. Each of the four would become mere statistics in news stories on the return of the death penalty in America. The words of the forty-fourth Psalm welled within me: "We are being massacred all day long, treated as sheep to be slaughtered."

Many people were active in the effort to stop Robert Wayne Williams's execution. Unlike Bob Sullivan, Robert Wayne had a supportive family who would be with him through the ordeal. My role was simply to be with the family. I arrived in New Orleans on Monday, December 12. The execution was set for shortly after midnight in the early morning hours of December 14. I disembarked from the plane and hitched a ride with some reporters going to Baton Rouge.

The clemency board had voted against Williams 3-2. The decision, the latest in a series of one-vote margins, sealed Robert Wayne Williams's fate. A young black man tried before an all white jury in Baton Rouge, a man without a prior felony conviction, a man with a court appointed lawyer, and a man with a serious drug dependency at the time of the robbery was going to be the first person killed by the state of Louisiana in its electric chair since 1961. In Louisiana, which billed itself as the "Dream State," the dream was now a nightmare for the Williams family.

I visited with Rose Williams on the evening of the twelfth. She and other family members had visited with her son most of the day. He was in good spirits despite the gravity of his situation. Clearly everyone in the family leaned on Rose for support. Her quiet strength radiated forth to all.

Rose and I went to the home of the leader of the local Amnesty International group who had spent an hour with Governor Treen earlier in the day. As I listened to him recount the meeting, I had to hold my cynicism in check. He felt the governor was really wrestling with the case, especially with the defense Robert Wayne Williams received at his trial. I had been down this road too many times before to set any store by a governor who indicated his concern. I had met with Governor Graham in Florida, corresponded with Governor Winter in Mississippi, tried to move Governor Clement in Texas, and now I saw the same situation developing through the "concern" of Governor Treen of Louisiana. In each situation, the political decision was made, overriding the moral/religious dimension of the state's taking a human life.

I had arranged to call Rose early Tuesday morning, and did so. She really wanted someone to try to find a member of the victim's family, to see if one of them would make a public statement on Robert Wayne's behalf. Since the victim's son had asked for the death penalty at the clemency hearing, I had little hope of changing his mind. But I promised Rose I would try.

After spending the entire day unsuccessfully searching for the victim's family, I headed back to the home of the Amnesty International leader. I was anxious to discover if Governor Treen had issued a statement regarding Robert's case. And I was impatient from my frustrating and unsuccessful day of trying to locate the victim's family.

When I arrived at the house, I was informed that the governor had issued his statement regarding clemency for Robert Wayne Williams. He stated he would not intervene, and did the usual public posturing about review in the courts being fair and complete. He indicated it was not his prerogative to overturn the court's decision, and closed with what was becoming a routine and nauseating exercise of Southern governors: invoking the will of God to support such action.

The governor's statement infuriated me. He knew as well as I that he could intervene and that he had authority to do so. And the closing remarks about "The Invisible One" who would judge us all sent me over the boiling point in anger. In no way, shape, or form could I discern God's action in this unmitigated evil event of state-sanctioned murder. To invoke God's blessing for this action was the epitome of hypocrisy and duplicity.

I was already at the Williams's house when the members of Robert Wayne's family returned from their last visit with him. Eventually Rose Williams entered in the company of her children and mother. She looked worn and weary but still had a determined expression on her face. She had just seen her son for the final time.

We talked briefly about Robert Wayne. He had spent his last hours ministering to his family. He encouraged them not to be burdened by his killing. He had special words for each one, trying to speak to their pain and sorrow. His words were a precious gift to those with him, a gift no one would be able to take away.

The family had decided to participate in the protest organized against the execution. Although we would be late, they were determined to join the vigil outside the governor's mansion. The worship service was over by the time we arrived, but a picket line was strung out on the sidewalk. Rose shook the hand of everyone at the vigil, thanking each person for coming out to bear witness against her son's killing. After half an hour of silent protest, a number of us journeyed to Angola for the protest there.

The family discussed whether to make a press statement and decided to do so. I was glad because I wanted the citizens of America to glimpse the strength and suffering that this family was displaying and the ordeal that they were enduring. Rose made a statement to the assembled media just outside the main entrance to Angola. One sentence lodged itself in my mind: "If God can forgive, why can't man?" The prison was illuminated by floodlights and the glare of television camera lights. At the conclusion of her statement, Rose and the other family members joined the protesters in a circle of more than fifty people. We held hands and proceeded with our planned religious service. Under the very nose of death we gave testimony to the Lord of life.

The service concluded at about 11:45 with each of us remembering Robert Wayne and sharing a story about him. It was a moving and fitting ending to the service, and it enabled us to express thanksgiving for Robert Wayne.

As we huddled in the cold with the wind whipping our scarves and coats, the unexpected news of a temporary stay of execution came. The governor had extended Robert Wayne's life for one hour so defense counsel could rush its papers to the U.S. Supreme Court for a ruling. We adjourned to the automobiles for warmth, and watched and waited.

I sat in the car with Rose, thinking, "Oh, God, be with Robert Wayne. Let him know this delay is caused by our desperate fight to keep him alive. Give him the courage for this extra hour." I had no hope that the Supreme Court would actually do anything about this case. I told Rose not to be hopeful about the stay because it was simply a last-ditch effort.

At 1:15 A.M. a minister emerged from the prison gates. He looked shaken. He had been with Robert Wayne Williams until he was killed. His presence outside meant the state had accomplished what it had set out to do—Robert Wayne was dead.

We arrived back at the Williams's home around 3:30 A.M. I was exhausted, emotionally drained, almost numb from the experience. The love and closeness the Williams family shared now burst forth in grief. Weeping and wailing echoed throughout the house, and I watched helplessly as one relative after another broke down in tears. Rose moved from person to person, going to her mother first, and then other family members. She was comforting each of them. She refused to be overpowered by her own grief. Rather, she ministered to those whose pain caused them to break down. I was astounded at her strength and her gentleness. Simply observing her renewed my strength.

The next day I returned to the Williams's house. Although it had been only a few hours since I had left, I was struck by the transformation in the mood of people as I greeted them. The family had united through Rose to endure the loss and persevere in the work against the death penalty. The abiding Christian faith at the core of this family held them together like glue.

I could sense Robert Wayne's presence in the room as his children and their cousins scampered about our feet. There was some gentle teasing and an occasional burst of laughter. The children reminded us of the simplicity and endurance of God, even in the face of the power of the state. They stood as visible examples of a determination to continue no matter what havoc was visited upon their family. The time passed swiftly amid the love of this family and soon it was time to bid Rose and her clan farewell. One of the friends of the family volunteered to take me to the bus terminal, so I hugged my friends and promised to stay in touch and to continue together in our fight against people being killed in the death chamber.

As my bus rolled through the Louisiana countryside and onto the causeway across Lake Pontchartrain, I could still hear the piercing wail of Robert Wayne's aunt shortly after he was killed:

"No more Robert Wayne! No more Robert Wayne! No more Robert Wayne!"

CHAPTER NINE

JAMES HUTCHINS
North Carolina
March 16, 1984

In the fall of 1983 James Hutchins was just another man on Death Row in North Carolina with his case pending appeal. But then North Carolina Attorney General Rufus Edmisten launched a full-court press of legal maneuvers that forced the Hutchins case in front of other cases so that Hutchins would be the first prisoner slated to be killed by lethal injection in North Carolina.

This meant that Governor Jim Hunt, who was in a bitterly fought race for the U.S. Senate with incumbent Jesse Helms, would be asked to decide clemency on James Hutchins, who had been convicted of killing three police officers. This would be more politically palatable to Hunt than ordering the death of the condemned prisoner who had been scheduled to die next: Velma Barfield, a grandmother who was slated to be the first woman to be executed in North Carolina in more than twenty years. It would also work to the advantage of Attorney General Edmisten, who hoped to succeed Jim Hunt as governor. The voters might balk at killing a grandmother (even one convicted of murder), but who would object to executing a cop-killer? Killing Hutchins first was a more pragmatic political decision.

— ▼ —

I had known James Hutchins for four years. He was on Death Row when I met him. I had found James to be confounding and charming, independent and sometimes cantankerous. He loved to talk about his hunting and fishing in the mountains.

In early 1983 James was, as he put it, "baptized by the Holy Ghost." Whatever happened to him, an extraordinary transformation took place. His stubbornness and pride seemed to disappear, and he stopped focusing on himself and turned instead to helping his fellow prisoners.

171

He became the leader of an evangelical brotherhood on North Carolina's Death Row, an unofficial lay minister serving his fellow prisoners.

The fight for James Hutchins's life raged on through the early months of 1984. Those weeks were a battle marked by complicated legal deliberations, appeals to the courts and to the public, last-minute delivery of legal papers to gain time for the next appeal, and heated confrontations with bureaucrats and politicians. Just as important, the Senate race between Governor Hunt and Senator Helms was heating up and turning nasty.

As I went to Raleigh for my March 12 meeting with Governor Hunt, I knew the situation was grim. The conventional political wisdom in Raleigh, North Carolina's capital, said that Jim Hunt would never commute the sentence of a convicted cop-killer while Hunt was running the political race of his life, not in the conservative state of North Carolina. And certainly not when running against incumbent Jesse Helms, arguably the most conservative member of the U.S. Senate. As in almost every death penalty case with which I had been involved, political ambition seemed almost certain to override mercy.

At 10:00 sharp I was ushered from the anteroom in the old state capitol into the governor's office. Governor Hunt rose to greet me. He was shorter than I had expected. He was well dressed and immaculately coiffed. Every hair on his head seemed to have been meticulously fastened in place. His detailed grooming made me uneasy. It indicated a man who was deeply concerned about appearances. Hunt's careful attention to his image didn't bode well for James Hutchins. Commuting the death sentence of a man convicted of killing police officers would not enhance a politician's public image.

But Hunt and I shared a common religious and cultural heritage. Both of us had been born in eastern North Carolina and raised Southern Presbyterians. I wanted to talk with him not on a political level, but from a religious standpoint.

Hunt and I sat down to talk.

"Governor Hunt, I would like to couch this discussion in terms of our mutual Christian faith. I am sure we would agree the crimes James Hutchins committed, although done in anger, were heinous. The question is how do we respond to someone who has committed heinous crimes. I believe we receive our guidance on such a grievous matter from the Christian gospel, and in light of the teachings of Jesus, we make our response. This is quite a different response than we may feel necessary to make as citizens, or even as chief executive. The issue before us is whether we are to take another human life, and I believe Jesus of Nazareth definitely instructs us that to do so would not be to follow his teachings.

"Second, I want to discuss James Hutchins as a person, not merely as a killer. I have known James for almost four years and I will be honest with you. Of all the people I know on Death Row in the South, James Hutchins was often the most difficult to visit. He could be irascible, ornery, stubborn, and often exasperating. Yet all of this has changed through a dramatic transformation that not only I, but his friends, family, prison guards, and the warden can attest to as having occurred. In the last year he has become the leader of an evangelical brotherhood on Death Row through his conversion to the Christian faith. In a profound sense, James Hutchins is not the same person who killed three law enforcement officers."

As I described the genuine conversion experience of James Hutchins, the governor sat forward in his chair listening to me.

"Well, Joe, I certainly appreciate what you are saying. For me the decision involves more than just the fate of an individual life. I have to be concerned with the society as a whole. As chief executive I have to determine what is best for all the people and how our laws can be used to reduce criminal activity."

I began to experience déjà vu. It seemed as though I had slipped back into Governor Graham's office in Tallahassee, Florida, in March of 1979. I was confronted with the same earnestness, the same appreciation for my work, and the same thinking that led to John Spenkelink's execution.

"Governor Hunt, I am reminded of a similar conversation I had with Bob Graham shortly after his inauguration as Governor of Florida. Governor Graham indicated he believed the death penalty was a deterrent. I understand you share that belief and your statements this morning lead me to remind you of what happened in Florida. Governor Graham signed John Spenkelink's death warrant and John was executed. According to the F.B.I. Uniform Crime Reports, the murder rate rose some 14 percent in Florida the quarter after John Spenkelink was killed. I would urge you to consider the possibility that the state's killing an individual sends out a message that killing is sanctioned by the state. Rather than a deterrent, the possibility exists that the state's killing people suggests approval of the act to some minds. I believe this understanding is just as tenable as any notion that executions are a deterrent."

The discussion proceeded for another ten minutes, but it was becoming increasingly clear to me that the governor was not going to intervene to stop the execution of James Hutchins. We ended our conversation and shook hands. I walked outside to the clearing skies of rain-soaked Raleigh. There was much to do for James Hutchins despite my feelings that Governor Hunt had already cast his die against our efforts.

James had been through a crisis in January and had come within minutes of execution. The events had annealed members of James's lawyer's office and me in a short period of time. I walked back to the office with a sense of familiarity. Now James's lawyer, Joe Cheshire, had delegated parts of the case to other members of his firm. Two of them had gone to Richmond on March 9 to argue Hutchins's case before a three-judge panel of the Fourth Circuit Court of Appeals. Although we were still awaiting a decision, the arguments had not gone well. We clearly needed to turn our attention to fashioning clemency papers for the governor.

As we worked on the clemency papers throughout the day, one of the lawyers was able to translate into legal jargon the points I felt we should make in the clemency overture. Late in the afternoon, he looked up from his typewriter and said, "You know this is hopeless, Joe."

"It probably is," I said, "and my meeting with the governor left no room for encouragement. However, it must be done. I believe in miracles, and perhaps the Lord will grant us yet another for James Hutchins."

The lawyer smiled. "I can only recall one incident in history that stands out in my mind as a clear instance of the Lord intervening. Attila the Hun was at Rome's door ready to sack it. He rode out alone to a meeting with Pope Leo I. There is no record of what transpired in that conversation, but Attila the Hun turned his army around and did not pillage Rome." He smiled, shook his head, and went back to typing.

The morning of March 14 proved to be warm and clear, a herald of spring. I spent the morning in the law office helping to put finishing touches on the clemency papers. Joe Cheshire had a 5:30 P.M. meeting scheduled with Governor Hunt, and we wanted him to personally deliver the clemency papers to the governor.

One of James's lawyers and I drove to Central Prison to visit James Hutchins. As we signed in, the guard gave us a message to contact the law office before seeing Hutchins. We walked across the lobby to the pay phone.

As the lawyer dialed the number, I stood next to her, fearful the word would be that the Fourth Circuit Court of Appeals had turned us down. "What is the word?" She nodded her head and then repeated the information for my benefit.

"They turned us down on all issues."

My heart sank. There was no recourse except a futile appeal to the U.S. Supreme Court or the equally dismal prospects of clemency. My native state of North Carolina was going to kill James Hutchins at 2:00 A.M. Friday morning.

We were quiet as we made our way into the prison to visit James Hutchins. We rode the elevator to the second floor visiting area and entered the booth where Hutchins was waiting for us, separated by a glass window and wire mesh. After exchanges of greetings, James's lawyer came to the point. "Mr. Hutchins, I had a message when we arrived at the prison to call my office. I did so. They informed me that the Fourth Circuit had called to inform us of their decision. They ruled against us on all issues."

James Hutchins's reaction was immediate. "Well, it's no use then. Stop everything. Don't go to the Supreme Court or the governor. I am tired of people saying no to me, and I won't beg anyone for my life."

For the next hour James Hutchins verbally attacked his former lawyers and his current lawyers. No words would suffice to explain the political reality of this case. As the lawyer wept next to me, my insides knotted at the suffering and pain of the two people with me. Finally, James reassured his distraught lawyer.

As James calmed down somewhat we moved the conversation away from his understandable anger and toward plans for the next day, the final day of his life. After an hour we bade James Hutchins good-bye, with a promise to see him the next day.

We returned to the law firm, where I had several messages asking me to return phone calls. The North Carolina director of the SCJP had called to report that she had found a portion of the North Carolina Administrative Code which stated the condemned person was entitled to a hearing before the parole commission. Several lawyers thought that requesting such a hearing would enable James to obtain a stay of execution. But James Hutchins no longer wished to pursue his appeals on any level. He had informed his lawyers to desist all litigation on his behalf. He had realized he was going to be killed, and he was weary of people saying no to him. A phrase he uttered during our visit echoed in my mind: "I ain't going to beg nobody and I don't want anybody to beg for me." He was a proud son of the mountains who was unwilling to face yet another denial.

I returned another telephone call and learned some rather frustrating news. The call was from the minister of Myers Park Presbyterian Church in Charlotte, who was also the first moderator of the newly merged Presbyterian Church U.S.A. This minister had been seeking an audience with Governor Hunt, an active Presbyterian layman. The minister was on his way back to North Carolina from Alaska and had altered his travel schedule to meet with Governor Hunt on Thursday afternoon.

He told me that he had called Governor Hunt's appointment secretary to confirm the meeting. The secretary informed him the governor planned to announce his decision at Thursday noon. The minister responded that he still very much wished to meet with the governor and he hoped the decision could be delayed until their meeting. The secretary then put Governor Hunt on the telephone. The minister relayed the gist of the conversation:

"Joe, he was in the similar position of Governor Winter of Mississippi last summer. We talked about deterrence and the need for upholding the law of the state. We talked for twenty minutes, and I reminded him of the denomination's statement against the death penalty and the fallacy of the deterrence argument. He concluded with his offer to meet with me tomorrow, but he didn't really see the point of it since his decision would be public by then. If you would like, I'm still willing to come."

I responded: "As much as I would like you to be here, I think the politician has once again upstaged us. Given his timing on his announcement, I am afraid he has pulled the rug from under us. Thank you for your efforts, and I appreciate your willingness to come up."

On Thursday morning I compiled a list of things we needed to take care of for James Hutchins. I met with Joe Cheshire to go over the list and to ask him to fight for all of the items. (1) A contact visit between James Hutchins and his wife. (2) No autopsy on the body since James had strong religious objections to such an examination. (3) A final communion to be served to James. (4) Trying to limit the time James was strapped to the gurney, awaiting the poisoned injection, with the saline solution running through the I.V. (5) Find a witness for the execution who could be there for James in his last minutes.

Joe Cheshire was amenable to all the suggestions and began calling immediately. He began with the warden and moved up the entire Department of Corrections chain of command. The only major problem was the contact visit. The policy decision of not allowing a condemned prisoner a final contact visit with his wife stemmed from the general rule of no contact visits at the prison, a cornerstone of correctional policy in North Carolina. After discussing the matter with the warden, the Secretary of Corrections, and the governor's legal aide, Joe wanted to bring it to the governor's attention when Governor Hunt called the law firm before the press conference to inform him of the decision on clemency. We waited in his office for the governor's call. It came shortly before 1:00 P.M.

Joe Cheshire leaned forward in his chair, his elbows on his legs, listening to Governor Hunt talk on the telephone. I heard Joe reply, "I understand your position, Governor, and I am not going to argue with you." As soon as he uttered those words, I knew all my fears were confirmed. James Hutchins, denied commutation, would die at approximately 2:00 A.M. Friday morning. He had thirteen hours to live.

Joe finished the conversation by mentioning the autopsy and the contact visit requests. The governor seemed agreeable to each request. I cynically considered our ability to obtain these little things for James Hutchins and his wife once the big issue of his life had been decided against us. Once the basic decision of killing James Hutchins was made, we were able to achieve little crumbs for James. I suddenly felt nauseated and angry.

I walked the block over to the state capitol to make Governor Hunt look at me when he made his announcement to the press. Unfortunately, he was finished by the time I arrived. I was left standing outside the door, frustrated, as press people streamed by me to report the story. My chest was constricted and I wanted to cry and scream. Instead, I walked.

The beauty of the creation was a decided contrast to the internal turmoil I was experiencing. Intellectually, I was prepared for the governor to deny James Hutchins's request for clemency. Emotionally, I was in a roiling boil at the announcement. A warm, gentle breeze caressed me as I walked back to the law office in the sunshine of the early afternoon. I couldn't help considering the loveliness of the weather at the many prior executions. It rarely rained. It seemed the Lord was trying to signify that no matter how ambitious governors continue to be, no matter how many individuals are destroyed by the evil of state-sanctioned murder, no matter how despairing I find myself on each occasion of state killing, we are supported through a strength we cannot muster for ourselves. Finally, I paused for a prayer, asking strength for James Hutchins and his wife, as well as for those of us sucked into the vortex of death.

Dr. James David Barber, a noted political author, joined me for a 3:00 press conference to discuss the failure of North Carolina to provide a clemency mechanism for James Hutchins. For over two years we had tried to establish a process for an orderly consideration of clemency, but to no avail. Governor Hunt had individuals shuttled into his office in January and March to discuss this situation. This enabled him to publicly posture that he had seen everyone who wanted to express an opinion about James Hutchins's fate. This was not true, and in the clemency papers we submitted was a list of fourteen individuals who wanted to testify to the governor, most of whom had not yet met with him. By refusing our repeated requests for an orderly process, the governor reduced us to frantically arranging last-minute appointments and making individual pleas, reducing any cumulative impact of a consideration of the extralegal matters involved in clemency. This placed us in a chaotic situation of trying to determine who had appointments, when the appointments were, and what the issues were to be discussed. At the press conference Dr. David Barber and I denounced this inadequate and ineffectual manner of dealing with clemency.

At the end of the press conference I left for my 4:00 visit with James. The lawyers had already given the press the news of clemency denial, so I was anticipating a discussion of personal and spiritual matters. I also wanted to say good-bye. This would be our final visit.

At the prison I was greeted by Kristin Paulig, a staff member of the SCJP in North Carolina and a close friend of the Hutchins family. Kristin introduced me to James's sister-in-law. She had been at the prison all day offering support to the family. Kristin indicated the booth where James was cloistered. I opened the door.

I introduced myself to James Hutchins's wife.

"Should I go while you visit?" she asked.

"No, please stay. I'll sit on the stool next to you, and we both can visit for a spell."

She smiled, and we turned to talk to James who was on the other side of the glass.

James and his wife reminisced, sharing stories with each other. As I listened to the warmth conveyed between these two people—especially James gently teasing his wife about her lack of a sense of direction when driving a car—I almost wept. The caring, the love expressed in the terms of endearment—James called his wife "mama," and she called him "daddy"—encircled me and brought me into the center of their family bond.

I recalled a statement of James's wife that I had incorporated into the clemency papers: "My family was opposed to me marrying an ex-con [Hutchins had done time for manslaughter], but I knew James Hutchins loved me and I loved him. I have these deformities [glass eye and transplanted palate in her mouth], but James took me in his arms and loved me anyway."

James's wife had a speech impediment due to her altered palate. Often the words came out slurred, difficult to understand. I noticed

James had no trouble understanding her meaning, even if the words were not clear. He saw her through the eyes of love, and I realized the power of that love as I sat and listened to them talk.

I asked James about the extensive injuries he had received through an accident while cutting wood with a chainsaw. "I thought he was going to die," his wife responded. "He couldn't eat for over two weeks. He just lay there, and I did all I could to care for him."

James showed me the faint scar on his forehead where his face had hit the chainsaw, and the deep scars on his legs from the surgery that enabled him to walk again. Then we talked about the time James cared for his wife when the hot water heater in their house blew up, scalding her severely.

The affection in their voices, the appreciation for each other in times of need, and the fun they had together when James tried to orient his wife beyond the bounds of their little mountain town were manifested in their animated conversation in which I occasionally took part.

At 4:30 James's wife stood to leave. "I'll see you tonight, Daddy. And you eat supper."

James nodded his head but said: "I don't feel like eating anything."

She gently scolded him and they compromised. Before she left the booth, she and I agreed to meet when she left the prison that night after the execution. I reminded her of our efforts to set up a contact visit.

Kristin Paulig and James's wife and family left the visiting gallery and stopped by the warden's office. When asked by the warden if she had requested a contact visit, James's wife responded that she hadn't because she didn't know that she could. She went on to request one, saying she had not held her husband's hand in four years. The visit was arranged.

My last fifteen minutes with James Hutchins were filled with small talk as each of us grasped for a way to say good-bye. Hutchins raised his gray-whiskered face raised toward me, and the clear gray eyes looked directly into mine. "Joe, I want to thank you for everything you have done for me and my family. I'd really appreciate it if you would be sure they were making it okay from time to time."

"Of course," I replied.

The door to the visiting booth opened behind me, and the guard poked his head in to say we had five minutes. James glanced down at his watch. "Be sure my wife gets the watch and wedding band, also any papers, and my Bibles."

We talked a bit about the afterlife. It was soon 4:45 and time for me to go. "Good-bye, James. I'll see all this stuff is taken care of, and thank you for being my friend."

I smiled, and James and I placed our palms together on the glass partition. It was a gesture of farewell, and as we rose, I heard James Hutchins say, "Good-bye."

I returned to the law office briefly to see how we had progressed in obtaining the five final requests we had made on behalf of James Hutchins. All but the matter of the autopsy had been granted, and we should know about that by the next day. I left the office to walk over to the vigil strung around the state capitol where the governor's office was located.

As in January when James had nearly been killed, more than one hundred people surrounded the capitol in a protest of the Hutchins execution. The event had begun at 4:30, and by the time I joined in at 5:30 it was a most impressive sight. People had come from as far west as Asheville and as far east as Wrightsville Beach. A somber, reverential mood characterized the protesters, and we stood in silence until 6:30.

We moved to the Church of the Good Shepherd, a few blocks west of the capitol. The setting sun silhouetted the downtown buildings as we walked to the church. We had a pizza supper in the church basement, then went upstairs for the worship service at 7:30.

The service at the church was quite moving. One by one people stood and announced the names of the victims of a person on Death Row, the victim's family, the person on Death Row, and the condemned's family. At the conclusion of the service, the thirty-six individuals representing the condemned of North Carolina and their victims gathered under a beautiful banner proclaiming life, beneath a rainbow of colors. They recessed from the church on a march to the prison. Two people, holding the banner high between them, led the marchers.

As the marchers disappeared into the spring night in Raleigh, I left my pew to go comfort James Hutchins's wife. She and her sister had entered after the service had begun, and I could tell she had been moved by the outpouring of concern for her family. As I approached her I sensed she needed embracing, and I opened my arms to her, pulling her to me. She wept.

I do not recall how long I stood comforting her. Her sobbing was muffled by my shoulder and by her handkerchief, which she clutched to her face. I said only what I felt: "We love you. We love you and James."

I thought of the 4:00 A.M. phone calls this woman had endured: "Is this Mrs. Hutchins? We're going to dig up your husband's body and throw it on the courthouse yard."

The harassments she and her children faced in the small mountain community where they lived were cruel. To have suffered so much abuse, not for what they had done but for being kin to James, was one of the heartbreaks of this situation. For a precious hour all of that painful past had been healed by the love and concern manifested in the worship service.

I escorted her to a back room in the church to be sure the press left the area before we brought her out. She had a 9:30 contact visit scheduled with her husband and she had decided to remain inside the prison, as near James as possible, until the execution occurred. As we sat together on two dilapidated folding chairs, the suffering she had endured poured forth in the tears that streamed down her face.

Shortly after nine, Kristin Paulig reminded us that we needed to go to the prison for the contact visit. I hugged James's wife and told her that after the execution I would meet her at the convent where she was staying. I watched them drive away toward Central Prison.

I drove to the Catholic Center where I sat, drank coffee, and made small talk with people who gathered prior to joining the vigil outside of the prison. I needed some time to relax before joining in the protest which would last until after the killing at 2:00 A.M.

I rode the bus to the prison at 11:00 P.M. and joined more than two hundred protesters on a grassy knoll that faced the prison. Many people had candles or flashlights and were signaling with the lights to the prisoners inside. The men inside signaled back through the windows with cigarette lighters or burning matches. We kept flashing signals to one another, acknowledging our concern and witness for life in an impromptu semaphore.

The spring night had become cold, and I was grateful for my winter coat. I made my way through the gathering several times, stopping to converse with friends. As I approached the top of the knoll, I saw Roger Smith making his way to join us from the street. We embraced each other for a long time, seeking to impart courage to each other in this difficult hour, and I thanked him for coming.

He explained his unexpected appearance: "My wife and I were sitting at home wondering what to do. Our fifteen-year-old son said 'We ought to go and join those folks.' He was right, so we came on down."

I scrutinized Roger's countenance to be sure he was okay. Of all the people gathered, he had represented James Hutchins for years, and it was possible he was feeling sorrow at his former client's approaching execution. As I gazed into his eyes, I saw the sorrow, but I was grateful for his presence among us. He introduced me to his wife and son, and we talked briefly as Roger went to join his brother further down the hill.

I wandered away from the crowd, wanting to be alone while James Hutchins was killed. I assumed by now he was strapped to the gurney, the saline solution pouring into his veins, waiting to become the third person to die from lethal injection in the United States.

We had no communication to the inside, so we could only surmise when the execution was completed. The official spokeswoman of the Department of Corrections appeared to address the media assembled below the prison in the visitor center. I knew James Hutchins was dead as I watched her leave the administration building and walk down the sidewalk to the press.

As the spokeswoman addressed the press, I was surprised to see James's wife and Kristin Paulig walking down the walk toward the parking lot. James Hutchins's wife was erect, holding her head high, and dabbing her eyes with a handkerchief. Fortunately, no reporters followed them, and they made it uneventfully to their car.

I stood in silence at the bottom of the hill, praying for us all. After a few minutes and some comforting hugs from friends, I left for the convent.

The Sisters of Notre Dame Convent had been extremely gracious and supportive of the Hutchins family. The sisters had welcomed them into their community and provided for their every need. As I approached the rear entrance of the convent, I felt awkward ringing a convent doorbell at almost 3:00 A.M. But I buzzed as instructed and a Sister opened the door immediately. She escorted me down the corridor to the room where James Hutchins's wife sat on the davenport, softly talking and crying.

I sat beside her and embraced her. She, her sister, Kristin, and I talked among ourselves. Although James's wife was disconsolate, her strength radiated through her sorrow. I knew that though broken-hearted, she would survive this ordeal.

As we sat in the small room, quietly sharing the pain of the evening, Mrs. Hutchins made a statement that haunted me with its familiarity. "If God can forgive James, why can't the state of North Carolina?"

I could not answer her question. It was the same question asked by Rose Williams on a cold, blustery night outside of Angola Prison in December of 1983, as the state of Louisiana executed her son: "If God can forgive, why can't man forgive?"

CHAPTER TEN

JAMES ADAMS
Florida
May 10, 1984

James Adams was born in 1932 into a poor black family near Covington, Tennessee. In the heart of a land of plenty the Adams family struggled to survive by hunting and fishing and by working the land. Despite the size of the family—fourteen children spread over eighteen years—it was a close clan. Sometimes the family had little food during the cold winter.

Willie Lawrence Adams, five years younger than James, has a vivid memory of childhood. "I would wake up some mornings before light and look down through the cracks between the floorboards. I could see the hens nestin' underneath the house. As soon as one laid an egg, I would hurry to get to it so I could eat it. We was always lookin' for somethin' to eat."

In 1962 James Adams, a thirty-year-old black man, was accused of raping a white woman. He was appointed a lawyer since he had no money to hire one himself. There was no physical evidence introduced by the state's doctor to confirm the allegation of rape. James Adams insisted he raped no one. The jury had the word of a white woman versus the word of a black man.

The jury was composed of twelve white males selected from a jury pool of five hundred white males. The "key man" system was the primary method of jury selection in nearby Dyer County. The jury commissioners simply called upon everyone they knew to be in the jury pool. Whatever citizens were needed to supplement the pool were chosen from the public utility records. Very few people who were black in Dyer County had public utilities in 1962. Although blacks represented 14.2 percent of the population of the county, none was in the jury pool when James Adams came to trial.

James Adams was paraded in shackles from the jail to the courtroom and remained chained throughout the trial. The prosecution and his own defense counsel repeatedly referred to him as "nigger." Born and raised in west Tennessee, James Adams knew what the word of a black man was worth in front of an all-white male jury on a charge of raping a white woman. Indeed, he was dispirited and remarked to his family, "I ain't gonna take it. I ain't gonna take it." When James was found guilty and given ninety-nine years in prison, his mother trailed him out of the court room, beseeching him. "Son, please take it. Don't do nothing crazy. Do the time and come home."

In 1971, after he had served almost ten years, Adams applied to Tennessee Governor Winfield Dunn for executive clemency. The Pardon and Parole Board reviewed Adams's record and found him to be an exemplary prisoner. The report hinted that the board members had some reservations about his trial as well:

> The Board finds that for the past five years, Mr. Adams's institutional record has been exemplary. It feels that due to the circumstances surrounding the crime and his conviction, as related to the Board, he has served an adequate number of years for the offense committed. The Board, therefore, recommends that his sentence be commuted to Time Served with the Special Condition that he be under the supervision of a State Probation and Parole Counselor for a period of ten years after the date of his discharge from prison. The Board further recommends that a Special Condition of this commutation be made, i.e., he is not to enter Dyer County, Tennessee, under any circumstances during his period of supervision.

But the district attorney who prosecuted Adams protested any parole or commutation, and the governor yielded to the prosecutor's objections. Adams was encouraged to reapply in one year. The Tennessee Commissioner of Corrections wrote to Adams saying that he "would be willing to speak to the governor on your behalf."

Adams maintained his exemplary prison record. With self-taught skills as a mason and carpenter he helped build a picnic area where prisoners and their families could visit. The Corrections Commissioner wrote to James Adams saying, "The attitude and quality of work has certainly been outstanding and all of us in the Department of Corrections are most pleased to see men like yourself respond in such a splendid manner."

A year later, in May of 1972, the Pardon and Parole Board once again recommended that James Adams be granted clemency. Once again the district attorney who had prosecuted Adams more than a decade before blocked the parole.

Prison officials had demonstrated their faith in Adams and their high regard for him by giving him trusty status and assigning Adams—a man convicted of rape—to work at a girls' institution, where he performed his duties without incident. James had done everything the corrections system had expected of him—had done everything he was supposed to do to earn the right to be released. Twice he had been at the point of being paroled, and twice the door to freedom had been slammed in his face by a prosecutor who seemed personally determined to keep Adams behind bars forever. James Adams had no reason to believe the prosecutor would ever yield.

In January of 1973 James Adams escaped from the Tennessee State Prison by driving off in a prison vehicle.

James made his way home to Covington to visit with his family. Law enforcement officers apparently made no attempt to locate him at home. It was as if a tacit agreement had been reached to let him go. After working near home, he worked odd jobs across the South for ten months. Then James once again encountered the law.

On November 12, 1973, Edgar Brown was discovered fatally injured in his home in Ft. Pierce, Florida. Police surmised Brown had been attacked and during the struggle received fatal head injuries from a fireplace poker.

James Adams was arrested for the murder on the basis of circumstantial evidence. His car was identified in the vicinity of the victim's house on the morning of the murder. Belongings of the victim and his family were found in the trunk of the car.

At the trial James testified he had lent his car to a friend and her male companion on the morning of the crime. The car trunk had a defective lock and could easily be opened without a key. The only prosecution witness who actually saw someone leave the house at the time of the crime talked with the person who exited the house. The witness positively stated James Adams was *not* that person. Indeed, he said that the person he conversed with was darker-skinned than James and had no moustache. He also stated he heard a woman's voice inside the house before seeing the man leave the premises.

Despite the conflicting testimony, James Adams suffered the social reality of being a black stranger charged with killing a prominent white person in a rural county in Florida. James Adams fit the recipe for the death penalty regardless of the facts surrounding the crime.

Studies conducted by Professor Samuel Gross and Robert Mauro of Stanford University demonstrate that a defendant convicted of killing a white person is eight times more likely to receive the death penalty in Florida than someone convicted of killing a person of color. If the accused perpetrator is black, an even higher factor of probability of receiving the death penalty emerged.[1]

In spite of his continued statements of innocence, and strong evidence supporting his claim, James Adams was found guilty of first-degree murder. The judge asked him if he had anything to say upon hearing the jury's verdict.

"All I would like to say is one thing," James Adams replied. "Mr. Brown's murderer is still out there. I didn't do it!" The second phase of the trial commenced with the same jury deliberating whether to give James Adams life or death. In this penalty phase of the trial, the prosecutor presented James Adams as a violent rapist convicted of a terrible assault in Tennessee. Indeed, the rape of a "white . . . married lady" and the resultant ninety-nine-year conviction and escape were presented as aggravating reasons for the jury to impose death. Not a word was mentioned about the systematic exclusion of blacks from the jury, nor of the lack of evidence to substantiate the first conviction. Nor was any mention made of James Adams's exemplary prison record in Tennessee. Rather, the jury was presented the portrait of a hardened, violent criminal. The court-appointed defense counsel presented no mitigating evidence.

The jury voted for death by electrocution. The aggravating circumstances cited by the judge in imposing the death sentence relied heavily on the Tennessee conviction and escape.

After the trial it was discovered the prosecutor had withheld the results from the state laboratory analysis of a hair sample taken from the hand of the victim. The hair sample taken from James Adams did not match it.

It is impossible to escape the conclusion that James Adams was sent to Florida's Death Row because he was a black male, poor, illiterate, and a handy victim of the white criminal justice systems of Tennessee and Florida. There was reasonable doubt about each conviction, which should have prevented incarceration on either charge. The Gross-Mauro study of racism demonstrated that if James Adams had been accused of murdering a black person in St. Lucie County, he would have been much less likely to have even been charged with first-degree murder, much less receive a death sentence.

The racism of the criminal justice system sent James Adams to the Florida State Prison and to Death Row in the spring of 1974.

The guard escorted in a well-muscled man who waited patiently as the guard switched his handcuffs from behind his back to in front at his waist. We shook hands.

"James, I'm Joe Ingle from Nashville, Tennessee. I understand you are from Tennessee too."

James smiled back at me and quietly responded, "Yes, I am."

Our time together sped by. The modest, strong, soft-spoken man across from me shared his tale of wrongful conviction in Florida and talked about his time at the Tennessee State Prison. James Adams was determined to improve himself, even under the deplorable conditions of Death Row. He was teaching himself to read and write at the age of 47. He recounted the painful process of learning to recognize each letter and then struggling to put them together. He was being aided by a pen-pal, the young daughter of his minister. The girl was also learning to read and write, and she and James provided mutual support and encouragement to each other by exchanging correspondence.

When it was time for me to move on to other visits, I said good-bye to my friend James and promised to send him some postage stamps. He said he would write to me and ask me to bear with his cursive style since he was just learning.

"No problem," I said. "Your handwriting cannot be any worse than Doug McCray's."

Doug, our mutual friend on Death Row, referred to his own scribbling as "ghetto hieroglyphics." James and I laughed and bade each other farewell.

Of the fourteen children in his family from west Tennessee, James had become only the second to read and write. He had done so under the most adverse circumstances imaginable. I was proud to call him my friend.

The months passed with correspondence and visiting. During one visit, and years after the incident had occurred, James informed me that one of the guards had tried to kill him. Although I was accustomed to the violence of prison life, this was shocking, even at the Florida State Prison. James said a guard used another prisoner, a "runner"—a prisoner who had access to the area outside the cells to run errands—to poison him by putting Drano in his food. James said he stopped eating after he became violently ill, and was carried unconscious to the medical facility for prisoners at Lake Butler.

In the spring of 1984, Richard Burr, lawyer for James Adams, filed a civil rights complaint in the Federal District Court in Tallahassee on behalf of his client. The petition described the incident of the poisoning and the event leading up to it:

> Shortly after the assignment of Mr. George Young [a prisoner] to Death Row, defendant Rex Bailes [a guard on Death Row] conspired with Mr. Young to assault Mr. Adams. Specifically, defendant Bailes said to Mr. Young about Mr. Adams: "He is giving us a hard time, you know, why don't you just straighten him out, you know." Because of similar orders from defendant Bailes on previous occasions (with respect to other prisoners) Mr. Young believed that defendant Bailes had just ordered him to kill Mr. Adams. Mr. Young agreed to do so, and thereafter put Drano crystals in Mr. Adams's food daily for approximately nine days.

The facts of the poisoning of James Adams were clear from the records of the Florida Department of Corrections. Although filed almost five years to the week after the assaultive behavior against James Adams, no statutory time limit had expired. It was simply a question of whether, for the first time in his life, James Adams would receive a modicum of justice from the criminal justice system. But Federal

District Court Judge Stafford was unlikely to grant time for an orderly presentation of the facts of the case for one very real political consideration: Governor Bob Graham signed James Adams's death warrant, affixing May 9, 1984, as an execution date. Although Richard Burr had filed the complaint on James Adams's behalf before any death warrant was signed, Judge Stafford did not set a hearing to investigate the poisoning. It was just another case on an overloaded calendar. Governor Graham's signing of the death warrant dramatically altered the status of the case. Judge Stafford set a hearing for Friday, May 4, 1984. It was clear Judge Stafford wanted to dispose of the case before the May 9 execution date so a stay of execution could not be obtained pending the outcome of the civil litigation.

Friday, May 4, was a day of travel for the family of James Adams. They journeyed by car from Tennessee to Gainesville, Florida, some thirty miles from the Florida State Prison in Starke. As the family arrived in Gainesville, Judge Stafford was denying relief in the civil suit focusing on the poisoning attempt. Later that same afternoon, Judge Gonzales also issued a denial of a stay of execution for the criminal conviction despite the presentation of evidence of the unconstitutional composition of the jury in Tennessee and the Gross-Mauro study, which indicated discrimination in the Florida death penalty law on the basis of the race of the victim.

The relatives of James Adams were staying in a hotel and with James's supporters throughout Gainesville. A small community of resistance against the death penalty had grown up since John Spenkelink's killing in 1979, and the members were generous in their hospitality and financial assistance for the Adams family. The highlight of Saturday, May 5, the day of their final visit, was James demonstrating his ability to write for the members of his family. The family was delighted that James had taught himself a skill that most of them had yet to master. Dr. Michael Radelet, a professor of sociology at the University of Florida, barbecued chicken for the entire family on Saturday evening. Throughout the unusually cool Florida evening, they visited with one another and with supporters from the community of resistance.

Monday morning found all of James Adams's family back home in Tennessee except Willie Lawrence, who had decided to stay to be with his brother. The final legal appeal was now in the Eleventh Circuit Court of Appeals, and the judges were being contacted to decide whether James Adams would live or die.

I flew to Tallahassee Monday morning to join in the Assembly of Conscience, a protest of James's execution organized by the SCJP Florida project and led by the Reverend Joseph Lowery, president of the Southern Christian Leadership Conference. Dr. Lowery was deeply concerned about James Adams's fate as a Christian brother and as a fellow black man. He led the Assembly of Conscience into the state capitol and up to the Great Seal of Florida, set in the floor down the hallway from the governor's office. Joining Lowery were Rose Williams and her family, traveling from Baton Rouge, Louisiana, to lend their presence and voices to the protest.

I was delayed in the Atlanta airport and missed the Assembly of Conscience demonstration. But at the airport I met the chairman of the National Conference of Black Lawyers, who was also flying down to join the protest at the capitol. Our plane's late departure for Tallahassee gave us time to review the record of the case. He had an appointment with Sidney McKenzie, the governor's legal counsel, and invited me to accompany him.

We arrived at the state capitol just as the Assembly of Conscience concluded and the crowd of more than one hundred was dispersing.

A special joy for me was the occasion to reunite with the Williams family who had traveled from Baton Rouge. I had not visited them since Robert Wayne Williams's execution in December, and we hugged one another and then went off to have lunch together.

As Rose Williams, her mother, Rose's son, and I shared a meal of sandwiches in a Tallahassee delicatessen, I was overcome with love and thanksgiving for them. They had driven all night for the assembly in the capitol, with Rose and Jerry taking time off from work to be there. They had come to speak and bear witness about the death penalty from a painfully personal perspective. Robert Wayne Williams's grandmother, seemingly indefatigable in her resolve not to allow her grandson to have been killed in vain, quietly spoke of their journey to Tallahassee and of the Assembly of Conscience. They also shared their attempts to involve the black people of Baton Rouge in fighting the death penalty.

We finished our lunch and carried take-out orders back to the office where Willie Lawrence Adams, James's brother who had addressed the morning gathering with a powerful prayer, and several volunteers remained working.

Arriving back in the office we learned there was yet no word on the appeal from the Eleventh Circuit Court of Appeals.

I tried to prepare for the meeting with Sidney McKenzie, since I knew all too well what to expect from past experience with Florida officials. McKenzie ushered us into his office where we were joined by Art Weidinger, another counsel to the governor, who took notes during the meeting.

For the better part of an hour the lawyer from the NCBL politely, articulately, and firmly informed McKenzie of his concerns about the execution of James Adams. He went over the Florida conviction, highlighting its dubiousness and dwelled on the evidence of the Gross-Mauro study of racism in the application of the death penalty. He was brilliant in his presentation. I watched Sid McKenzie closely for a response. The telltale mannerism McKenzie revealed was a refusal to make eye contact with the man arguing for James Adams's life for more than a few fleeting seconds. This was a clue to me that even if we walked through the door with a signed confession of someone else who admitted committing the crime for which James had been convicted, the political decision had been made to kill this particular black man: James Adams.

I voiced my concerns as a citizen of Tennessee about the 1962 rape conviction in Dyer County, Tennessee. I pointed out that without the aggravating circumstances of that conviction and subsequent escape, the prosecutor in Ft. Pierce would not have been able to portray James Adams as a dangerous, violent, escaped rapist. This portrait of a hardened criminal most certainly affected the jury's decision to impose the death penalty.

McKenzie said, "As you know, under Florida law you only need one aggravating circumstance to impose the death penalty." This technical, lawyerly point was true but not applicable in this case, because there was considerable doubt as to whether James ever committed the first crime.

"Mr. McKenzie," I said, "if you take out the rape and escape as aggravating circumstances, if you imagine an adequate defense lawyer who introduced some of the mitigating facts available rather than doing nothing, as this court-appointed lawyer did, it is quite simple to envision the jury returning a life verdict rather than death. Are you going to kill James Adams because he was poor, black, and falsely convicted of rape twenty years ago?"

After the meeting ended, the lawyer from the NCBL and I returned to the SCJP office. I needed to go to Gainesville, where I was spending the night.

Willie Lawrence Adams and I drove a rental car through the evening to Gainesville.

"Joe, what does it mean? Explain the courts to me again."

"We are waiting for the Eleventh Circuit Court of Appeals to decide," I said. "After their decision, whichever way it comes down, it will be appealed to the U.S. Supreme Court. Our best shot is in the Eleventh Circuit. The Supremes seem to be in a killing mood."

After reminiscing about his childhood in west Tennessee, exhaustion overtook Willie Lawrence. As he nodded off to sleep, I sang to myself to stay awake, and drove hard for Gainesville and the home of Michael Radelet.

Michael Radelet's brilliant research on the death penalty marked the sociologist as a rapidly rising star. We had met but didn't know each other well. I was grateful for his hospitality toward Willie Lawrence and the remainder of his family, housing Willie over the weekend, and I anticipated the comfort of a home rather than the sterility of a motel room in Starke.

Mike, Margaret Vandiver, Willie Lawrence, and I stayed up late talking. We shared memories of each of the men killed by the state of Florida since 1979—John Spenkelink, Bob Sullivan, Anthony Antone, and Arthur Goode—and we prepared ourselves for the next few days' events. The collective storytelling served to knit us together closely as we articulated the pain, the love, and the character of men now dead and our relationship to them. Soon it was 2:00 A.M., and a long day awaited us.

On Tuesday morning Willie Lawrence and I went to Mike's office and answered press inquiries. In the early afternoon, as we were being interviewed by a local television station, Margaret Vandiver burst into the room.

"We have a stay!" she exclaimed. "We have a stay from the Eleventh Circuit!"

I embraced Margaret, and Willie Lawrence wept with joy. Willie led an impromptu prayer of thanksgiving. I called Scharlette Holdman, director of the SCJP's Florida project in Tallahassee.

Scharlette said the Eleventh Circuit Court of Appeals three-judge panel voted 2-1 to grant a stay of execution for James Adams. The opinion cited the Gross-Mauro study with its evidence of racial discrimination in the administration of the Florida death penalty law. Since the Eleventh Circuit was deciding a similar issue in a Georgia case, *Spencer* v. *Georgia,* the panel decided to halt James's execution pending resolution of the *Spencer* case.

"Scharlette, do you know what this means?" I asked. "By implication all executions of blacks in Florida will hold pending the resolution of *Spencer.* If James wins, all black people on Death Row win! I know I shouldn't raise my expectations until we get by the Supreme Court, but this is wonderful!"

"I know, Joe," Scharlette said. "It is wonderful. That means Alvin will be safe [Governor Graham had set the execution of Alvin Ford for May 31], and we will at least have a month. I talked to Dr. Lowery and he is delighted, and I have a call in to James's lawyer. It's just wonderful!"

We laughed and rejoiced over the stay of execution. James Adams, despite all the power of the state of Florida, would not be killed the next day.

Evening found us enjoying the cool weather in Mike Radelet's back yard. But our initial exuberance faded and the tension had already begun to build in each of us as we awaited news from the Supreme Court. Surely the Court would uphold this stay of execution; Justice White had blocked a Georgia execution in December so the discrimination issue could be heard by the Eleventh Circuit. As we sat and talked, the mourning doves filled the air with their haunting cooing.

Margaret Vandiver agreed to drive Willie Lawrence and me to the prison for our 8:00 P.M. visit with James. James's minister would meet us inside the prison. We received word that representatives from the West Palm Beach Public Defender's Office would also be there. They were part of the legal team headed by Dick Burr which won the stay of execution for James. James's woman friend from Jacksonville would be the final member of the support group.

Willie Lawrence and I didn't get into the prison until 8:30. After security checks, we were shown into the narrow visiting room and greeted by everyone visiting James. After exchanging hugs and introductions, I sat in the chair offered me in the visiting booth and peered through the glass window that separated me from James Adams. We placed our hands on the glass in a gesture of greeting, and I gazed into my friend's smiling countenance.

"Good to see you," James said. "I'm glad you could come. How are you doing?"

The softly modulated accent came though the microphone and it seemed each word spoken was gently cradled before being released. The hours of disciplined practice as James learned to read and write had also enhanced his speech. Each word was clearly articulated and well chosen.

For four hours we took turns talking with James. The visitors got to know each other. I enjoyed getting acquainted with James's woman friend and with one of his lawyers as well as with the Presbyterian minister who had visited James for years. As the orange juice and soft drinks flowed from the prison canteen, I pushed my apprehension about the pending Supreme Court decision to the rear of my mind and enjoyed the pleasure of good friendship.

As we neared the midnight conclusion of our no-contact visit, Willie Lawrence asked James if he would like a prayer. James said he would, and we joined in a circle next to the glass partition, holding hands. As the circle reached the glass, James raised his manacled hands to the glass separating us, placing each palm down on the glass and linking up a complete circle with the hands that rested on the other side of the glass. We remained standing as Willie Lawrence dropped to his knees and began to pray.

The sing-song cadence of Willie Lawrence's prayer filled the room. The words of thanksgiving, of request for further strength, poured forth in the psalmody of prayer. King David of the Psalms would have appreciated the soaring, inspiring rhythm of this prayer, and I felt myself carried away on its wings. When we concluded with our firm "Amen," I bade James good-bye with a promise to see him the next night. I left the prison, transported on the strength of the experience of grace Willie Lawrence's prayer provided.

Margaret Vandiver had returned to drive me back to Gainesville. Willie Lawrence, the woman friend, and the minister remained with James for a contact visit. I chatted briefly with the lawyers before Margaret and I left.

The experience of the last two days, from the governor's legal counsel to my visit with James in the bowels of death inside the Florida State Prison, culminated in Willie Lawrence's prayer. I felt brimming over as we drove toward Gainesville. I expressed my feelings about the evening to Margaret.

"James was concerned about me tonight. He wanted to know if I could keep doing this, keep enduring the awfulness of friends being isolated and killed. I found myself telling him, 'James, I wouldn't want to be anyplace in the world but here tonight. I wouldn't want to do anything but be here with you.' I meant it, Margaret. No matter what happens to James, this is where I am meant to be. To what end, I don't know. But this is where I'm meant to be and whom I am meant to be with."

We arrived in Gainesville and pulled into Radelet's driveway. I was spent, ready for sleep. A suspenseful day awaited us.

On Wednesday morning I arose and showered. The smell of frying chicken greeted me as I dressed. Willie Lawrence had set up shop in the kitchen and was frying chicken and cooking vegetables for us to take to the office. Lunch promised to be a feast!

We drove to Radelet's office and talked to one another and the press as we awaited news from the Supreme Court. I was increasingly worried as the time passed. The afternoon crawled by. We wondered what was going on in the minds and hearts of the nine black-robed judges in the Supreme Court chamber in Washington, D.C. We left for the prison at 7:00 P.M. to be sure to arrive on time for our 8:00 visit.

As we arrived at the Florida State Prison, its pastel green was shrouded in twilight. The electric chair in Q wing had claimed four lives since 1979, and I hoped James Adams would not be the fifth.

As Willie Lawrence and I entered the visiting room I sensed the tension in the air. After welcoming hellos, I pulled an attorney aside to see if the Supreme Court had ruled during the forty-five minutes we had spent on the highway driving to prison. He was solemn and confirmed my fears that although the Court had not ruled, a telephone conversation with Dick Burr indicated Burr was increasingly pessimistic. I turned to James.

Sitting in the chair looking through the glass, he greeted me. He seemed reflective, somber.

"James, you know what is going on?"

He nodded.

"I think we all fear the worst," I said, "that the Supreme Court will lift the stay of execution. I just want to be sure you are okay. It's been an emotional roller coaster the last couple of days."

"I'm all right, Joe. It has been up and down, but at least I have another day. A whole twenty-four hours of life is a precious gift. I would have thought some judge somewhere would have seen I didn't belong here, but they didn't. So I'm just waiting. I don't expect much. I'm just glad I'm here with my friends and my family."

Moving away from the booth so someone else could talk, I choked back my tears. James was such a brave man! I walked over to the corner of the room, fighting to control my emotions.

Midway through the visit the word came that the Supreme Court had lifted the stay of execution. James Adams was set to die at 7:00 A.M. the following morning. James received the news stoically, a catch in his voice betraying his disappointment as he talked about it.

Our time dwindled quickly. Each of us took turns sharing a few minutes with James. I pulled the chair up close to the window and gave him a faint smile.

"James, has there been any other time in your life when you thought you were going to die?"

His dark eyebrows came together as he concentrated, trying to recall.

"Yes, I remember now," he said. "I was a youngster, maybe barely a teenager. I really felt I was going to die. I was real sick."

"Can you remember anything else about it?" I asked.

"It was like a dream, Joe. It was like a dream. I was walking away from my body. I could look back and see Momma, Daddy, everyone around my bed. But I was leaving them all. I knew I was all right, but I couldn't let them know. Then I felt them pulling on my ankles, on my feet, bringing me back. Then I was back."

James looked up and smiled. "You know, I haven't thought of that dream in years. I knew I was dying, but they dragged me back. Where I was heading I don't know, but there was light. A bright light. That's what I was moving toward when I came back."

There was little I could add to the conversation. Whatever the dream meant to James, it became a buoy for him to hold onto in those last few hours. Maybe there was a bright light, a white light. I didn't know. What I did know with all my trembling soul was that James Adams was in the hands of the Lord. No matter what happened in that electric chair, God had made his Spirit felt through the life of James Adams. As I considered the good James had done for others even in this hell-hole of an institution, I knew "Tennessee" Adams would be home shortly.

James asked me to come back up to the window. We talked a bit; he thanked me for my friendship. Then he said:

"I don't mind the dying. It's the killing, the slaughter which bothers me."

As I beheld a man who would be killed in seven short hours, and who knew it so well, I found myself replying: "James, I'm going to take your story out of here. I am going to tell it wherever I can. It needs to be told. People need to know what is going on in this country. Until my dying breath your story will be alive in me, and I will tell it."

We circled up for a final prayer. Once again, Willie Lawrence dropped to his knees. The sorrow, the grief, came tumbling out in a psalm of love for his brother and our friend. I looked up during the prayer, blinking a tear back. I gazed at James and saw two tears rolling down his cheeks. As I watched the tears tracing a path on his ebony skin, I wept.

We closed with "Amazing Grace" and each person bade James good-bye. Willie Lawrence and I left, and he wept as I led him to the parking lot. James's minister remained behind for a contact visit and would go back to Q wing to be with James until 4:00 A.M. James's friend from Jacksonville had been unable to come to the prison.

Margaret Vandiver met Willie Lawrence and me in the prison parking lot and drove us back to Gainesville. None of us had much to say. We arrived at Mike Radelet's house and stayed up making desultory conversation as we sought to integrate the reality of James's upcoming killing into our spirits.

We lay down to rest for a few minutes before rising at 5:00 A.M. to drive back to the prison. All we could do now was bear witness against this injustice. Dawn broke the sky as we assembled in the cow pasture across from the Florida State Prison.

A local United Church of Christ minister led us in a somber but hopeful service. At its conclusion, we all turned to the prison and waited in silence.

I prayed for James Adams, for his family, for the three friends witnessing James's killing, for the killers hired by the state, and for all who through their silence had tacitly conspired to kill James Adams. Especially did I pray for my dear friend Dick Burr, James's chief lawyer, who had labored so diligently on his client's behalf.

The door opened at Q wing and a guard raised a white handkerchief. This was the signal that killing was done.

The witness van drove from the prison to the pasture, and the press besieged the witnesses for stories. One of the witnesses told me James's final words.

"I'd like to say to the men on Death Row, keep on fighting because it [the death penalty] is wrong and immoral. I have no animosity toward anyone. I have only love. That's all I have to say."

NOTE

1. Samuel R. Gross and Robert Mauro, "Patterns of Death: An Analysis of Disposition in Capital Sentencing and Homicide Victimization," *Stanford Law Review*, vol. 37 (1984): 27-153.

CHAPTER ELEVEN

DAVID WASHINGTON
Florida
July 13, 1984

Pee Wee. It was a nickname coined in the streets of Miami, and one that David Washington brought with him to Death Row at the Florida State Prison. But David Washington was not a pee wee. His six-foot frame was well conditioned, and he was acknowledged as one of the best basketball players on Death Row. His smooth, creamy, caramel skin and dark eyes were regularly accompanied by a warm smile. As his many friendships in Miami confirmed, Pee Wee radiated a genuine charm.

The events that sent David Washington to Death Row culminated in the killing of three people. A product of Liberty City, the black ghetto in Miami, David was a street-wise youth. But he never used his social background as an explanation for his crimes. Rather, he readily admitted his responsibility to the police and to the court. He turned himself in. He threw himself on the mercy of the court, waiving a right to a jury trial, and the court had no mercy. David Washington was sentenced to three consecutive death sentences.

In my visits with David Washington over the years, I found a deeply troubled soul. David would be so depressed over what he had done that he would simply remain quietly in his cell for days. If my visit coincided with one of his retreats, he would probably not come out to talk. He would remain in his cell, reflecting over the lives of the people he had murdered.

In the course of one visit, Pee Wee struggled to explain why he had not come out for my last visit.

"Joe, I want you to know it has nothing to do with you. Sometimes I just get back there thinking about those people I killed and I don't say nothing to nobody. I just sit there for days, waiting for it all to go through me so I can feel right again."

In a sense, it was as if those three people were inhabiting David Washington's soul. He probably remembered them, what he had done to them, in a way only their families could understand. A conversation with Pee Wee often seemed like a talk one would have with someone who had lost a family member to murder. David Washington never forgot his victims, and his struggle became accepting himself and learning forgiveness for what he had done. It was a difficult pilgrimage of the soul that Pee Wee had commenced. Sometimes he was simply overwhelmed, and he wanted me to know that at those times he could not do otherwise than he did: remain in his cell and wait it out.

But when Pee Wee was sociable, there was no kinder and more enjoyable presence in the entire prison. He resonated a sweetness of character and a true humility in our visits. He and I hardly discussed the legal proceedings of his case. He had accepted his guilt on a personal level and whatever the courts did really had no effect on those feelings. The guilt and responsibility he experienced were real, no matter what any court would do to him. Thus almost all our visits were personal and spiritual in nature. We came to care a great deal for each other.

It is often stated that when the lives of the saints are examined, their souls become windowpanes to God. This means the saints were able to become transparent so that others could experience or see God through their lives. The sufferings they endured enabled others to see God at work through them. In a very similar manner, the suffering of David Washington in his cell served as a reminder to others on Death Row, and those from the outside who came to know him, of the presence of the victims in his life and also in ours. Pee Wee became a windowpane through which we came to see God at work preserving and reconciling the world. Destroying life, whether by random street killing or by the electric chair, must be struggled against. Responsibility for such deaths must be borne by those involved with them, because it is only in coming to see our complicity and responsibility for murder that guilt can prod us onto a level of forgiveness and reconciliation that transcends the wrongful deed. David Washington taught this painful lesson by example as he lived out his days on Death Row at the Florida State Prison.

Pee Wee came to Death Row in November of 1976. The first person he talked to upon arrival, the person who took him under a protective wing, was John Spenkelink: "I was ignorant when I came to Death Row. I didn't know nothing about it. John Spenkelink spent time with me. He explained the way things worked, introduced me to the guys, eased my way. He was a real friend to me and a lot of the guys. He was quiet, calm, a real leader. If we wanted changes made we came to John. He made sure things were done right."

So, with the help of John Spenkelink, David Washington became familiar with the routine of Death Row: the countless hours locked in a cell, the television or radio blaring, the conversation, and worst of all, the waiting. Simply sitting there feeling for his victims, David was unable to explain to himself or his God why he had murdered. He would often cry. Weeping for what he had done, he quietly sobbed as a consequence of the guilt he felt for those killings. As the years passed, the suffering David Washington endured remained his faithful companion. He made his peace with God; he had sought forgiveness and felt it given. But he could never forget what he had done. The suffering remained with him.

In the summer of 1984, the U.S. Supreme Court announced its ruling in *Washington* v. *Strickland*. The Court had chosen Pee Wee's case to establish guidelines for ineffective assistance of counsel. The decision was adverse for David and others on Death Row since it established lower standards for defense counsel in capital trials. We knew it was now a matter of days before David Washington went to the electric chair.

David's first lawyer, who had appealed David's case for years until the ruling against him in the Supreme Court, stepped aside and allowed his former colleague, Dick Burr, to fight to save David's life. Burr began by filing a petition in state court. Dick Burr discovered an issue in David Washington's case and filed a successor habeas corpus petition. The prosecutor had utilized a closing argument to the judge that Burr considered prejudicial.

In mid-June, in the wake of *Washington* v. *Strickland,* Governor Bob Graham signed David Washington's death warrant. The execution was set for Thursday, July 12. I arranged to travel to Florida and visit Pee Wee on the night of July 9.

Before I arrived, Margaret Vandiver, an active opponent of the death penalty, had visited with David to be sure he had everything he needed. Margaret visited the Florida State Prison regularly. On one occasion, she wore a rose so David could smell and touch a flower for the first time since 1976. During the course of another visit, David confided to

Margaret his worry that he had not done the things he should have done religiously, in terms of certain observances of ritual. He hoped God would not hold this against him. Margaret responded: "I do not believe you will miss getting into heaven or being united with God because you failed to say certain precise formulas in prayer or maintain certain exact observances."

David nodded his head and said: "You know, Margaret, I certainly don't want to be executed, but I am tired of all this. I feel like an animal in a cage, and people keep coming by and poking me with sticks. They have done everything to me they could do. This is my third death warrant, and I am tired. I want out, one way or another. I do not choose death, but if it comes, I accept it. I am like a tormented animal tired of abuse by my keepers."

In the courts Dick Burr had obtained a stay of execution from the trial judge on Friday, July 6. The state was appealing the case to the Florida Supreme Court. The Florida Supreme Court met and urged the judge to lift the stay of execution, utilizing imperative judicial language. By remanding the case back to the trial judge with an either/or ultimatum, the Florida Supreme Court was in effect saying they didn't care whether this legal issue was legitimate or not. The message was: It is time to kill David Washington, and let's get on with it. When I arrived at the Florida State Prison at 8:20 P.M. on July 9, we were awaiting a response from the trial court judge to the Florida Supreme Court's demand.

As I was making my way from the prison gates to the cell where David was being held, David received a call. The call was to inform him that the death sentences had been dissolved. As I entered the cell, Margaret told me the news. I was stunned.

I sat down and visited Pee Wee. We placed our palms against the glass window in greeting. As the evening progressed, the effects of being free of the sentences of death for the first time in eight years were evident in him. He was lighthearted, joyous, laughing, and teasing me unmercifully. The joy and happiness we experienced were rarely felt in the bowels of the Florida State Prison. We did talk seriously about the state's appeal to the Florida Supreme Court, and David had a very realistic appraisal of his chances. He expected the state to prevail on appeal, but he would experience that when it came. This night, for the first time since we had met, David Washington was unburdened of the death sentences. We celebrated until visiting time was over at 10:00 P.M. As Margaret and I left the prison, we reflected David's joy. Seldom had I exited the house of death so joyous.

Driving back to Gainesville, we discussed prospective events in the courts. We all agreed that despite Dick Burr's miraculous work, the Florida Supreme Court would probably reinstate the death sentences. But it was as if David's dwelling wholly in the present had communicated itself to us. We would let tomorrow take care of itself. The night was for celebration.

Perhaps Margaret Vandiver put it best as she discussed David's attitude toward the courts.

> David received news about the legal proceedings very gracefully. He was glad there were people who cared about him and who were making the effort for him, but he had no attachment to the results of what happened in court. He had a tremendous serenity, a kind of holy indifference, as to the outcome of any of the legal proceedings. It was not the most important thing going on with him. He never manifested more than a polite interest about the legal issues. At the same time, he received news of the legal efforts gratefully but in no way could anything that happened in the court disturb what was happening in him.

On Tuesday, July 10, I spent the day at the Florida State Prison visiting men on Death Row. It was an enjoyable time of making new acquaintances and renewing old friendships. But by the conclusion of visiting hours, I was spent from eight hours of visits.

I was visiting some friends that evening when the telephone intruded at 10:30 P.M. It was Margaret Vandiver: "Joe, we just heard from the Florida Supreme Court, and it's bad news. They've reinstated David's death sentences."

I was not surprised, but the news was piercingly painful.

On July 11, Federal District Court Judge Spellman granted David Washington a stay of execution until 6:59 A.M., July 13. This would enable David to pursue his appeals through the courts and still maintain the execution within the parameters of the death warrant. Although Judge Spellman was to rule against David's appeal, he issued a certificate of probable cause, indicating the appeal had merit. While the legal course was followed by Dick Burr from court to court, I had no hope of a reversal of the Florida Supreme Court's decision to kill David Washington. I sought to maintain the holy indifference to the legal proceedings that David manifested in order to minister to his family and to him.

On the evening of July 11, Margaret Vandiver and I joined eleven members of David Washington's family for a visit. From 7:00 P.M. until 10:00 P.M. we crowded into the non-contact visiting area to talk with Pee Wee through the glass separating us. Three small children, ages three through five, enlivened the occasion by talking to their uncle through the glass. David teased them, put happy smiles on their faces, and sought to uplift all our spirits. His stepfather was a quiet, strong man whose large stature radiated a strength for the family. David's mother relived some of the time she had shared with her son. David spoke intently to his younger brother, who was clearly having a difficult time. At one point David asked me to be sure his brother made it through the planned events. But of all the family members gathered in the room, the poignance of David's twelve-year-old daughter was most painful. She had not seen her father in years, and she had a difficult time expressing her love amid the horror. She broke down several times, and it was only David's constant kindness and encouragement that kept her intact.

During our three-hour visit, I joined David's brother at the window that provided a view of the prison and the parking lot. He was standing, silently crying, while gazing toward Q wing, which housed the electric chair and holding cells. I spoke quietly to him. After several minutes, he stopped crying long enough to tell me he just couldn't take it. I assured him there was no reason he should bear the awful burden placed upon him; it was an insane situation and the important thing was to remember David's request that he not do anything stupid. He nodded, and we stood together in silence.

On the night of Thursday, July 12, all of Pee Wee's family returned, with the exception of his brother. Unlike the previous night when we knew there would be another day, the finality of the night enveloped all of us. The three children wept most of the visit, not fully understanding why they were so sad. David would summon each individual to the glass and talk. By seeking to comfort his loved ones, David poured himself out to each person. At one point, Pee Wee asked Margaret and me to come to the window. Margaret Vandiver recalls the moment:

> David said that apart from his family, we had shown him more love than anyone else. He tried to express his gratitude and told us also of his concern for us. He was worried because we were being hit so hard by every execution and personally involved with each one. We immediately let David know how much he and the other men had given us and that we were doing what we were doing because we wanted to do it. He had given us more than we could ever return to him, and more than the state could take away by killing him.

During the course of the conversation David mentioned how much Margaret's assurance that formula and ritual would not pave the way toward God meant to him. I echoed the sentiments, and we talked about love's being the uniting reality through life and death. It was clear that spiritually David was at ease and greatly comforted, despite a lack of formal ritual or a spiritual adviser in the usual sense. Although David could not express what brand of religious or established doctrine applied to him, he radiated the love of one forgiven and forgiving on the deepest level possible.

At midnight, David's mother, daughter, and I moved to join David for a one-hour contact visit. The remainder of the family and Margaret stayed on the other side of the partition separating us. They would occasionally communicate by tapping on the window, but for the most part they simply observed us as we visited.

After each of us hugged Pee Wee, we sat in chairs around him. He proceeded to minister to each of us as he had done throughout the night. He began with his mother: "I ain't believin' this! I ain't believin' you're crying! You've always been the strong one. I never expected this. Now come on, we can't have this. You dry those tears and sit up straight." His mother, forcing a smile through her sobs, looked at David and spoke: "But you're my baby. You're my baby." David, his voice catching, almost overcome with tears himself, embraced her despite the handcuffs. There were no words to be said.

David's primary concern was his daughter. He agonized over what she was enduring. He sat her on his lap, like a child, her lanky body draping him. She was crying hard, the tears streaming down her face, and David spoke to her: "I want you to make me proud. I don't want you messin' up like I did. You listen to your grandmother and do what she tells you. I want you to do better than I did. I didn't listen, and you see what happened to me. Now I want you to get your books, to study. School is important, and I want you to do well. Don't you be makin' the mistakes I did, thinkin' school wasn't important."

As Pee Wee spoke softly to his daughter seated on his lap, he wiped her tears away. I sat in a chair, stricken by the pathos of the moment. A father was saying good-bye to his daughter, imparting advice to help her survive in the world after his killing. He was trying to leave a legacy to stand fast with her through the years, since he would be gone. As I looked at her stricken face and gazed at David's mother, I heard a soft sobbing. I looked to the glass and there peering through the glass was one of David's nieces. Her face was pressed against the glass, a torrent of tears flowing down her cheeks. As I saw her and felt her tears, I realized she and I were equally unable to fathom the events at hand. We were both bearing witness to a final parting, but neither of us understood it. Why was Pee Wee going to his death? The dispenser of so much love and grace, the sufferer of such grief, was going to be taken from his loved ones. I could not stop the tears welling in my eyes.

Soon it was almost 1:00 and we were saying good-bye. David once again thanked us for our friendship. As we filed out the door, each of us hugged David one last time. The guards handcuffed David's hands behind him and led him down the hallway toward Q wing. As I watched his retreating form, clothed in the faded orange t-shirt and light blue trousers of a Death Row prisoner, I gazed about me. His daughter was sobbing, watching her father leave for the last time. The small children were near hysterics, his mother's shoulders were heaving with sorrow, and his stepfather tried to comfort all. As David neared the door that would take him from us, I called down the prison corridor: "We love you."

Several others yelled out their love also. Then David Washington looked back over his shoulder, beholding his family for the last time. His expression was tender and sorrowful. His gaze rendered us speechless, and a gentle smile creased his smooth face. Then he was gone.

We remained transfixed. None of us moved. It was as if by holding the moment, by not moving, we could keep David with us. We stood planted in the middle of the prison corridor like fixtures. Then the head of the execution team walked through our midst down the hall. The spell was broken, and we stumbled out into the parking lot, wailing, grief-stricken, and inconsolable.

The events of the night had left me numb on an emotional level. My soul had been seared so completely that there was no pain. My sensitivity had been deadened by the overwhelming sorrow I had experienced. I reacted by functioning despite what I had seen and endured. After David's family left, I suggested to Margaret that we go to the motel in Starke and locate the Miami *Herald* reporter who had interviewed us earlier in the day. He had kindly offered bed space to us, and we were too tired to attempt the drive back to Gainesville.

The drive into Starke found me focusing on my friend, and David Washington's lawyer, Dick Burr. Burr was slated to witness the execution, and I had agreed to join him. But now I wanted to discuss the decision with him. Although we wanted someone in the witness chamber for the condemned during every execution, I did not want Dick Burr to be that person. He had too many other death cases, and we simply could not afford to lose him to the emotional fallout of watching his client be killed. And I also knew that I did not want to see David killed after sharing the intensity of the last hours with him and his family.

We found the reporter and woke him up. He gave Margaret his extra bed, and I made space on the floor. But before sleeping I had to contact Dick Burr. The execution witnesses would be gathering outside the prison at the witness van in three hours. I called his office and then his home. Dick's wife gave me the number where she thought he was staying. I tried it, and the hotel desk informed me that neither he nor his colleague was registered there. For the next thirty minutes I tried likely hotels in Jacksonville, Starke, and Gainesville. My efforts were to no avail. I finally lay down for some sleep before rising at 4:30 to rendezvous at the prison with Burr at the witness van.

At 5:00 A.M. I was outside the prison. I observed the witnesses assemble but did not see Dick Burr. A guard informed me I was not on the official witness list and could not enter the prison. Frantically, I scanned the faces of the other witnesses as they climbed into the prison van. I did not see Dick Burr. The van drove off and passed through the roadblock at the junction. The witnesses were going to eat breakfast in the prison before David Washington was to be killed in less than two hours. This state amenity nauseated me.

It was after 5:30 and the eastern sky was beginning to light with a hint of dawn. I paced up and down the road, fearful that Burr was already in the prison and about to endure this horror alone. I prayed, stupefied by exhaustion and worry, not knowing what else to do.

At 6:30, I walked through the cow pasture to assemble with others arriving to protest Pee Wee's execution. As I awkwardly approached the group gathering in a large circle to participate in a vigil, Margaret joined me. As we filed into the circle with the other fifty people, I glanced around to see who else would be in our circle that I might know. As my eyes traveled around the vigil circle, I saw the bearded face and curly reddish-blond hair of my friend Dick Burr. I was deeply relieved.

A Gainesville United Church of Christ minister led the service of song and remembrance of David Washington. Shortly before 7:00 we concluded and faced the prison. We remained silent as the minutes passed, approaching the 7:00 A.M. electrocution.

Shortly after 7:15, the door opened from Q wing and the white handkerchief was waved. It was a signal to the world that the execution was complete. Pee Wee was dead.

CHAPTER TWELVE

TIM BALDWIN
Louisiana
September 10, 1984

The Louisiana State Penitentiary at Angola sprawls across eighteen thousand acres in northeastern Louisiana. Surrounded on three sides by the Mississippi River, the prison is as isolated from the rest of the state as the prisoners are isolated from the consciences of the people of Louisiana. In the spring the plantation-style prison with its far-flung work camps is normally quite active with prisoners working in the fields. On May 24, 1982, however, the prison was unusually quiet and subdued. Tim Baldwin was scheduled to die in the electric chair the next day. If his final appeal was denied, Baldwin would be the next person executed in Louisiana.

Tim Baldwin and I sat talking together on Death Row awaiting word on his appeal from the Fifth Circuit Court of Appeals. Although the oppressive heat permeated the visiting area on Death Row, we hardly heeded it. We talked through a wire-mesh screen about the chain of events that had brought Tim Baldwin to Death Row. The chain of events began on the night of April 4, 1978, in Monroe, Louisiana, the night when Mary James Peters was beaten and robbed.

Mary Peters was the eighty-five-year-old godmother of one of Tim Baldwin's children. Although she regained consciousness in the hospital and was questioned about who attacked her, she could not identify the assailant. This circumstance combined with several others to raise questions about Baldwin's guilt:

1. The van parked outside the house during the robbery was gold or brownish gold according to neighbors. Tim Baldwin drove a black van.
2. The man observed through a window inside the house was described as a young man wearing a short-sleeved shirt. Tim Baldwin, who always wore long sleeves to cover the numerous

tattoos on his arms, was thirty-eight. He did not look like a young man.

3. Although Baldwin was in the midst of what he later described as a "mid-life crisis"—he had run off with a thirty-five-year-old former high school sweetheart—it was difficult to understand why Baldwin would have attacked and beaten a woman whom he had worked for on occasion, and whom he clearly was fond of since one of his children was Mary Peters's godchild.

4. Despite his affair, Baldwin loved his wife, Rita, and their children. He had returned—before he was incarcerated—to visit them on occasion, and Rita clearly desired his return to the family.

5. After Baldwin's trial a receipt was discovered from a motel in El Dorado, Arkansas, some seventy miles from Monroe, Louisiana. The receipt established Baldwin's presence at the motel on April 4, the day of the murder. Baldwin stated he checked in shortly *before* midnight. It was inconceivable that he could have attacked Mary Peters in Monroe at 11:00 P.M., driven over seventy miles to El Dorado, and arrived at the motel by midnight.

Tim Baldwin hadn't been able to afford a lawyer, so he was appointed one by the court. The lawyer had never handled a capital case and did an extraordinarily poor job of defending Baldwin. Baldwin's appeal was based on the ineffectiveness of his trial counsel. It seemed that innocence, guilt, truth, and justice were irrelevant to a criminal justice system couched in a legalistic battle of defense versus prosecution. As in virtually every death penalty case in which I had been involved, the defendant who is too poor to hire a competent lawyer ends up facing the executioner.

Tim Baldwin, like John Spenkelink, had a naive faith in the American criminal justice system. I could not comprehend why these two men, each of whom had personally seen this system function when they served time for previous convictions, still believed that justice would prevail. John Spenkelink, in turning down a plea bargain and opting for a jury trial, gambled with his life and lost. The same fate might await Tim Baldwin shortly, but he deeply believed his faith in the system would prove justified.

I had helped bury John Spenkelink, and I knew of too many similar examples of a misplaced faith in the adversarial justice system to share Baldwin's optimism. The state relentlessly brings its power to bear in death penalty trials. Nine out of ten times the defendant in capital trials cannot even afford a lawyer, much less the necessary investigators and expert witnesses. In these cases, the death penalty is the inevitable punishment. I feared Tim Baldwin was about to become another casualty on the list of those who trusted in the American system of jurisprudence to do right.

As Tim and I waited for word from the court, he told me about his family. Each of his seven children had a special place in Tim's heart, and the deep love he shared with his wife, Rita, had led to their reuniting despite the walls and bars that separated them. "You know, Joe," he told me, "if it happens tomorrow, it happens. I can't do too much about it. But if it does happen I'm worried it's gonna mess up my son's graduation from the Air Force Academy. He's worked hard, and I'm proud of him. The last thing I want to do is mess up his graduation by having those people kill me. He's come in to be with the family, and I'm afraid I'm ruining the proudest moment of his life."

Tim Baldwin told me about his son's graduating from the Air Force Academy in just a few weeks. Tim had even gone so far as to suggest that his son change his last name to avoid the stigma of bearing the name of an executed man. The love of this man for his family seemed extraordinary to me, but upon reflection I realized it was the common, all too human love any father would feel for his family when facing such an ordeal. I was deeply touched.

As the afternoon dragged on amid increasing heat, the plywood door behind Baldwin suddenly opened. An associate warden peered in and said:

"You got a stay. You can go back to the cell now."

Tim Baldwin smiled, and we looked at each other with relief. I promised to find out the details and have his lawyer call him. We bade one another good-bye, placing our hands on the wire-mesh screen that separated us.

Calling from the pay telephone outside the building that housed Death Row, I reached the SCJP Louisiana project director in New Orleans. He confirmed the stay of execution from the Fifth Circuit Court of Appeals and explained that the state was not appealing to the U.S. Supreme

Court. He also agreed to call Baldwin's lawyer to be sure she had called Tim. Finally believing the good news, I thanked John and hung up.

The four-hour drive from Angola to New Orleans gave me the chance to gradually release the tension of the last few days. Tim Baldwin was such a likable guy. I was thankful our friendship had been granted a reprieve and we now had months, if not years, for deepening our relationship.

Tim Baldwin had served time previously for non-violent offenses. He was a hard worker, a man as good as his word, an "old school convict." The convict, as opposed to the inmate, prides himself on loyalty and honor. The convict does not "snitch" on fellow prisoners or curry favor from the prison administration. He does his time and lives by the convict code. Such prisoners frequently draw the respect of prison administrators who look to these convicts for leadership.

I turned up the radio so I would not fall asleep as I drove. As usual in an execution crisis, I had not rested enough during the frenetic few days prior to the reprieve. As relief of the stay of execution relaxed the tension in my body, weariness began to creep in. I struggled to focus on the highway as I approached the lengthy causeway across Lake Pontchartrain leading to New Orleans.

The babbling on the radio penetrated my consciousness. A New Orleans radio talk-show host was taking calls from his listeners about Tim Baldwin's stay of execution.

The callers denounced the courts for granting the stay of execution and generally attacked Tim Baldwin and all those who defended him. It was typical of the public sentiment for the death penalty that prevailed in the South. No caller mentioned that the evidence strongly suggested Tim Baldwin was innocent.

The talk-show host, infused with the venom of his callers, said that they "should have put Tim Baldwin in the electric chair and fried him. Not only Baldwin, but this SCJP guy also. They should have strapped him into Baldwin's lap and pulled the switch on both of them."

— ▼ —

The months passed by as Tim Baldwin and I corresponded, visited, and talked by telephone. The closeness that bonded us through the ordeal of his near execution cemented our relationship.

The more I investigated the robbing and killing of Mary James Peters in West Monroe, Louisiana, the more convinced I became of Tim Baldwin's innocence. Some extremely unusual proceedings occurred at Baldwin's trial, and the irregular nature of the trial convinced me that it was not a fair one.

Although familiar with numerous capital cases, I had yet to encounter the unique jury selection employed by Baldwin's trial judge. The defense used its challenges of prospective jurors until the jury pool was exhausted. Then the judge ordered the bailiff to gather people off the street and bring them into court. The bailiff coerced several groups of people into the courtroom for further jury selection. The impaneled jury was then sequestered until the conclusion of the trial. For the jurors who were arbitrarily picked off the street, seated on the jury, and then sequestered in a motel, the experience must have seemed like a governmental kidnapping. It wasn't hard to imagine their outrage, resentment, and eagerness to complete the trial as quickly as possible so they could return to their homes.

The district attorney relied heavily on the testimony of the traveling companion of Tim Baldwin and his woman friend at the time of the murder. The district attorney took the stand to testify he had not arranged a plea bargain with the traveling companion in exchange for his testimony. Despite this assurance to the judge, the traveling companion's own testimony revealed him to be guilty of accessory to the murder before and after the fact. Yet he was never charged for any involvement in the crime. He walked away from the Baldwin trial despite his own testimony of his involvement in the murder of Mary Peters.

The district attorney stated another remarkable fact while on the witness stand. When asked if he knew anyone on the jury, he looked at the jury box. The jury foreman raised her hand and stated:

"I know you."

"I'm afraid you have got me at a disadvantage," the district attorney said. "I don't recall."

By refusing to acknowledge his relationship with the jury foreman, and by stating no deal had been cut with the man who was traveling with the couple in exchange for his testimony, the district attorney succeeded in establishing the witness and himself as reliable witnesses in the court's eye.

The police and district attorney were under a great deal of public pressure to solve the *Mary Peters* case—the murder of an elderly woman in West Monroe, Louisiana. This public pressure helps explain some sloppy police work performed in the eagerness to convict Baldwin of the crime.

Neighbors of Mary James Peters, while trying to identify the man they saw leaving the house, pointed out someone other than Tim Baldwin in a police lineup. Mary James Peters, who regained consciousness before her death, testified that she did not know her assailant, although she was well acquainted with Tim Baldwin.

The police alleged a safe was taken from Mary Peters's home and that Tim Baldwin's fingerprints were found on it. The safe was only discovered on the morning of the trial, in a canal with three feet of water. The witness's description of where the safe was located led the police to it. Tim Baldwin's fingerprints were not found on the safe, nor on any murder weapon. Baldwin's fingerprints were found in Mary Peters's house, but he maintained he visited her the evening prior to the murder.

The real blow against Tim Baldwin was the testimony of his own stepdaughters, who were called as prosecution witnesses.

After Baldwin was arrested, police kept the two stepdaugters up late at the police station, threatened them, and implied that they could not go home until a statement was made. Each stepdaughter made a statement. The statement Michelle Baldwin made (despite being so intoxicated she had passed out earlier in the evening) was the one she repeated on the witness stand. Michelle believed she had to repeat exactly what she had told the police even though she had made the statement under duress. (Such was not the case.) Her sister simply indicated that she could not recall what she told the police.

Summoned by the prosecution as a witness, Michelle testified that her stepfather called her the night of the murder and said, "I've done something I can get Old Smoky for." "What's Old Smoky?" Michelle asked. "The electric chair," he said.

This devastating allegation by Tim Baldwin's stepdaughter seems overwhelming at face value. But the family story that lay behind this statement was an important part of the puzzle.

Tim Baldwin, in sustaining an affair with his old high school sweetheart, had left Rita and their children. Although he returned to visit, Michelle was very upset with him. She feared Tim would kidnap the twins, Rita and Tim's youngest children, and take them with him. Michelle even instructed the school authorities not to allow anyone, especially the twins' father, to remove them from school. She did so in her role as surrogate parent. Michelle acted as her siblings' surrogate parent because her mother, Rita Baldwin, was in jail. Rita and Tim had forged a check, and Rita Baldwin was arrested for it. Rita was put in jail from February 9 until April 13, 1978, and then released for time served. At the time Michelle gave the police a statement concerning her stepfather, their relationship was deeply estranged. Michelle was acutely resentful of the pain Tim Baldwin had forced upon her mother through the affair as well as her mother's incarceration for the bad check. As the oldest child remaining at home, Michelle had become the custodian of Tim and Rita's children. Although a loving and responsible person, concerned with the welfare of her siblings, she was only eighteen years old at the time of Rita's incarceration. Her testimony at the trial came from the perspective of a resentful stepdaughter who was experiencing the pain Baldwin had forced upon the family by leaving them.

The final piece of evidence against Tim Baldwin was the police discovery of a bank bag and bonds belonging to Mary Peters in Tim's van. This discovery was not made on Saturday night, when he was arrested, but only after he gave the police permission to search the van on Monday morning. At this point, the black van had been in the possession of the police since Baldwin's arrest. When I asked Tim Baldwin about the bank bag and bonds, his response was interesting.

"All I know is that they weren't there when I was arrested, and suddenly they turn up two days later. You figure it."

A person facing a murder charge does not give the police permission to search his vehicle if he knows they will find evidence to use against him. The time lapse in the search of the van, the heavy pressure on authorities to solve the murder, and the circumstantial evidence turned up thus far in the proceedings suggested the police would have had a strong motive to help the prosecutor by planting evidence.

Police officers testified that the 164 securities worth $27,000.00 were found in the back of the van. The black van Baldwin drove had no partition between the front seat and the rear of the vehicle, so it had an unobstructed view from the front to the rear. If securities were there in the back of the van, anyone looking in the rear from the front of the van would have easily discovered them. But the police stated that although they drove Baldwin's van from El Dorado, Arkansas, to Monroe, Louisiana, the bonds were not discovered until Baldwin gave them written permission to search the van on Monday, April 6. This incredible account of the discovery of the bonds was unchallenged by Baldwin's lawyer at the trial.

Tim Baldwin came to trial July 24. Jury selection, including pulling people in off the street to supplement the jury pool, lasted until July 26. The trial ended on Saturday, July 29, with the jury deliberating from 11:39 A.M. until 2:00 P.M. This two-hour-and-twenty-minute period included a lunch break. The jury returned a verdict of guilty. The judge immediately began the sentencing phase to determine whether Tim Baldwin would receive a life in prison or a death sentence. After hearing approximately fifteen minutes of testimony from Rita Baldwin, and from Michelle, the jury received the judge's final instructions and retired. After deliberating almost two hours and twenty minutes the jury returned a recommendation for the sentence of death.

Tim Baldwin, a man convicted on the dubious testimony of a witness and the incriminating remarks of his estranged stepdaughter; a man unidentified by the victim, despite the fact that Mary Peters was the godmother of his child; a man eye witnesses failed to identify in a line-up because he was older and had shorter hair than the assailant; a man who was at a motel seventy miles away just an hour after the crime was committed; a man tried by a jury, some of whom were pulled off the street and into the courtroom, was condemned to die in Louisiana's electric chair.

The long and winding road of the appellate process now began.

As time passed, the rift between Tim Baldwin and his stepdaughter Michelle mended. For Tim there was nothing more important than his family, and he was determined not to mention Michelle's testimony to her or other members of the family. As he said to me in the course of one of our visits: "Michelle had too much to drink that night and was scared. The cops kept her up until almost 6:00 A.M. trying to get a statement. She finally gave one. I don't know why and really don't care. She did what she had to do. We just all need to pull together now and put the past behind us. The family is what is important."

The restoration of his relationship with Rita was of utmost importance to Tim. Rita visited regularly with the children, and the close-knit family was emotionally intact once again despite its physical separation. The entire episode with his high school sweetheart was simply a bemusing memory for Tim. His energy and time focused on Rita and the children. The woman friend was serving a twenty-five-year sentence in the women's prison in St. Gabriel, Louisiana. She had been convicted in a separate trial as Tim's accomplice in the murder. Her conviction, like Tim's, rested on the testimony of their traveling companion, who admitted his complicity in the murder, but who remained a free man.

Tim's son graduated from the Air Force Academy and made his daddy a proud man. The other children got on with their lives.

In 1983 Rita Baldwin learned she had advanced lung cancer. Her doctor did not expect her to live out the year.

In reflecting on his wife's illness, Tim Baldwin remarked, "You know, Joe, that near execution in May was hard. But compared to Rita being sick and me being unable to help her, it's nothin'. All I can do is sit here and worry. I can't be with her when she needs me. God, I've put that woman through so much and here I am in a lousy cell, not helpin' a bit. I feel terrible."

Rita Baldwin's illness grew progressively worse. In the summer of 1983, she was hospitalized. Tim telephoned me and asked me to try to arrange a visit for him to the bedside of his dying wife.

The Louisiana Department of Corrections denied SCJP's request for a final visit between Tim and Rita Baldwin citing "security problems." "Security" had always been available for the eight sentencing dates Tim Baldwin received over the years, since each date had required Tim's appearance in the courtroom in West Monroe. But now that Rita Baldwin lay terminally ill in a hospital bed, security could not be provided for a condemned husband to visit his dying wife. Although other states allowed Death Row prisoners a visit with a dying loved one, Louisiana refused to do so.

When Rita Baldwin died on September 2, 1983, part of Tim Baldwin died as well. Tim was never quite the same after Rita died. He showed a reluctance to become involved in our discussions about other prisoners or conditions on Death Row. Regarded as a leader by Death Row prisoners in Louisiana, he began to defer initiative to others. The death of his wife took the heart out of him.

The U.S. Supreme Court ruled that proportionality was not required in death penalty cases in the autumn of 1983. This ruling, *Pulley* v. *Harris,* adversely affected Tim Baldwin's best friend on Death Row, Robert Wayne Williams. Events picked up momentum, and Robert Wayne had a near brush with execution in late October 1983. Then another date was set for December 14, 1983, and Robert Wayne Williams was killed in the Louisiana electric chair. In a three-month period Tim had lost his wife and his best friend.

The political situation in Louisiana changed with the incumbent David Treen losing to former governor Edwin Edwards. In his prior tenure as governor, Edwards had indicated he had significant concerns over the death penalty issue. Hopes rose on Death Row and among those fighting the death penalty that Governor Edwards would prove more considerate of death penalty cases when he assumed office in March, 1984.

As is the case in the majority of death penalty cases, the lawyers representing Baldwin at trial dropped the case after he was convicted. A prominent Baton Rouge lawyer agreed to assume the role of local counsel with the assistance of the NAACP Legal Defense Fund in New York. Now that Baldwin had excellent counsel, the question became whether they could overcome the original conviction through the appellate process.

The stay of execution granted Baldwin in his near brush with death in May 1982, was given pending the result of the establishing of standards for defense counsel in capital trials. The stay of execution resulted from the excellent appeal work of Baldwin's attorneys. Unfortunately, the standards for effective defense counsel set by the U.S. Supreme Court in its June 1984 ruling in *Washington* v. *Strickland* were minimal. Given these modest performance standards required by the Court, it seemed unlikely that Tim Baldwin's trial counsel would be ruled to have been ineffective, despite their inexperience and ineptness.

Governor Edwards had hardly settled into his job when he was confronted with the execution of Elmo Sonnier on April 5, 1984. Although Edwards allowed the execution to proceed on schedule, the general sentiment was that he simply did not have time to acquaint himself with the facts of the case. The next clemency decision would be a true test for the governor, and it could very well be Tim Baldwin who provided Governor Edwards with an opportunity to stop an execution.

Another attorney was recruited to prepare Baldwin's case for clemency. He diligently prepared for a hearing before Governor Edwards's appointees to the pardon board, and he sought an interview with the governor. As the clemency undertaking gathered momentum, SCJP launched a petition campaign. The letters, mailgrams, and cards that poured into the office of the Pardon Board on Baldwin's behalf represented a national effort to commute his sentence to life in the light of his dubious conviction. The first warning signal that such an effort might fail came in June 1984.

Governor Edwards appointed a former judge as his legal counsel. This man, an arch conservative, remarked to the press in Baton Rouge in mid-June that Baldwin was "as likely to get clemency as the son of Sam [the infamous mass murderer]." This blatantly biased remark by the governor's legal counsel, who would be advising him on clemency for Baldwin, indicated the depth of his desire to execute Tim.

August 7, 1984, was the date of Tim Baldwin's hearing before the Louisiana Board of Pardons, appointed by Governor Edwards after he assumed the governorship in March. No one believed the pardon board would make a decision to commute unless Governor Edwards communicated such a verdict was acceptable to him.

The governor's legal counsel ordered that the Pardon Board hearing be moved from the board's offices in Baton Rouge to the penitentiary at Angola. Moving a supposedly objective clemency hearing to the penitentiary that held the man and the death chamber designated to kill him clearly changed the atmosphere in which evidence was presented.

The attorney who worked on clemency had performed yeoman's work in preparing for Baldwin's hearing. In a lengthy oral presentation he reviewed the forty points he had submitted in writing to the board as grounds for a recommendation for clemency to Governor Edwards. In pointing out the 154 commutations of death sentences in Louisiana in the past one hundred years, he established the clear precedent for such an action. His most powerful points were centered on the failure of adequate representation at trial by Tim Baldwin's court-appointed lawyers. He presented twenty affidavits by people who would have willingly testified on Baldwin's behalf at trial as character witnesses. The people represented a range from a sheriff to a Catholic priest. Each affidavit portrayed Baldwin's virtues as a hard worker, as a gentle man, as a devoted family man, and communicated the affiant's disbelief that Baldwin could have committed such a crime. All of these people would have testified at trial if contacted by the trial attorney, but none of them was called to testify. The lack of witnesses on Baldwin's behalf at the sentencing phase of the trial increased the likelihood of his receiving the death sentence.

The motel receipt from the White Sands Motel in El Dorado, Arkansas, was also presented. It was dated the day of the murder. For the first time before any official body, Tim Baldwin could document his whereabouts on the day of the murder. One witness, a park ranger, established his presence at a state park in Mississippi until noon on April 4. The motel receipt placed him at the motel before midnight on the night of the murder. Neighbors of Mary Peters testified that a young couple left Mary Peters's home after 11:10 P.M. April 4. The white couple, unidentified in the police investigation, drove a goldish or goldish-brown van. If the couple were the older couple of Baldwin and the woman, they would have had to drive a black van over seventy miles in less than fifty minutes to check into White Sands Motel before midnight, so the motel receipt could be dated April 4. It was hard to conceive of such a scenario.

Tim Baldwin testified at the pardon hearing. A proud man, he would not beg for his life. He also was clear in his instructions to his family that he did not want them to beg for his life. Rather, he sought only justice, and he reasserted his innocence.

After four hours of testimony the Pardon Board adjourned to confer and make a decision. They deliberated approximately an hour. The board returned and announced that by a vote of 4-1 it would not recommend that Governor Edwards grant clemency to Tim Baldwin.

Since Governor Edwards had the final decision and authority in the matter, those active in organizing to save Tim Baldwin's life redoubled their efforts after the Pardon Board's decision. The governor's office was flooded with mail and calls urging him to halt the execution and to meet with Baldwin and grant clemency. An indication that this effort was having an effect came when the governor started making comments about Tim Baldwin's case in his news conferences.

As the summer waned, the trial court judge set an execution date of September 10, 1984. The efforts for clemency mounted and the calls to the govenor for clemency dramatically increased. As the demands on Governor Edwards increased, he began holding press conferences on the Baldwin case. In one press conference he said he opposed the death penalty but was sworn to uphold the law. This dodge of the power to grant clemency with which he was vested did nothing to halt the organizing effort on Baldwin's behalf. Indeed, if the governor was opposed to the death penalty we wanted to provide him an opportunity to prove it by granting clemency.

As we generated thousands of petitions on Tim Baldwin's behalf, I wondered what it took to stop an execution through executive clemency. When would any politician, especially Governor Edwards, who stated he opposed the death penalty, say "no" to the politics of death and commute a sentence? I hoped and prayed he would begin with Tim Baldwin.

On August 28, 1984, an extraordinary event occurred. Governor Edwards summoned Baldwin's lawyer to the governor's mansion in Baton Rouge. The lawyer discussed the Baldwin case with the governor. The two men then boarded a helicopter for a flight to Angola so Governor Edwards could personally interview Tim Baldwin.

Tim Baldwin described the visit with Governor Edwards: "I didn't know he was coming. All of a sudden the guards told me to get ready, I was going to the warden's office. When I got to the warden's office, in shackles and chains, the governor and my lawyer were there with the warden. We were introduced by the warden, and we all sat down. He asked questions about the case, and I answered them. It went as well as I could expect. I was really glad he met with me."

I received a telephone call informing me of the meeting with the governor. It appeared that Tim Baldwin was finally going to get the break he deserved. But then I learned the governor was also going to the women's prison to visit Tim's former woman friend. He would not be accompanied by Baldwin's lawyer, but by the woman's lawyer. This news worried me.

Governor Edwards was first and foremost a politician, and second a Catholic. Although Pope John Paul II had spoken against the death penalty when he interceded on Bob Sullivan's behalf in November of 1983, I knew the governor was looking for an out so he could avoid granting clemency. The woman could well provide him the reason for not granting clemency.

The woman, tried separately from Tim Baldwin, received a life sentence for the murder of Mary Peters. She, like Baldwin, was a victim of the testimony of the third party who was with Tim and her when the murder was committed. She had refused to testify against Tim at his trial. Indeed, her failure to testify against Tim was one reason the prosecutor asked the jury to recommend that she be sentenced to death. But the jury brought back a sentence of life imprisonment rather than the electric chair.

At first glance, it appeared that the woman would have no reason to impair Tim's clemency bid. But I was concerned because two dramatic changes had occurred since the trial in 1978. Tim's fling with her had ended, and he was reconciled with Rita. He regarded her as a good friend, but nothing more. The romantic bond that had once united them was now severed. Second, she was facing the reality of doing hard time before being eligible for parole. A life sentence in Louisiana usually meant twenty-five years. She had served six years and knew the difficulty of prison life. A gubernatorial intervention could shorten her time considerably. Strictly from a viewpoint of her own self-interest, she might benefit by giving Governor Edwards the excuse he was so clearly seeking not to commute Tim Baldwin. The fact that Baldwin's lawyer would not be present to examine any statement she might make to the governor—a statement that could be harmful to Tim—deeply concerned me.

On August 29, Governor Edwards met with the woman. The governor discussed the murder of Mrs. Peters with this prisoner while her attorney was with her. By agreement, no statement was made by either party about the contents of the conversation.

Thursday afternoon, prior to departing for a long Labor Day weekend, Governor Edwards announced his decision on the question of commutation to life imprisonment for Tim Baldwin. At a specially called news conference, Governor Edwards stated: "I have completed my investigation. . . . I have found no reason to interfere with the due process of law."

The governor went on to state a misrepresentation of his role in the clemency process: "I am not supposed to interfere unless I find new evidence indicating that an error was made or some legal reason for a new trial. I did not find anything in my investigation, as exhaustive as it was."

Within one year the woman received a reduction in her sentence from Governor Edwards. She was subsequently paroled.

Governor Edwards's decision came ten days prior to Tim Baldwin's scheduled execution. Although a last-ditch petition would be filed with the courts on a good legal issue, none of us had any hopes of success. For the first time since the long legal ordeal began in 1982, I felt sure Tim Baldwin would be killed by the state of Louisiana in its electric chair.

Although Governor Edwards had squashed hope for clemency, I was simply not going to accept his denial. As the days sped toward the execution date of September 10, I asked religious leaders in Louisiana to reach Governor Edwards. I implored the Catholic bishop and archbishop, Edwin Edwards's spiritual shepherds, to ask Governor Edwards to reconsider in light of Pope John Paul II's opposition to the death penalty. Each man had discussed the issue of the death penalty with the governor previously; neither held any hope that further discussions would be of value.

As the final efforts to halt the execution proved fruitless, I arranged to journey to Louisiana to be with Tim. As in 1982, we would be facing his probable execution. Unlike 1982, this occasion did not hold forth even the remote promise of a stay of execution.

On Saturday, September 8, the entire Baldwin clan assembled to visit Tim Baldwin except one of his daughters. The family spent the afternoon visiting and the occasion gave Tim an opportunity to impart the love and advice he wanted to share with each of them. The final visit was a painful but loving encounter. The visit provided the opportunity for the final healing of the rift between Michelle and Tim that stemmed from the trial in 1978. It heartened Tim considerably to see his family together, and he instructed them again of the importance of sticking together and looking out for one another. He did not want quarrels or past problems between them to continue. Since he couldn't be there with them to hold them together as their father, he communicated his fervent hope that they hold on to each other no matter what adversity awaited them.

On Sunday, September 9, I went to the Louisiana State Prison at Angola for my final visit with Tim. Staff members from the Louisiana Coalition on Jails and Prisons, Tim's daughter who had not visited on Saturday, and I were scheduled for a 3:00 P.M. to 6:00 P.M. visit. At the end of the visit I would remain with Tim until he was executed shortly after midnight.

We were cleared by security and driven in a state car by a guard to Camp *F*. Camp *F* is the housing unit where the condemned are taken a few days prior to execution. The electric chair and holding cells are in Camp *F*.

We were led into a foyer that had a metal door with a screen in its center. Tim was on the other side of the screen, sitting in a chair and manacled.

We exchanged greetings and launched into conversation. Tim was deeply concerned about his daughter and talked forthrightly.

At one point, I glanced at the daughter, who sat with her head bowed. The tears were rolling off her face into her lap as Tim talked through the screen to her about what her life should be after his death in a few hours:

"Now, look-a-here, I don't mean to upset you or hurt you. It's just that you and the family are all that I have left. Rita is gone, and it's up to all of you now. I'm not going to be here to help you anymore, and I want you to understand one another, love one another, stay together as a family. I know it is hard. I know you don't get along with Michelle or understand why she says some of the things she says, but try to understand it from her point of view. It's tough raising a family, and she's had to do that from when she was young. She really does love you and is trying to help you."

I leaned back in my chair, breathing deeply to choke back the tears. As Tim's words to his troubled daughter tumbled out I listened, knowing he had to get it all said by the 6:00 P.M. deadline for the conclusion of the visit.

As Tim talked with his daughter, I slipped away to talk to the guard in command of the shift. I asked the guard if Tim and his daughter could be allowed a final embrace at the end of their visit. The guard returned to say the warden had approved a final embrace at the conclusion of the visit.

At 6:00 the guard opened the door separating father and daughter, and they embraced. The tender, tight hug, despite Tim's handcuffs, seemed unending. Finally, they parted. Tim returned to his cell, and I joined him outside his cell door for the final six hours of his life.

As Tim ate the bacon, lettuce, and tomato sandwiches he had requested as his last meal, we talked about the recently concluded visit. His concern for his family was moving. He took his responsibility as a father seriously.

Tim was on his second sandwich when the warden came to the cell door. The warden had a drooping moustache and inhaled King Edwards cigars constantly. He had recently come out of retirement to return as warden of the L.S.P.

The warden simply wanted to know if "Tim had everything he needed." The visit was brief but cordial, and he soon departed. He had mentioned the "schedule," and Tim nodded that he understood what to expect. I inquired of Tim what the order of events was to be.

"I get to make my phone calls at 8:00. I'm gonna call my family in Ohio and Monroe. Then at 9:00 they come to shave my head. At 11:00 the priest will come for communion. They're gonna do it just after midnight."

As I sat on the chair gazing through the cell bars, eating french fries Tim had given me, I shuddered at the schedule. I remembered an evening about five years before. It seemed like yesterday that some of our supporters and I were having dinner with the warden in his home atop a hill overlooking the prison. I remembered the warden talking about the electric chair having been folded up in his garage. His wife wanted to paint it and turn it into a planter. We laughed at the prospect in 1979. Now, in 1984, that same electric chair would char Tim Baldwin under the supervision of a man who once considered converting it into a planter.

Tim was nervous. He confided his fear to me while maintaining a brave appearance for the guards. He desperately wanted to be able to make a last statement but was worried: "My knees will be knocking so bad I won't be able to think." He pulled several pages of writing from a folder and proceeded to go over it with me. It was a final statement he wanted me to issue to the press.

The time passed swiftly as we discussed the final statement. He stopped to make his phone calls and as he did so I reviewed his words. By the time he completed his phone calls I had some suggestions to make. It was approximately 8:40.

The tone of Tim's remarks was bitter and at places sarcastic. Although such was reasonable to me since I shared his anger at an innocent man's being killed by the state, I simply asked him if he wanted to lower the intensity of the anger somewhat for the public. He agreed, and we made some minor changes in his statement.

At about 9:15 the death squad arrived to shave his head. As we observed these seven men enter the walk and proceed toward the cell, Tim remarked: "They're big enough, ain't they?" Chuckling at Tim's humor, I noticed each man looked like a retired professional football lineman. The contrast between the men of the death squad and Tim, who was all of 150 pounds and small of stature, was striking.

During the fifteen-minute head-shaving ritual, I was in a large room outside the cellblock. As I paced back and forth, I was approached by a guard. The man asked, "Will you take a message to Tim for me?" Struck speechless by the request, I nodded. "Tell him I'm just doing my job. It's nothing personal."

As I gazed into his troubled eyes, I realized how utterly bizarre this entire process was. Here was a guard, one of Tim's killers, asking me to deliver a message so he could be absolved of his deeds. And the terrifying aspect of the guard's words was that they were true! He *was* just doing his job. He probably liked Tim personally and wanted Tim to know that only because of his job was he in the death house that night. He wanted Tim to understand, and perhaps to forgive him.

As the death squad exited the walk I returned to Tim's cell, bracing myself for his appearance. I found him gazing into the mirror over the toilet, with his back turned to me. As I saw his reflection in the mirror, saw his freshly shaved scalp, vulnerability and helplessness were translated in a glance. Silently we both felt his imminent doom.

Tim turned and came back to sit on the bed. In addition to shaving him, they had put diapers on him. The surge of electricity that would kill Tim would convulse his body, wrenching every muscle, including the sphincter muscles that emptied his bowels. The disposable diapers peeked above his hips. "They put two big Huggies on me," he said, forcing a smile at the ludicrous situation in which he found himself. A grown man, diapered, shaved, stripped of his dignity in preparation for his killing. In order to kill him the state was transforming him to an expendable infant, bald and diapered. A disposable man in disposable diapers.

We finished going over his final statement. As the reality of his killing neared, his naive belief that the United States criminal justice system would not really kill him finally dissolved. Although he maintained a sense of humor to his death, he was a bitter man.

"You know Joe, I guess I should count myself a lucky man. The governor has decided he's against the death penalty; the attorney general is against it, four of the five members of the clemency board are against it. What more could a man ask for?"

Tim had put his finger on the bizarre nature of his fate. All of those individuals claimed to be against the death penalty, yet they were going to let him die. The emotional roller coaster of the last month, which culminated with Governor Edwards meeting personally with Tim in the warden's office and his denial of clemency one week later, had been a numbing experience. The scenario had been too much for any of us to comprehend. We had just endured and fought desperately to keep Tim alive. Now we knew the fight was over.

Tim and I talked until 11:00 P.M. He was concerned about his family, his friends, about me.

"Joe, you should be home. You can't keep doing this. What does your wife think?"

"Tim, I wouldn't want to be anywhere else right now except with you. God knows I wish we weren't here, but Becca and I both strongly feel I am in the right place. We love you, Tim."

The Catholic priest came in for the last rites and communion. I walked to the far end of the cellblock and talked with the young guard who had been stationed there throughout the evening. Since I knew Tim had no prior relationship with the priest, I hoped he would be brief.

At 11:30 I observed the priest returning his rosary beads to his pocket. I walked up to the cell, standing at the priest's left shoulder. I saw him smile at Tim and remark, "You know, my son, it won't hurt." I had to restrain myself from lifting the man up and throwing him against the bars and shouting: "It won't hurt! How could you say that! If it won't hurt, maybe we can have you take Tim's seat in the electric chair."

After the priest had left us, Tim, sensing my anger, ministered to me. "Don't worry about it, Joe. He was just trying to say something comforting." The words brought me up short, and I understood. All night long this man before me had been humiliated and demeaned as he was prepared for killing. Yet he not only understood those whose actions were directed against him, he forgave them. In his last half hour on this earth, his concern was for those around him—priest, guard, warden, friend. Although bitter at the state for killing him, he had transcended his feelings in a manner that, while not denying those feelings, did not allow them control over his behavior.

At midnight the warden appeared. "It's time, Tim." Tim stepped through the opened cell door, hobbling down the corridor with manacled feet and hands. I followed behind as Tim, accompanied by the warden and the death squad, crossed the foyer. He was marched through a large room crowded with people. He then proceeded to the death chamber. The warden positioned the microphone before Tim. Looking out through the glass at the witnesses, Tim remarked: "I was afraid I would be too nervous to say anything. But I do want to say something. I am an innocent man. You are putting an innocent man to death. It takes a special kind of person to live with themselves to do that."

I prayed a prayer of thanksgiving as Tim spoke. He had been so concerned he would be unable to speak, but now he spoke flowingly, eloquently. I watched them escort him to the electric chair. It stood on a raised platform, like a throne. The throne established for the king of death who welcomes another sacrifice. As he stepped up, I called out: "I love you." I wheeled and left the room with the sound of the generator rising in my ears.

— ▼ —

Tim Baldwin's Final Statement
(As dictated to his friend and
spiritual adviser, The Reverend Joseph Ingle)

I've always tried to be a good sport when I've lost at something and I see no reason not to leave this world with the same policy. After all, it was a hell of a battle.

I therefore congratulate all those who have tried so hard to murder me. I definitely have to give them credit as it takes a very special kind of person to murder an innocent man and still be able to live with themselves.

It's over now, so you can drop the pretense and I can't blame you if you in society are upset with the district attorney and the police—after all, that wasn't a very smart move when the district attorney and the police refused to release the records—they as good as admitted I was innocent.

Shame on you! You almost blew it. People were starting to get curious.

But who am I to condemn anyone? After all, I was just a human being like anyone else.

To the Citizens of Louisiana:

I now have my own life to account for, and yes, you'll have to account for yours, also. No, sorry to say that politics, money, nor social status will help you.

So I'd suggest you start thinking about a good excuse as death comes at the darndest times. I only wish I could hear how you tried to excuse your part in my murder.

I imagine there will be a lot of fingerpointing. It seems to work here on earth when someone asks where the blame lies. But I just don't think it's going to work up there.

I love my family, and I hope the media will respect my wishes to leave them alone. They have been through enough.

Until tonight, I have always had faith in the criminal justice system even though I have been on the wrong side of the law from time to time.

After what is being done tonight, I don't think they can hold their heads up when they say "justice."

I want to publicly thank everyone who has worked so long to keep me alive. They know who they are, and I urge them to keep up the fight until society becomes civilized by abolishing the death penalty.

CHAPTER THIRTEEN

VELMA BARFIELD
North Carolina
November 2, 1984

The terrain of eastern North Carolina is Kansas flat. Agriculture reigns king in the geographic area known by cartographers as the coastal plain. The sandy loam soil is fertile, and on a drive to the North Carolina shore in the summer one is surrounded by legions of corn, battalions of soybeans, and an army of tobacco.

As a native of eastern North Carolina, this section of the state etched itself on my soul. Its laws of segregation, torpid summers, bountiful harvests, and intertwining family relationships are well known to me.

It was only when I attended St. Andrews Presbyterian College, in Laurinburg, that I saw eastern North Carolina from a distance that provided perspective on the region. In the turbulent years from 1964 to 1968, St. Andrews provided a maturation period, a time to explore myself and my state. As I stretched my wings to fly into adulthood, I entered the social realities of civil rights, the Vietnam War, and poverty. As I struggled for manhood amid the vicissitudes of the era, a woman in an adjacent county struggled to survive with the memories of sexual abuse and the all too common violence that afflicts poverty-stricken families trying to survive in a prosperous country. Unknown to me at the time, the life of the woman, Velma Barfield, was inextricably bound to mine.

It was in the slow paced environs of Robeson County, North Carolina, that Velma Barfield came to trial for the murder of Stewart Taylor. Although not on trial for three other murders, she freely confessed responsibility for killing Dolly Taylor Edwards, John Henry Lee, and her mother, Lillian McMillan Bullard.

The murders occurred over a seven-year period of time. Velma Barfield was a well known member of the community and not suspected. Indeed, the murders were presumed to be death by natural causes until the suspicious family of Stewart Taylor provoked an autopsy, revealing his death by arsenic poisoning. Evidently, Velma Barfield bought rat poison and placed it into the food or drink of her intended victim. Gradually, the arsenic accumulated in the person's body until death occurred.

The shock of the accusation and trial of Velma Barfield reverberated throughout the county in 1978. It was difficult to envision the matronly woman, who shopped at the A&P market and worked spinning yarn, as a killer. After all, the woman was a grandmother!

Velma Barfield had a court-appointed lawyer who had never defended anyone in a capital case. The perfunctory defense was no match for the prosecutor's portrait of Velma Barfield as a cold-blooded murderess who enjoyed watching her victims die. On December 2, 1978, the trial judge sentenced Barfield to death by asphyxiation.

In the fall of 1979, Velma Barfield's conviction was upheld by the North Carolina Supreme Court. Her court-appointed lawyer was eager to drop the case, and those who had come to know the quality of her representation were equally anxious to locate another lawyer to represent her.

In December, 1979, Richard Burr of the Southern Prisoners' Defense Committee journeyed to the Women's Prison in Raleigh, North Carolina. He discussed with Mrs. Barfield the possibility of becoming her lawyer. He recalled the conversation:

> We spent three or four hours talking the first time we met. We both liked each other a great deal. We left the interview feeling that we were glad we had run into each other.
>
> After meeting Velma, I thought that if she had committed those crimes, they were committed under circumstances in which her mental and emotional states were seriously altered from the way they were when we were together. The person I saw was kind, sensitive, and loving. There was no hidden agenda with Velma. Whenever you were with her, she was who she was. From what I understand, that's how she lived her life in prison. So, from the very beginning, I believed that when she committed those crimes it was not the Velma Barfield, mentally and emotionally, that I was seeing and getting to know.

Richard Burr had experienced the loving, kind, doughty grandmother that many people knew and loved. This Velma Barfield was inconsistent with the person who killed four people. The problem became one of trying to overcome the trial record, which portrayed Velma Barfield as being a cold-blooded murderess, and replacing it with an accurate personality portrait of the woman who committed these crimes, along with an explanation of why she did so. Burr discussed the approach he took:

> I knew she had been evaluated before trial by two court-appointed psychiatrists. I was also aware that testimony had been given by her own psychiatrist, who treated her for depression for several years. As I became more familiar with the trial record, read the psychiatric evaluations, and received medical records made during her hospitalizations, I began to feel that the pre-trial evaluations were inadequate.
>
> Basically, the pre-trial evaluations concluded that she suffered from functional depressions and personality disorders. I felt that there had to be more, because there was a long history of prescription drug abuse.
>
> Furthermore, as I became acquainted with Velma, I learned more about her childhood and the difficulties she suffered as a child. Tragically, she and the other children in her family were victims of violence and sexual abuse.

As time passed and a relationship of trust grew between Dick Burr and Velma Barfield, Mrs. Barfield alluded to the history of abuse. Unfortunately, none of this was on the court record. The appellate courts were looking at a record fashioned primarily by the prosecutor who portrayed Velma Barfield as a murdering witch. In order to begin presenting an alternate view of the woman he represented, Burr turned to a psychiatrist. He evaluated Velma Barfield in September 1980, and presented his findings to the state superior court in late November of the same year.

In the appellate process, one opportunity is eventually given in either state court or federal court for a full evidentiary hearing. In this context, the psychiatrist testified in the state court. Burr commented on the diagnosis:

> [The doctor] felt that he never quite understood Velma. Basically, he believed that she suffered from three disorders. The first was a

multiple prescription drug abuse disorder that had been present for more than ten years at the time of the homicide. It was coupled with, as he put it, an underlying personality disorder that allowed her to put poison in a person's food or beverage without feeling any appreciation for the consequences of what she was doing. The third disorder was depression.

[He] thought that she suffered from an organic-based depression; a depression caused by some chemical or other physiological dysfunction in her brain. This dysfunction, as he explained in court, could be psychotic in proportion. It is like the depressive side of the manic-depressive disorder. [He] did not see the manic side, but there was depression. This depression had been diagnosed by her treating physician as well. Despite identifying these disorders, [he] never felt that he had put together a complete picture of Velma Barfield.

The week-long post-conviction hearing held in late November 1980, proved critical to Velma Barfield's appeal. A portrait contrary to the prosecutor's portrayal was now a part of the court record. Reflecting on the hearing, Dick Burr shared his frustrations:

I was not experienced, at the time, in putting together mental health histories. I did not know nearly as much about the interrelated incidents in people's lives, or symptoms and emotional states, which I later might have been able to come up with to help [the doctor] piece it together. So, I didn't know where to go with [him] because he seemed to be at a dead end. Certainly, at that point, I didn't know how to help him get out of it. I felt the evaluation was incomplete—but I did not know what to do about it.

Burr's reference to "incomplete" incisively described my own relationship with Velma Barfield. My visits with her in the Women's Prison in Raleigh were invariably delightful. She was witty and a caring grandmother. She knitted, doted on her grandchildren, and enjoyed family visits every weekend. After spending several hours visiting with Velma Barfield, I always left the prison feeling that she cared for me. I realized that I was coming to regard her with the love that I have for members of my own family. Yet, she was undeniably a murderess. I frankly did not know if we would ever discover why she committed those crimes. Without that knowledge, I feared we would not be able to persuade the courts or the governor to spare her life.

As Velma Barfield's appeal continued, the reality of the death penalty in the South shifted dramatically. In 1981, there had been one execution in the United States. In 1982 there were two executions, and in 1983 there were five executions. In the spring of 1984, James Hutchins was the first person in North Carolina to be executed in approximately twenty years. The death machinery was functioning with increasing efficiency, and it was primed to obliterate Velma Barfield. Yet the question that remained unanswered was how this woman, who was known and loved by many, both inside and outside the prison, could have poisoned four people. It did not seem to bother Velma Barfield as it did those of us who knew her. Dick Burr commented:

> Velma always seemed to have a hopeful attitude about things. She balanced her hope with what we realistically expected from a particular proceeding in the courts. She was always better able than the local lawyer recruited to assist in the case, or me to sustain a real sense of hopefulness and optimism about the outcome of her case. She felt that with [us] representing her, she was represented by good lawyers and that it would make a difference. She had not been represented by good lawyers at the trial and she had the fairly simple belief that was all it would take. Right up until we had no more legal proceedings to pursue, she never gave up her sense of hopefulness about her life.
>
> I think her sense of optimism was rooted in more than hopefulness about the outcome of her case. I think she had some real resolution in her life, so she was able to maintain hope without ever being overwhelmed by despair. It was as if she believed that if she didn't succeed in the courts, that it was not the end for her anyway.

Dick Burr was fighting to keep his client alive with all the tools the law provided. He had come to love Velma deeply in the four years he represented her, and although he did not share her profound Christian faith, he admired the strength it provided for Velma. Yet for Dick Burr, if Velma achieved the after-life, she would first be killed by the state of North Carolina—an unacceptable final solution that he sought desperately to avoid.

Burr described the next step in the effort to save Velma Barfield:

> We felt that all of our efforts should be put into the clemency plea. I
> did a lot of strategy planning. . . . Jimmie and Lao really put a
> massive effort into clemency from March until September, 1984.
> We put together a huge clemency presentation involving people
> who cared a great deal about Velma. It included people who had
> known her a long time, or who had come to know her since she was
> in prison. These people spoke about Velma's many qualities that
> deserved life, and about how much she had meant in their lives.
>
> The most moving and impassioned of the pleas were from people
> at the Women's Prison. Velma had touched each of these people,
> including the warden. Velma grew where she was planted, and
> sank deep roots in that prison and touched a lot of lives. Women at
> that prison loved her like a mother or sister. She was not a convict
> at that prison, but a part of everybody's life in a very important
> way.
>
> One of my favorite stories about Velma and the prison, from
> when I first met her, was the way she referred to the guards. She
> called them "the help." The term struck me profoundly because I
> had been used to, in all my death penalty cases and prison cases, a
> sharp antagonism between the guards and prisoners. For a
> prisoner to call guards "the help," showed a remarkable inversion
> of power relationships. In fact, there was nothing affected about
> Velma. I mean, that statement was as genuine as anything else
> Velma ever said. You know, she knew these folks were there to
> make a living and to do their job. She treated them with dignity and
> respect and received it in return. I never heard a bad word from
> Velma about any of the guards at that prison.

In preparing the clemency presentation for Governor Hunt, Burr
determined that another psychiatric evaluation was appropriate. He
sought an explanation for the anomalous behavior of this charming
grandmother who had killed four people. In the three years that had
passed since Velma's initial evaluation, Burr had learned a great deal
about evaluating condemned people. A key in the learning process was
working with Dr. Dorothy Otnow Lewis. Dr. Lewis, on the faculty at

New York University and Yale University, combined brilliance with a gift for diagnosis that provided an invaluable framework for understanding violent behavior. In the summer of 1984, Lewis and Burr spent the day at the North Carolina Prison for Women in Raleigh evaluating Velma Barfield. Burr recalled the interview:

> The most difficult experience for her to talk about, an experience that she had never talked about before, was the extent to which she was a victim of sexual abuse by male members of her family. She began to talk about her life in detail, particularly about the time after the onset of her depression, which she dated approximately twelve to fifteen years before the homicide.
>
> Patterns in Velma's earlier life began to emerge—patterns of manic episodes. They were not major manic episodes, but were known in the psychiatric literature to be associated with the development of a manic-depressive disorder—eating binges, buying sprees, outpourings of emotion, outpourings of rage. For the first time, a person's life that previously had not made complete sense to anybody began to make sense.
>
> Seeing Velma as a person suffering from a bipolar mood disorder or a manic-depressive disorder, made a tremendous amount of sense to me. It explained how she could fluctuate between behaving like a normal person and behaving like a psychotic person. However, that is the character of a manic-depressive disorder. You are usually somewhere in between the poles, but you do have those sharp poles, either of which can be the psychotic state. It was during the course of that discussion when Velma said she was glad that this had finally come to an end, because she was afraid that she was going to poison her grandchildren. She didn't know why she did it, but she did it, and it was not something she could stop. That statement fit in sensibly with the bipolar disorder.

In late September, 1984, Velma Barfield's lawyers met with Governor Hunt for over an hour to discuss the case. This meeting occurred six weeks before the election for the U. S. Senate in which Governor Hunt challenged the powerful incumbent, Jesse Helms. Jesse Helms had spent $15,000,000 to maintain his seat, and the large lead once enjoyed by Governor Hunt had been lost. In fact, the polls indicated that he was trailing Senator Helms. In this context, Dick Burr recalled the discussion with Governor Hunt concerning Velma Barfield:

> We sat in the outer part of his office for approximately an hour and a half. We were supposed to have two hours with him, but I think we ended up having only a little more than an hour. He impressed me as somebody who was very well organized. He was familiar with many of the details of the case. The governor had obviously spent a good part of that week seeing family members, friends, and interested parties from both sides of the case.
>
> The governor was very cool, detached, and formal in dealing with us. He asked some incisive questions. But nothing, in fact, made a real impression on him. I did not get a sense that anything had.
>
> I was hopeful that the whole process had made an impact because the governor had heard some powerful pleas. He saw the warden at the Women's Prison who had made a tearful plea. He also heard powerful statements from women at the prison in support of Velma's life.
>
> Although the pleas focused on the goodness of Velma's life in prison, the governor kept saying that it was not enough. He seemed to believe that for someone to have lived a good life after she had committed a murder was not a reason to grant clemency. This astounded us. But it all became clear once he made his statement denying clemency.
>
> The governor said something to the effect that nothing warranted overturning the verdict of the jury and the sentence of the judge. Furthermore, he concluded that nothing suggested that either of those decisions was wrong. It was clear that he focused on the need for new evidence in her case; the need to show that something was wrong with the legal process. He did not focus on what we actually put forward as the heart of the clemency, which was that she was a decent human being who deserved to live because her life had meaning for a number of people. He did not see that as a reason for granting clemency.

After the matter-of-fact interview with Governor Hunt, it came as no surprise that he denied clemency to Velma Barfield on September 27, 1984. The trial judge had previously set the execution date for November 2, 1984. Rather than taking the high road and refusing to decide Velma Barfield's case until after the political race of his life, Governor Hunt practiced the politics of death when he speedily decided the fate of Velma Barfield.

Velma Barfield never had a chance. Apparently, she would become the first woman executed since the historic 1976 Supreme Court decisions. Suddenly, the vortex of death loomed before all who cared for Velma Barfield and sucked us toward a November 2 killing.

— ▼ —

After the denial of clemency, one faint hope remained for keeping Velma Barfield from the executioner. If a legal issue could be uncovered that had not yet been litigated because it had only recently been discovered, then a habeas corpus petition could be sought to stay the execution.

This maneuver was effective in the past because trial lawyers often did not know the proper issues to raise. In Velma Barfield's case, the issue that arose was whether or not she was competent at the trial. The Southern Coalition on Jails and Prisons North Carolina project director found that the issue of her competency at trial had not been litigated. Significantly, medical information indicated that the prescription drugs to which Velma Barfield was addicted had a prolonged withdrawal period. This indicated that Velma was in acute withdrawal at the time of trial. This could explain some bizarre behavior on her part. For instance, she laughed at the prosecutor, wore inappropriate clothing while hospitalized, and had erratic mood shifts upon arrival at the Women's Prison. Thus the decision became whether or not to raise this newly discovered issue after the clemency denial.

After Governor Hunt denied clemency, Velma's children strongly felt that the end was near. They simply did not believe they could endure another round of litigation with raised expectations, only to lose once again. They had persuaded the local counsel to oppose any further legal action. On the other hand, I felt strongly that the competency issue deserved litigation and might result in a stay of execution. Clearly, it was Velma's decision. Dick Burr flew to North Carolina to discuss the legal situation with Velma Barfield. Burr recalled their discussion:

I went back to North Carolina to see Velma on October 22 to go over the potential issues with her. I had talked with a psychiatrist in Atlanta who was going to provide very helpful corroboration of the effect of her withdrawal and its relationship to competency to stand trial. We were documenting the evolution of the medical knowledge in order to show that information relevant to her competency to stand trial simply was not known at the time of her trial, or even at the time of her first state and federal collateral proceedings.

At that long afternoon meeting, Velma seemed as though she wanted to pursue the issue. Her local counsel cautioned her to think about it overnight and talk with her children, because their position had been that unless there was nearly a guarantee, they did not want her to litigate the issue.

The next morning we returned to the prison and she was just as serene as could be. She said, "I want to do it. I couldn't live with myself or die with myself if I knew I had given up, and I'm not ready to give up. I think I owe it to everybody on Death Row not to give up, and I don't want the state to have the last word in this case." Velma was fired up and ready to go.

I think Velma's children felt bad about her decision because they didn't get the guarantees they wanted. Velma, however, did not feel bad about it at all. You know, she really separated herself at that critical point from her children and decided what she had to do. It was just a beautiful, beautiful time with her that morning. She was just on fire.

We started early Monday morning, October 29, in the state trial court. We wrangled a hearing there the next morning. We lost there and took it to the North Carolina Supreme Court. We didn't get an argument there, so it was hard to get any sense of that court. Then, on Wednesday, we had a hearing with Judge Dupree in the Federal Court for the Eastern District of North Carolina in Raleigh. The hearing began in the afternoon. We argued for a stay of execution in order to conduct an evidentiary hearing on Velma's competency to stand trial. We finished about 5:00 P.M. and waited for word.

I entered into this last-ditch drama to save Velma Barfield in the late afternoon of October 30. Arriving at the federal district courtroom, I observed Dick Burr present his arguments before Judge Dupree. After

Burr completed his arguments he left the courtroom for a nearby law office. While we waited for Judge Dupree's ruling, we ordered food and made plans for the journey north on Highway 1 to Richmond, Virginia, the home of the Fourth Circuit Court of Appeals.

At 7:30 P.M. we were summoned back to the courthouse for a copy of Judge Dupree's order. As expected, Judge Dupree ruled against Velma Barfield. However, he granted a certificate of probable cause indicating his belief the appeal had merit. It was time to drive to Richmond.

At 8:30 A.M., November 1, 1984, the oral arguments in *Barfield* v. *Woodard* began. Velma Barfield's execution was set for 2:00 A.M. on November 2, 1984. Given that only seventeen hours remained before the scheduled execution, coupled with the conservative posture of the U.S. Supreme Court regarding the death penalty, the three-judge panel of the Fourth Circuit Court of Appeals would probably decide the fate of Velma Barfield.

After the state completed its argument, Dick Burr stood and walked to the podium for his argument. He began to set the stage, describing the convoluted history that had brought Velma Barfield's case before the court at the last hour. But before he even finished chronicling the development of the competency issue, one judge commenced an *ad hominem* assault on Dick Burr that totally shocked me. The judge was utterly disrespectful of Burr's position as he harassed him from the bench. My astonishment soon gave way to anger. I knew that the judge's outburst meant that Velma Barfield was doomed.

Another judge finally interjected and began a soliloquy that saddened me as much as the first judge angered me. Basically, the second judge stated in a five-minute peroration from the bench that he would like to do something, but the Supreme Court had tied his hands. Listening to him, a man I knew and respected, sign his conscience over to the state because of his oath to uphold the law, drained my anger, and gloom descended upon me. I sat through the remainder of the hearing, aghast and depressed. Velma Barfield was truly going to be killed even though she was no more responsible for her crimes than any other psychotic. Richard Burr recounted the events in court:

> The judge hastily said: "The Supreme Court has tied our hands." I think my response was, "It doesn't have to come out that way in this case because we have presented an issue that at the very least

requires a full evidentiary inquiry, but Judge Dupree did not let us have it." I seem to remember the judge not making any response to that. I don't think there was any doubt in our minds what they were going to do.

After the hearing the clerk informed us of the decision against Velma. A written order would be forthcoming, so we adjourned to Bob Brewbaker's law office. Bob was a close college friend who once again came through in an emergency situation by providing us with an office and telephone for the remainder of the day.

We called the attorneys in Raleigh who were communicating the latest development in the courts to Velma Barfield, who remained on death watch at Central Prison. They agreed to take the news to the prison and share it with Velma personally. Mary Ann Talley, one of the attorneys, also agreed to counsel Velma to file a petition for *certiorari* to the U.S. Supreme Court. Dick Burr, Adam Stein, and I began seeking issues to frame for the Supreme Court.

As the afternoon progressed, we awaited a written opinion from the Fourth Circuit panel in the forlorn hope it would give us yet another opportunity to appeal to the Supreme Court. At 4:30 P.M., we moved to the conference room adjacent to the clerk's office in the Fourth Circuit, because the appeal was to be delivered to us there. Shortly after 5:00 P.M. the order was delivered. We read it. There was nothing to appeal. Our last gasp of hope was gone. Velma Barfield had nine hours to live.

Due to the time it took to prepare the order, Dick Burr opted to ride back on the state plane with the attorney general's staff in order to visit Velma one last time. Adam Stein and I would drive back and join the hundreds of people gathering in protest outside of Central Prison.

After returning to Raleigh, Dick Burr went directly to the prison for a final contact visit with Velma Barfield, who seemed unafraid and serene. He commented:

> I arrived at the prison about 8:00 P.M. I had arranged earlier with Mary Ann to buy two roses for Velma for me to give to her, and Mary Ann had done it. I picked up the roses at the prison and took them in to see Velma. Mary Ann was already in with Velma and I went in to see her. It was so surreal. We were having a contact visit, sitting in the room with her, and I gave her the roses. We

hugged each other. I couldn't talk to her. Mary Ann sort of carried the conversation, Velma talked, and finally toward the end of the time I just told her how much she meant to me as a person, and as a lawyer.

I guess it wasn't in Velma's character to be angry. Nevertheless, I wish I'd had the strength to say to her, "Velma, it's wrong. I think it's wrong. I think you ought to claw and kick and scratch and scream." You know, that would have been the Velma who said, "I don't want the state to have the last word in this case." That would have been the Velma who said go ahead and go back to court. But, Velma had been convinced that the doors to the execution chamber were the gateway to heaven. So, instead, Velma kept talking about that.

People, however, have to face their death in their own way and nobody faces it the same. They are not dying, you know. They are being killed. They are not coming to the end of a natural process, they are being murdered. They don't scream because their soul is in anguish, they scream because what is happening to them is wrong. That bothered me a lot. The whole serenity of the night bothered me a lot.

Later, Dick Burr joined Velma's children in an associate warden's office to wait for the execution. As they looked out from Central Prison, they beheld hundreds of people gathered in silence with candles illuminating the darkness. The protesters were gathered on a grassy knoll across a creek bed from the prison, a mere three hundred yards away. A visible witness against the barbarity perpetrated on Velma Barfield was made with a simultaneous affirmation of the worth of Velma's life, regardless of what the state of North Carolina decided.

As someone who had joined the throng about 10:00 P.M., I felt honored to bear a candle in tribute to a woman I held so dear. The anger I felt at the entire scenario ebbed and flowed as the night progressed toward the inevitable denouement at 2:00 A.M. I alternated between pacing the hillside alone and talking with friends.

The people gathered across the street in support of Velma Barfield's killing burst into a chant as the time neared 2:00 A.M. "Kill the bitch! Kill the bitch!" The refrain shattered the night air with its hatefulness. I noticed one of Velma's brothers separate himself from those gathered at the hilltop, and walk to the curb of the street that separated the protesters and celebrators. He peered into the night like a watchman in a lighthouse, absorbing all around him as the chant for his sister's death repeated itself again and again. It was as if he were trying to comprehend the hate, the spite these strangers felt for a woman they had never met. Finally, he shook his head and returned to the crowd on the hill.

After the execution, Dick Burr, Mary Ann Talley, and I met as we had planned. The three of us talked, shared events of the night, and sought each other out to affirm our own liveliness amid the macabre machinery of deliberate death. As the clock neared 4:30 A.M., exhaustion overtook us.

In reflecting on the events and years with Velma Barfield that led to the dreadful night of November 2, 1984, Dick Burr shared his feelings about the tapestry of relationships Velma had knitted together: "You know, the thing that is true in all of these cases, but was truer with Velma, was that in working in these cases you always meet other really fine folks. But in Velma's case, there were multitudes of such people. . . . It's the fabric in which we were woven together. Velma was the seamstress, the weaver. She was the weaver."

CHAPTER FOURTEEN

MORRIS MASON
Virginia
June 25, 1985

As spring gave way to summer in 1985, I found myself face to face with a terminal situation. Although I didn't know the person, I was familiar with his situation and life story. And I couldn't accept what was apparently going to happen to him.

The state of Virginia was trying to electrocute a manchild, Morris Mason, age 32, who had an I.Q. of 66 and was a diagnosed paranoid schizophrenic. The evaluation was not in question; it had been made by doctors who worked for a Veterans Administration hospital in Pennsylvania. The state of Virginia was seeking to kill a man who, when rational, had the mentality of the lowest 3 percent of the population in the United States. The scenario boggled the mind. A person was going to be electrocuted by the state despite evidence of his diminished mental capacity. Surely, I thought, the federal courts will stop this insanity.

When Morris Mason was taken from Mecklenburg Correctional Center to the Virginia State Penitentiary on Spring Street near downtown Richmond, he was escorted to the basement and placed in a holding cell near the electric chair. There he would wait to see if he received a stay of execution from the courts. During his several trips to the penitentiary, he would call the SCJP project director for Virginia, Marie Deans. Marie was working tirelessly on Mason's case to be sure the issues of his mental retardation and mental illness were presented to the courts. During one attempt to telephone Marie, Morris talked with her twelve-year-old son, Robert. Later Robert described the conversation with Morris Mason as "just like baby sitting." Morris Mason had few verbal skills, and an ability to reason only at a child's level, yet he was being treated by the state of Virginia as an adult fully responsible for his actions.

Morris Odell Mason was born in Philadelphia and brought at the age of five months to the Eastern shore of Virginia so his mother could raise him with her family. Northampton, the peninsula on which Morris Mason grew up, is famous for its clams, oysters, and produce. Indeed, over 85 percent of Virginia's produce comes from the verdant fields of the Eastern shore. Its isolation from the mainland creates a rural environment more reminiscent of the nineteenth than the twentieth century.

When Morris was five years old, his mother married a man by whom she had three daughters. Morris and his three halfsisters grew up near the community of Birdsnest.

Since Morris was six years old before his first sister was born, he was a protected child. His aunt Lauramer Amers described him in an interview with Rex Springston of the *Richmond News Leader:* "He didn't know how to fight. He was very much a coward. One time he came home from school crying. The other children had taken his books. . . . The kids he played with would take advantage of him. They would lie in wait for him to come to the ballgame on Sunday so they could take his money from him."

Morris was caught in various misdeeds while in school. The principal at Northampton Middle School told Springston, "Mason was constantly in trouble for such things as small thefts. Somehow, Mason was consistently ending up 'holding the bag' while other troublemakers escaped detection."

The warning signs of a troubled child were apparent. Morris was not bright enough either to do well in school or to get along with his classmates. So he became a loner. After the tenth grade, he dropped out.

Given the isolation of the Eastern shore, perhaps it is understandable that no one was alerted to Morris Mason's behavior problems. However, at age seventeen, he was involuntarily committed to Eastern State Hospital by his mother and authorities for repeated acts of arson. At that time, he was diagnosed as being "mentally retarded." Despite this evaluation, Morris was able to enlist in the Army. He was discharged a year later due to a back injury.

In January of 1974, Morris Mason began a period of six weeks in a Veterans Administration Hospital in Coatesville, Pennsylvania. Complaining of hearing voices, he was evaluated and diagnosed a paranoid schizophrenic. He left with a documented history of mental illness and mental retardation. But he was never to receive assistance for either condition.

Unable to adjust to society, Morris committed arson and was sent to prison. He served two and a half years and returned to the Eastern shore no more equipped to deal with life than he had been when he left. It was the spring of 1978, and Morris Mason remained on parole.

In May 1978, Morris Mason began a crime spree on the Eastern shore of Virginia. He spent several days in jail for defrauding an innkeeper. After his release, feeling he was rapidly losing control, Morris Mason called his parole officer twice asking for help. Finally, on May 12, he requested to be put in a halfway house because he couldn't cope with life. The parole officer set a meeting for later in the week. The appointment was never kept.

On May 13 Morris Mason attacked seventy-two-year-old Margaret Hand, bound her to a chair, killed her, and burned down her house. On May 14 he attacked two children aged twelve and thirteen, leaving one a paraplegic. He was apprehended the same day after setting fire to an unoccupied house. After the arrest, he also confessed to the May 2 murder of Ursula Stevenson. He was never tried for this crime because of a lack of evidence.

At his trial, Morris Mason pleaded guilty, waived his right to a jury trial, and was sentenced to die for killing Margaret Hand. He left the courtroom saying, "I'm the killer for the Eastern shore. I made the Eastern shore popular."

How was it possible for Morris Mason—with an I.Q. of 66 and previously diagnosed as a paranoid schizophrenic—to waive his right to a jury trial? Indeed, did Morris even know what a trial was or what kind of difficulty he was facing? These questions will never be answered because the trial court judge denied the defense counsel's request for a private psychiatric evaluation.

Given the remoteness of the Eastern shore, and the horror of his crime on the forty-mile-long peninsula with a population of fifteen thousand, the urge for vengeance was understandable. But simple justice demanded that some judge in some court stop these proceedings and determine whether or not it was proper to electrocute the mentally retarded and mentally ill.

Horrible crimes led Morris Mason to Death Row. But questions linger. How did this manchild go so long without help? Or, as Alice Brinkley Brown, who taught English to Morris Mason in junior high school, told Rex Springston: "The things he did were really terrible, but the state is partly responsible. This never would have happened if they had hospitalized him like they should have. . . . The boy needed help."

Joe Giarratano, a prisoner on Death Row in Mecklenburg with Morris Mason for four years, recalls being in the same housing pod and relating with Morris on a daily basis.

Morris Mason as I Knew Him

The only description that would aptly describe Morris Mason is that he was a child in mind who had no concept of reality. Morris was the same everyday, and always seemed to live in his own little world. Living with him was like living with a hyper-active eight-year-old. He could never sit still, and was always talking. If one ever wanted to know something about sports one could find out from Morris. Talking with him was like talking to a kid who knew everything there was to know about a particular sport he liked. He had absolutely no reading comprehension, and could barely spell his name. Morris would ask me, or one of the other men, to read his mail to him. He would also ask us to write out responses to the letters he would receive. Then he would copy the words down in his own handwriting: large block print letters.

Morris had no concept of death, and didn't have the slightest idea of what being on Death Row meant. Morris just existed here from day to day talking about sports. He always had a perpetual grin on his face, and was docile as a lamb for as long as I knew him. Even after his execution date was set, and the guards came to take him to the death house, he told us that he'd see us in a couple of days. He would stand for hours talking to anyone who would stand and listen to him, and his conversations were always the same. At one time or another he would always manage to get on our nerves, and one of us would snap at him. When that would happen he would go to his cell for a few hours, come back, and try to give you a carton of cigarettes so that you would not be mad at him. But, no one could stay angry with him—most everyone just felt sorry for him.

It was weird because he never seemed to sleep. No matter what time of day or night you could always hear Morris chattering away. He would call down to my cell at night to ask if I was awake, and it never mattered if I wasn't. He'd just keep calling until I was. I'd growl at him and he'd just keep right on talking. When he decided I was no longer listening he'd call someone else.

In a nutshell, that was Morris Mason: the same from one day to the next. When they executed Morris they didn't kill a consciously responsible individual: they executed a child in a man's body. To this day I do not believe that Morris knew right from wrong, or left from right for that matter. He just didn't want anyone to be angry with him. That includes the guards who worked the unit. The guards were always his best listeners: they had to be here for eight hours a shift anyway. And Morris would stand there and babble for as long as they would sit and listen. Back then conditions on the Row were pretty harsh, but nothing seemed to phase him. No one here, prisoner or guard, saw Morris as a threat. If he were here today he would still be chattering on about sports, and trying to please people in his own out-of-touch-with-reality way.

Joe Giarratano

On June 25, 1985, Marie Deans and I visited Morris Mason in the basement of the Virginia State Penitentiary. Morris was scheduled for electrocution at 11:00 P.M. Our afternoon visit was spent talking with Morris while he packed his meager possessions in a box. He showed us letters he'd received, proud to have been sent mail even though some letters urged his killing. All Morris understood was that people were writing to him, and usually that didn't happen. He was very tender with Marie and me. He gave Marie a bracelet when she started crying. Looking at her as a child would look at an unhappy mother, he sought to comfort her: "Don't cry. Don't cry. It's all right. It's for you. Promise me you won't give it away." Marie clutched the bracelet and promised.

Morris gave me a photograph of himself in his cell on Death Row. He showed us all the pictures he had. He was proud of the few things he could show off to us. As the afternoon progressed, I felt like a father to him. He so much wanted our approval and kept trying to take care of us.

The guards kept interjecting into the conversation, always trying to keep the mood light. Marie and I left for supper. We came back afterward, accompanied by Morris's lawyer. We talked sports through the evening. The lawyer and I shared sports enthusiasm with Morris.

At one point, Morris looked up and asked: "What does it mean to die?" Marie responded: "It means you'll be with your grandmother." That seemed to satisfy Morris, and he chatted on about basketball. Suddenly, he stopped and told Marie: "You tell Roger [another Death Row prisoner] when I get back, I'm gonna show him I can play basketball as good as he can." The concept of death eluded Morris as it does any child.

At about 8:30 the death squad came to shave him for electrocution. We had to leave. When we returned we found Morris lying on his bunk, the back of his shaved head glistening from the light outside the cell. He turned to us and sighed: "Oh, Marie, look what they've done to me now." The clothes they had given him dwarfed his small frame. The blue denim shirt and blue jeans made Morris look clownish.

We sat outside the cell, the minutes slipping away. Marie held Morris's hand. He asked us about death again. Before we could answer, his expression brightened, and he said: "Does it mean I get to order anything I want for breakfast?" For Morris, selecting his own meal after years of being fed in his cell represented the ultimate idea of heaven.

As Morris was struggling to articulate thoughts about death and dying, a shout and commotion came from the hallway leading into the basement. I was so intent on helping Morris verbalize his thoughts, I only dimly heard the noise. Morris's face was before mine on the other side of the bars. He looked over my shoulder in the direction of the voice. Suddenly, hatefully, he spat out a man's name. Surprised, I turned around to confront the warden of Mecklenburg Correctional Center, the location of Death Row over one hundred miles from Richmond and the electric chair. He was striding across the basement floor, yelling that he had to have a "private" conversation with Morris Mason. Marie and I stepped aside, and Morris greeted the warden's arrival with the enthusiasm of encountering a poisonous snake. The warden stayed about ninety seconds, asking Morris if he had a message for the men on Death Row. Morris mumbled a few nothings, and the man left. Puzzled, Marie and I returned to Morris after the "private" conversation was concluded.

It was 10:30, and we only had fifteen more minutes with Morris. Morris was absolutely determined to make Marie and me "proud" of him. He kept saying: "You tell the men [on Death Row] how strong I was. I'm gonna be strong. I'm gonna be brave. I'm gonna make you proud." It was like a litany. Morris was holding to this refrain, even as he trembled, to get through the next few minutes. "I'm gonna be strong. I'm gonna be brave. I'm gonna make you proud."

The overwhelming feeling of bidding good-bye to a child struck me. Marie and I were Morris's parents for his last minutes. We knew he would make us proud and that it was his gift to us.

At 10:45 the death squad assembled outside Morris's cell. Morris said to us: "I love you. Don't be sad. Don't cry." We told Morris we loved him too.

Marie and I exited through the basement door, walked up into the yard and through the administration building. Outside, the warden was holding court with the press, informing them of how "competent" Morris Mason was. Suddenly I understood why this warden had made his perfunctory visit to Morris. As Marie and I joined the candlelight vigil protesting the electrocution, he spoke for quite some time to the press about his ninety-second conversation with Morris. I saw why Morris Mason spat out his name with such vehemence.

Across the street, a cheering mob of seventy-five to one hundred people were chanting "Fry the nigger" and "Kill the coon." When the official word came that Morris had been killed, this ghoulish gathering filled the summer's night air with a cheer.

Echoing in my mind was Morris Mason's benediction:
"I'm gonna be strong.
I'm gonna be brave.
I'm gonna make you proud."

CHAPTER FIFTEEN

WILLIE DARDEN
Florida
March 15, 1988

As a child growing up in Pitt County, North Carolina, in the early 1950s, I saw the public bathrooms and drinking fountains labeled "white" and "colored." Black people could not eat with white people in restaurants. Black and white were legally separate and unequal.

Such signs were merely a part of life for Southerners, but the hatred and fear those signs represented were brought home to me at a very young age.

One of my aunts was driving me in her car through my home town of Greenville, North Carolina, one day in the early 1950s. As we stopped at a traffic light, a black woman wearing a multicolored dress walked in front of our car while crossing the street. I pointed to her and exclaimed: "Look at the beautiful dress the colored lady has on!"

My aunt turned, grabbed my arm, and yanked me up so that my face almost touched hers. Then, squeezing my arm so hard it hurt, her face contorted with emotion, she spat out the words: "Don't ever let me hear you call a nigger a lady again!" She pushed me backwards into the seat.

If such hatred, anger, and fear existed in the early 1950s, there was no doubt it flourished in the 1930s. The racial apartheid during the depression was particularly severe. Black sharecroppers toiled on white men's land. Lynchings were frequent throughout the South, and vigilante actions were swift and sure.

Into this world Willie Jasper Darden was born in 1933.

Willie Darden was the son of an auto mechanic and the great-grandson of a slave born in Greene County. In many ways, circumstances had not altered significantly for many of the black people of Greene County since slavery. The Reverend Leon White, born in Franklin County in 1932 amid the rural poverty common for so many black Southern families, recalls in an affadavit from Willie Darden's clemency petition: "In 1860, slaves constituted half the total population of Greene County; in 1930, blacks constituted half the total population. They owned only 4 percent of the taxable wealth in the state, and the average black family income was less than $1,000 annually. Four out of five black farming families were tenant farmers or sharecroppers."

Willie Darden was fortunate to survive infancy. North Carolina was fifth in the United States in infant mortality rate. North Carolina lost nine children out of every one thousand born. Willie's mother, who gave birth to him when she was fifteen years old, died in childbirth two years later.

Willie Darden was especially close to his maternal grandfather, the son of a slave, who homesteaded a "two horse" farm. Land was especially precious for black families, and as soon as he was old enough, Willie helped his grandfather farm.

Although Willie enjoyed learning, school had to take a backseat to farming. After his grandfather's death, Willie felt responsible for keeping the farm going, being "the man of the family," even though he was just a teenager. Willie managed to complete the eighth grade—quite an accomplishment in an area where black adults averaged a second-grade education. His aunt recalled, "Because I spent so much time with Willie, Jr., when he was a child, I was as close to him as if he were my own. He went to Sunday school every week with my children, and I know for a fact that that child was always solid as a rock."

The Zechariah School for the Colored provided a lot of the joy of learning for Willie. Willie was from a family his aunt described as "a first-class colored family in Greene County. The white families would hire our husbands and children to work in the tobacco factories during the season because [we] were known to be a hard-working and religious family."

Being black in the South meant you were regarded by white folks as either "a good nigger" or "a bad nigger." The line was not clearly drawn. However, once a black person broke the law, whites saw him or her as a "bad nigger."

Willie Darden became a "bad nigger" as a result of being placed in foster care after his grandfather died and his stepmother deserted the family. Forced to provide free labor for his foster family, Willie began to steal to get food and clothing. Eventually caught stealing from a mailbox, he was sent to the National School for Boys, a segregated facility. At the age of sixteen, Willie began his lengthy experience with prisons.

Upon release from the juvenile facility, Willie Darden did odd jobs.

Willie met his future wife in 1953. They dated for two years before marrying in 1955. In January of 1956, Willie Darden was arrested for trying to cash a $48 forged check. He was sentenced to four years in prison. His ex-wife recalls: "It broke my heart that they put him away so long because I knew that he had done it to buy us some food."

His experience in prison in North Carolina embittered him to the degree that he seemed determined to become a "bad nigger," just as white law enforcement sought to portray him. Menial jobs were all he had been able to find since leaving the security of home in Greene County. By the time I met Willie Darden on a visit to Florida State Prison in 1979, he had been on Death Row for five years. His first death warrant was signed by Governor Bob Graham on May 18, 1979.

Willie had been convicted of killing a man in a robbery of a furniture store near Lakeland, Florida. His life prior to coming to Florida State Prison was checkered with convictions for assault, forgery, and theft. The dark-skinned, proud man I came to know through visits to Death Row at FSP was a twenty-year veteran of prison life. Only as our friendship grew did this old-time convict trust me with the details of his childhood in Greene County. Willie Darden had mastered the art of survival in prison, where the fundamental rule was not to let anyone get too close to you. I was just another white man until the visits through the years cemented our relationship. I became Willie Darden's "homeboy," an affectionate term of black slang, meaning that he and I came from the same neighborhood. Although my birthplace in the hospital in Pitt County and Willie's in a farm house in adjacent Greene County were not far apart geographically, we both knew that the gulf that separated the white world, where I grew up, and the black world, where Willie grew up, was vast. For the gregarious Willie to call me "homeboy" was an endearment transcending the racial worlds that were created to separate us. We became good friends.

Not infrequently someone on Death Row will tell you he is innocent. Sometimes a review of the case record convinces you that such a claim is legitimate. As I came to understand the specifics of Willie Darden's case, the questions of Willie's guilt became too troubling to ignore.

The issues that begged for justice in Willie Darden's case were apparent to anyone with a modicum of experience in death penalty cases. Unfortunately, Darden had been represented by a court-appointed lawyer, a lawyer with a professional career to maintain after Willie Darden was long gone. So, with an inexperienced and unwilling legal counsel, Willie Darden went to trial for his life in January 1974.

Willie's was the only black face in the courtroom. There was a white prosecutor, a white judge, a white defense lawyer, and an all-white jury. "Joe," Willie told me, "when I looked around at all those white faces, I knew how it was gonna come out!"

A black male was charged with killing a white man. The racial overtones in a rural Florida environment made a fair trial virtually impossible. Clearly, a black male would pay for this crime. Events would show that it wasn't important to the authorities whether or not Willie Darden was the man who actually committed the crime.

Christine Bass, a woman living in Lakeland, Florida, came to the courtroom with information exonerating Willie Darden of the crime for which he was being tried. The only problem was that she was not given the opportunity to testify.

Darden's lawyer never called Christine Bass to the witness stand even though she would have testified that Willie Darden had been at her house from 4:00 P.M. to 5:30 P.M. on September 8, 1973. Darden's car had broken down near her house, and she allowed Willie Darden to call a tow truck from her house. He remained outside with his car until 5:30.

The defense lawyer had done no investigation into Darden's case, so he was unwilling to call Christine Bass. The police time of the crime wavered from 6:00 to 6:15, or even 6:30 P.M. There was no way Willie Darden could have left her home in time to commit the crime.

Every day of the trial Christine Bass hoped to be summoned to testify. She was never called. Darden was convicted on eyewitness identification but not linked to the crime by any physical evidence. Over the next decade Christine Bass shared the facts of Darden's whereabouts with anyone who would listen.

The widow of the man who was murdered in the robbery of their furniture store identified Willie Darden in a most peculiar fashion. After initially telling police that she could not remember what the subject looked like or what he was wearing, she identified Willie Darden. One day after her husband's funeral, she was led into a small courtroom where only one black person could be found. He sat at the defense table. The prosecutor asked if "this man sitting here" was "the man that shot your husband."

The other eyewitness, a neighbor who was shot while trying to assist the furniture store owners during the robbery, also identified Willie Darden in a rather odd manner. While in a hospital bed he was shown six photographs. Willie Darden's picture was the only one of the six photos labeled "Sheriff's Department, Bartow, Florida." The man chose Willie Darden's picture.

The discrepancies in the eyewitness reports—whether or not the assailant wore a moustache, the color of the shirt, whether or not the shirt was a pullover—indicated a good deal of confusion about the identity of the suspect. He was said to have been 5'6", 5'8", and 6' tall. The police, however, simplified the identification process by clearly indicating that Willie Darden was the sole suspect to the widow and the most probable suspect to the neighbor who witnessed the crime, as both agreed that the suspect was "colored."

Even under the best of circumstances in the rural South, justice is hard to come by for a black man accused of killing a white person. It is impossible to achieve when a poor defense is combined with a racially inflamed atmosphere in a trial before an all-white jury.

The prosecutor characterized Willie Darden as subhuman throughout the trial. "Willie Darden is an animal who should be placed on a leash." "As far as I'm concerned this animal . . . " In the summation, the prosecutor expressed a desire that he could "see [Darden] sitting here with no face, blown away by a shotgun."

The trial was held in Citrus County, Florida, in Inverness, but the change of venue from Lakeland didn't help. "The only black face in the courtroom," Willie Darden, was bound for a noose. On January 23, 1974, forty-year-old Willie Darden was sentenced to be executed by the state of Florida.

As the years passed, Christine Bass pursued Willie's case. Finally, in a 1979 post-trial hearing, she was able to get her statement in the record as to Willie's whereabouts from 4:00 to 5:30 P.M. on the day of the murder. Despite only meeting Willie Darden when he came to her house to use the telephone, she was haunted by her belief that an innocent man could go to the electric chair. The problem was that her story remained uncorroborated. It would remain so until 1986.

The problem with Willie's case was that even though evidence had emerged to establish his innocence, the failure of his court-appointed trial lawyer to unearth any of this in 1974 placed Willie in imminent danger. Governor Bob Graham had already signed two death warrants and had used the Darden case in public speeches as an example of the court's thwarting the death penalty. If Willie were now proven innocent, the politicians pushing for his death would be embarrassed. We feared that another warrant could well be a final one for Willie. Willie Darden was a marked man in the politics of the death penalty.

Governor Bob Graham signed Willie's third death warrant, setting the execution date for September 2, 1985.

In early September of 1985, I journeyed to Starke, Florida, to be with Willie and Felicia, his sweetheart who had corresponded with Willie and visited him faithfully for years. She was a kind-hearted woman who didn't understand the legal complexities of the death penalty. But she knew she loved Willie and wanted to be with him.

The legal status of Willie's case was simple. The U.S. Supreme Court would either stop the execution or allow it to proceed. There was no other avenue of aid possible.

On September 1, Felicia, Margaret Vandiver, and I gathered at Mike Radelet's home in Gainesville, Florida, before driving to the prison. We expected to hear from the Supreme Court shortly. It was the evening of September 1. The electrocution was set for 7:00 A.M., September 2.

As Mike, Margaret, and I planned who would ride with whom to the prison for our final visits with Willie, Felicia watched the local television news for word about Willie's final appeal. She heard the reporter announce that the Supreme Court had turned down Willie's final request for a stay of execution. We were startled by a piercing wail from her. She grabbed her purse and ran out the door toward her car. Stunned, we didn't understand what had happened until we glanced at the television. I ran to catch Felicia before she drove to the prison.

Felicia was behind the steering wheel as I slid into the car. I reached for her hand that clasped her key. "Felicia, don't drive this car. You're upset. You won't do Willie any good if you wreck this car trying to drive it."

Felicia sobbed in my arms, moaning, "They're going to kill Willie." I tried to comfort her. "Felicia, we haven't heard from the lawyers. Let's wait until they call before we reach conclusions. The press often makes mistakes with this crazy process."

Holding Felicia and trying to convince myself as well as the tearful woman in my arms, I kept hearing in my mind her wail when she had heard the news. It was so instinctive, so painful; it still reverberated through me. "Lord, give us strength," I prayed.

Felicia finally agreed to allow me to drive her to the prison. Margaret would follow shortly. We made the forty-five-minute drive to the prison in painful silence. There was nothing to say to ease her pain.

Arriving at dusk, we waited for Margaret, who arrived with the confirming word from the lawyers. The Supreme Court by a 5-4 vote had denied Willie's stay of execution request at about 6:00 P.M. We entered the prison for our last visits with Willie Darden.

Until midnight we would visit Willie through the glass barrier, speaking through a covered opening in the window. Then Willie would have a one-hour contact visit with Felicia. I would spend the remainder of the night with him, seated outside his cell until they came to shave his head for the electrocution.

Margaret and I wanted Felicia to have as much private visiting time as possible with Willie. We greeted Willie and moved to the far end of the visiting area. After spending almost an hour comforting Felicia, buoying her spirit, Willie motioned for us to join them.

We had brought a tape player, and our souls were caressed by the *a cappella* voices of Sweet Honey in the Rock. Their songs of oppression of blacks, of striving for freedom echoed in the room of the prison where several blacks had awaited their deaths. Given Willie's case history, his story could very easily have been put to verse and music for Sweet Honey in the Rock to sing.

Willie was determined to keep things upbeat. For Felicia, for us, or maybe for himself, he kept talking about "keeping up the struggle. Not lettin' these people defeat us."

A few minutes before midnight, we made ready to leave. Since I would be with Willie from 1:00 A.M. until 5:30 A.M., I eased out the door to a chair in the corridor outside the visiting area. Slumping against the chair's back, I shut my eyes to try to let this nightmare go away.

As I sat in the chair, I was startled by the sound of rapid footsteps. I was dumbfounded to learn that Willie had gotten a stay. Only six hours earlier the Supreme Court had turned him down. The questions tumbled out. "Who gave him a stay? For how long? Why?"

The story was that although denied 5-4 on Willie's stay of execution application, his lawyers realized that they could very well have the four votes needed to grant a *cert.* petition. The Court rules stated if four justices wanted to hear a case, it would be accepted. *Cert.* would be granted. Justice Lewis Powell, although unpersuaded by the merits of Darden's case, realized that four of his fellow justices felt very strongly about it. In order to prevent the case from being mooted because of Willie Darden's execution, he changed his vote. What at 6:00 P.M. was a 5-4 vote to deny the stay of execution request had become a 5-4 vote to accept the case for oral argument and briefing. As a matter of courtesy to his fellow justices, Justice Lewis Powell saved Willie Darden's life.

The months passed, and Willie Darden's case was argued in the Supreme Court. Fearing the ultimate outcome would be 5-4 against us, we redoubled our efforts for clemency.

Governor Bob Graham, after signing 155 death warrants and killing eighteen people, was elected to the U.S. Senate. His successor was Bob Martinez, the Republican former mayor of Tampa. Governor Martinez would decide Willie Darden's fate.

The adverse Supreme Court ruling came: 5-4 against Willie Darden. Justice Harry Blackmun was incensed about the injustice of the case. His dissent fairly crackled:

> Thus, at bottom, this case rests on the jury's determination of the credibility of three witnesses. . . . I cannot conclude that McDaniel's [the prosecutor] sustained assault on Darden's very humanity did not affect the jury's ability to judge the credibility question on the real evidence before it. Because I believe that he did not have a trial that was fair, I would reverse Darden's conviction; I would not allow him to go to his death until he has been convicted at a fair trial. I believe this Court must do more than wring its hands when a state uses improper legal standards to select juries in capital cases and permits prosecutors to pervert the adversary process. I therefore dissent.

Justice Blackmun even spoke about the case before the Eighth Circuit Court of Appeals judges in the summer of 1987: "If ever a man received an unfair trial, Darden did. He may be guilty, I don't know, but he got a runaround in that courtroom." Supreme Court judges rarely comment publicly on cases. Justice Blackmun was clearly upset.

In a chance conversation with the chaplain at the hospital where she worked, Christine Bass shared Willie Darden's story. The chaplain remembered that a minister friend of his, the Reverend Sam Sparks, had gone to see the dead man's widow shortly after the crime. He suggested they contact this minister to see if he could remember the time he went to the furniture store.

When the woman contacted the minister, she told him about Willie Darden's presence at her house from 4:00–5:30 P.M. The minister replied: "Then it couldn't be him that committed the crime." He was certain he was at the furniture store at 5:55 P.M. He calculated it took him over a half hour to get to the store after being notified of the crime. His testimony provided the missing link in the time sequence. Although the police had moved the time until as late as 6:30 P.M., the minister was at the store and the police were already on the scene at 5:55 P.M. Sparks's testimony, coupled with Christine Bass's statement, meant that Willie Darden, who had maintained his innocence since his arrest, could not have committed the crime. The new evidence claim stayed Willie's fifth death warrant.

Willie corresponded with people throughout the world. He had a particularly strong base of support in Holland. He kept himself busy writing and sharing his case with people everywhere.

The Southern Coalition on Jails and Prisons mounted a clemency campaign. Thousands of requests for clemency for Willie Darden poured into the governor's office. I was able to interest two network news magazines—"West 57th Street" of CBS and "20/20" of ABC—in Willie's story. Both broadcast episodes on Willie's case in January of 1988.

Amnesty International launched a world-wide campaign to gain clemency for Willie. Coupled with the clemency effort of the SCJP, Govenor Martinez's office was flooded with petitions. Included in the letters was correspondence from Dr. Andrei Sakharov, winner of the 1975 Nobel Peace Prize. Sakharov wrote:

I ask you to intervene in the affair of Willie Darden. I am convinced that capital punishment is an inhumane institution for which there can be no room in a civilized, democratic society.

Injustice, a mistake in relation to an executed person, cannot be set right. Moreover, capital punishment may not be applied in cases where there's at least a shadow of doubt of the legality of the sentence, or the unbiased nature of the legal system for racial or other reasons. I ask that the death sentence of Willie Darden be revoked.

The winter of 1987–1988 brought good news to my wife, Becca, and me. Our hoped-for adoption of our first child was going to materialize. We journeyed to Alabama to pick her up from the hospital. We arrived at Becca's parents' house in Huntsville, Alabama, to await the birth of our baby. On March 5, 1988, Amelia Gaston Ingle was born. She had to remain in the hospital until her bilirubin count came down to normal. Becca and I could hardly wait to bring her home.

On March 8, as I waited for the telephone call from the hospital telling us to pick up our daughter, the phone rang. It was Willie Darden's lawyer calling to tell me that Governor Martinez had signed Willie's seventh death warrant. The execution was set for March 15. The lawyer also told me that Willie sent a message. "Joe, don't come down here. Stay with Becca and your baby. I know how much this means to you."

Becca and I brought Amelia home from the hospital on March 9. After three wonderfully sleepless nights with our new daughter, I journeyed to the Florida State Prison on March 13.

During the evening of March 14 at the Florida State Prison, we heard from court after court that Willie's appeals had been denied. Yet we all maintained hope until the U.S. Supreme Court ruled 6-3 against Willie shortly after midnight. Willie had seven short hours to live.

Shortly after Willie's final visit with Felicia, we shared a brief service of penitence and communion. We then walked back to his cell on Q wing with several guards escorting us. As always with a condemned prisoner, Willie had his hands cuffed behind him for the walk. Upon reaching the cell he was strip-searched and given fresh clothes to wear.

Willie and I went through his voluminous correspondence. He didn't have time, due to the short period of the death warrant, to write to everyone. So he looked through his address book and indicated whom he wanted me to write to on his behalf. This effort consumed over an hour. I gave him two Jamaican cigars, and we smoked, talked through the bars of the cell, and reviewed his correspondence. Soon it was past 2:00 A.M. Willie spoke of his son and grandson, his love for Felicia, and teased me by referring to me as "Dad." For the first time since our friendship began, I was a father.

The early morning light began to peep through the darkness. Soon they would come to prepare him for killing. At 5:30 A.M. I knelt outside his cell, and we shared a final prayer. We discussed my presence at the execution. I had consented to his request to be there for him, and the guard arrived with a gray briefcase. We both knew that inside the unobtrusive briefcase were the tools to shear his head and leg so the electricity could pass unimpeded through his body. I told him I would see him later. And I left.

Willie had composed a statement for the press and his friends. He requested that I read it to the press assembled in the cow pasture outside the Florida State Prison.

After leaving Willie Darden to be barbered for killing, I joined the witnesses and media in the administration building of the Florida State Prison. After brief instructions, we walked back to the prison itself and were led to a large room that served as a cafeteria. It was approximately 6:00 A.M. We were treated to breakfast by the state of Florida.

I ate at a table alone. Everyone else was gathered two or three to a table. Small talk escaped me, and I sat in silence. My exhaustion, the adrenalin rushing through me from drinking Willie's strong instant coffee, and my own anger left me a silent spectator, lingering on the fringes of this bizarre morning ritual the state kindly provides for those gathered to do their duty. As I gazed about benumbed, seeking to comprehend the events that encased me, I noticed that the room was dominated by two huge flags, hung next to each other, about fourteen feet up the high ceilinged room. The two flags were the flag of the United States of America and the flag of the state of Florida. They were there in all their glory, representing governments engaged in the process of exterminating their citizens. The Florida flag, white background with red, criss-crossed bars, held the state seal encircled in the middle. Beneath the seal, the state motto proclaimed: "In God We

Trust." This state proclaimed to trust in God while it officially destroyed its citizens, not trusting in God to determine the length of their days? I almost burst out with laughter at the pitiful process with which I was caught up. Hannah Arendt was so right when she wrote of "the banality of evil."

At 6:45 A.M. we were assembled and briefed on what to expect upon entering the death house. We filed out of the room, down the corridor and outside.

Two white prison vans conveyed us to the tip of the spine of the Florida State Prison—the death house. The vehicles stopped outside the door to the witness room of the death chamber. The thirty or so people, representing media and law enforcement, clotted in the doorway. Slowly, we entered one by one.

Three rows of white, high-backed chairs facing the window to the electric chair quickly filled up. Seeking a place where Willie could see me when he was brought into the death chamber, I moved to the rear of the viewing area. I stood with my back to the wall at the far end of the witness room.

By the clock in the electrocution room, it was 6:58 A.M. We waited for Willie Darden to be brought to the electric chair.

I cynically thought that if you had seen one death chamber, you had seen them all. The electric chair faced us in the middle of the room. It was slightly elevated, giving it the appearance of an oak hewn throne. A throne for an offering to the god of slaughter.

Shortly after the second hand swept past 7:00 A.M., the door swung open in the rear of the death chamber and Willie Darden stepped across the threshold into the vortex of the killing machinery. He was manacled at his ankles, and his hands were cuffed to a chain around his waist. He moved slowly, but with erect posture and head held proudly high. He was led to the electric chair by the firm hands of the death squad members. They began the process of cinching the leather straps around his waist, legs, and arms. They parted the right trouser leg to apply the electrode that would conduct the deadly current.

As the fastening and strapping process ensued, Willie looked for me. Finding me in the corner, he nodded and gave me a smile. His countenance then surveyed the official witnesses. Slowly gazing at each one individually, he looked directly into their eyes. The chief of the killing team asked Willie if he would like to make a final statement. Willie replied, "Yes." In a clear, firm voice, Willie spoke from his heart without any notes. "I tell you I am not guilty of the charge for which I am about to be executed. I bear no guilt or ill will for any of you. I am at peace with myself, with the world, with each of you. I say to my friends and supporters around the world, I love each and every one of you. Your love and support have been a great comfort to me in my struggle for justice and freedom."

Willie looked at me, holding me fast with his gaze. I had removed the Committee of Southern Churchmen symbol that I wear around my neck. I held the symbol in my clenched fist before my face. Willie Darden and I looked into each other's eyes, the symbol uniting us in life and into death.

The guards tilted Willie's shaved head back against the chair at an uncomfortable angle. With his held head back, a chin strap was fastened around his jaw. Willie winced at it was tightened. Still maintaining eye contact with me, he then did a most extraordinary thing. He winked his left eye at me, lifted his left thumb upward, as if to assure me that he was all right. Then, as they dropped the black mask over his face, he waved good-bye with his left hand, even though his arm was strapped down to the infernal device. I almost lost control.

After his face was covered, I returned the cross to my neck and dropped my head in unceasing prayer. Repeatedly I prayed for strength for Willie, for acceptance of his soul, and for God to grant me some way not to lose my own soul in the next few minutes. Finally, I looked up again.

The scene that greeted me was eerily calm. Willie was strapped in the chair, two medical personnel opening his shirt to place stethoscopes on his chest to check for a heartbeat. They each leaned over Willie's body, then rose. Willie Darden's official killing was intoned over the microphone to us all: "The sentence of the court against Willie Darden has been carried out. He was pronounced dead at 7:12 A.M."

March 15, 1988

Dearest friends and supporters:

Writing this short message to you is by no means an easy task. There is much I would love to say to you, but I have not the time or the patience to write all that needs to be said.

Nevertheless, it is my sincere hope that each of you will know and understand the fact that my love for you is never-ending, that my respect for you and the friendship we came to know so well shall never ~~diminish~~ diminish.

The news I have for you is not good! But it is a reality and, therefore, a fact that will not be ~~against~~. What I am ~~trying~~ to say to you, without sounding angry or bitter, is that my struggle for justice and freedom has run its course. We, together, have fought a great battle. We stood like soldiers on the battlefield and fought our ~~side~~ and side! And we were far out-numbered, we gave our ~~enemies~~ enemies all the hell that could take.

But in the end we lost ---- or did we? On ~~second~~ second thought: hell no, we didn't lose. We won a victory! We lost the war but we had won many victories before we lost in defeat—didn't we?

Well I have been talking but still haven't told you anything you didn't know already. Well maybe it's because I can't find the correct words that would allow me to express my feeling to the fullest. I never said I was smart, you know. In any case, the U.S. Supreme refused to give me a new trial. And the decision left me standing between hell and the deep blue sea. But don't worry, in a few hours my heartaches and pain will be over and the state of Florida will have murdered an innocent man (me) in the electric chair. I have no fear of death, and surely my death will never change the that I am "Innocent!"

To those of you who have fought my case within

the Court System. I have nothing about of the greatest
of love and respect for. I am speaking about Mark E.
Olive, Robert Harper, Jimmy Lohman, Donna Harris,
Jenny, Larry, Schaulette, And all the CCR Crew.

But I do not forget Margaret Vandiver, Susan
Cary, Joe Ingle, Mike Radelet. And the many others
of you who was there for me when I needed you.

Further, My lovely lady Felicia, I you will
be with no matter I go, And certainly I will be there
with you when you walk through our own paradise.
I love with all of myself, darling.

I Shall Conclude here. So you Guys and
Gals be Sweet. Enjoy life. And keep on loving me.

In peace, love, struggle & Solidarity,

Your Brother Gatlin

CHAPTER SIXTEEN

A HOLE IN DEMOCRACY

It is tempting to pretend that minorities on Death Row share a fate in no way connected to our own, that our treatment of them sounds no echoes beyond the chambers in which they die. Such an illusion is ultimately corrosive, for the reverberations of injustice are not so easily confined. . . . And the way in which we choose those who will die reveals the depth of moral commitment among the living.

U.S. Supreme Court Justice William Brennan
McCleskey v. *Kemp*

I have been taught the values of the Judeo-Christian tradition and seek to follow them through my Christian faith. In addition, I have been raised to believe in the practice of democracy and share a belief in such a system of government. In acting as a follower of Jesus of Nazareth and as an American citizen, I find that the very values I have embraced through my religious heritage and political tradition place me at odds with American society and government. In order to understand the conflict between the reality I have experienced through working with the condemned and the values I have been taught, it is most helpful to simply step back and begin with a fresh consideration of the religious and political milieu in which the death penalty is situated. The French philosopher M. Merleau-Ponty described it best in the introduction of his book *Phenomenology of Perception*. In referring to Edmund Husserl's writings, Merleau-Ponty described the philosopher as follows: "The philosopher is a perpetual beginner, which means that he takes for granted nothing that men, learned or otherwise, believe they know."

Although I do not fancy myself a philosopher, I am an individual seeking to discover meaning amid experiences that totally contradict the traditions imparted to me. In order to achieve a viewpoint of the political and religious traditions that address the death penalty situation in America, I step back and begin surveying anew. And I "take[s] for

269

granted nothing that men, learned or otherwise, believe they know." So, let us begin at the beginning of democracy in America.

On May 11, 1831, Alexis de Tocqueville and his traveling companion Gustave de Beaumont arrived in New York harbor. The two young Frenchmen had journeyed to America to examine its fledgling experiment in democracy. Granted a leave from his magistrate post by the French government, Tocqueville's stated purpose was to observe the results of prison reform in America, the penitentiary in particular. He was also interested in observing American government at work. After traveling over seven thousand miles throughout the continent in nine months, Tocqueville returned home and penned *Democracy in America,* part I of which was published in 1835 in Paris. It was followed by part II in 1840.

Even though 155 years have passed since the publication of the completed *Democracy in America,* there has yet to appear a worthy rival to Tocqueville's masterpiece. Because he perceived the fundamental workings of democracy and conveyed them so clearly, we turn to him for analysis of the American system of government.

Although Tocqueville praised the American political experiment, certain aspects of the government alarmed him. One particular manifestation of democracy led him to fear that the minority would become expendable for the majority. Tocqueville described this phenomenon as "tyranny of the majority."

Chapter XV of *Democracy in America* is entitled "The Unlimited Power of the Majority in the United States and Its Consequences." After a brief presentation of the three branches of government (legislative, executive, and judicial), Tocqueville describes how the power of the majority exerts its will through all three branches of government. He concludes with the following observation: "The majority in that country therefore, exercise a prodigious authority, and a power of opinions which is nearly as great; no obstacles exist which can impede or even retard its progress, so as to make it heed the complaints of those whom it crushes upon its path. The state of things is harmful in itself and dangerous for the future" (p. 256).

In the last half of the first volume of *Democracy in America,* Tocqueville hoists a warning flag about inherent difficulties in government by democracy. Under the heading "Tyranny of the Majority," Tocqueville elaborates his fears.

> In my opinion, the main evil of the present democratic institutions of the United States does not arise, as is often asserted in Europe, from their weakness, but from their irresistible strength. I am not so much alarmed at the excessive liberty which reigns in that country as at the inadequate securities which one finds there against tyranny. (p. 260)

Here Tocqueville discerned what I call "a hole in democracy." He perceived that the real danger from tyranny rested in the power of the majority rule. It was a concern he especially had for the future of this young, growing nation he admired. "I do not say that there is a frequent use of tyranny in America at the present day; but I maintain that there is no sure barrier against it, and that the causes which mitigate the government there are to be found in the circumstances and the manners of the country more than its laws" (pp. 261-62).

Tocqueville was not convinced that the separation of powers into the three branches of government would prevent tyranny. Rather, he realized that the powerful influence of the will of the majority would be exerted throughout government. "In the United States the omnipotence of the majority, which is favorable to the legal despotism of the legislature, likewise favors the arbitrary authority of the magistrate" (p. 262). Tocqueville points out how such judges are selected, as is the head of the executive branch—the president—so no branch of government is immune from the "omnipotence of the majority."

In looking to the future, Tocqueville expresses concretely the fear of what the omnipotence of the majority might do:

> If ever the free institutions of America are destroyed, that event may be attributed to the omnipotence of the majority, which may at some future time urge the minorities to desperation and oblige them to have recourse to physical force. Anarchy will then be the result, but it will have been brought about by despotism. (p. 269)

To buttress his fear Tocqueville quotes from James Madison and Thomas Jefferson, who share his concern. The Jefferson quote has proven prophetic: "The executive power in our government is not the only, perhaps not even the principal, object of my solicitude. The tyranny of the legislature is really the danger most to be feared, and will continue to be so for many years to come. The tyranny of the executive power will come in its turn, but at a more distant period" (p. 270).

In order to balance chapter XV on the tyranny of the majority, Tocqueville follows with chapter XVI: "Causes which Mitigate the Tyranny of the Majority in the United States." Here the extent to which conditions have changed in the 155 years since *Democracy in America* was published are apparent.

The "central government" of 1835 has been dramatically altered by the technological revolution. It is now highly organized, bureaucratized and computerized. It is able to function, as Jefferson forecasted and Tocqueville feared, as an instrument to fulfill the will of the majority. The federal government of the United States is one of the most formidable forces in the world.

Using Tocqueville's analysis, today we see the will of majority manifested directly in the election of state legislators, Congress and the President. Whenever state court judges are elected, the judiciary is directly accountable to the majority. The only exception appears to be the federal judiciary, where judges are appointed by the President.

As of December 30, 1989, there are 752 federal judgeships in the United States of America. All are subject to presidential appointment. Of this total, 378 appointments to the bench were made by President Ronald Reagan. President Reagan and his Attorney General, Edwin Meese, were vociferous advocates of a law and order agenda and screened their appointments to be sure they matched their philosophy. Hence a law and order ideology, which includes favoring the death penalty, now predominates the federal judiciary. Since President George Bush also reflects a similar philosophy, the federal courts— including the U. S. Supreme Court, four members of which were appointed by President Reagan—will be less concerned with individual rights than with the state's right to exercise its authority through the legislature. In becoming deferential to legislative will, the federal courts became accountable to the majority will also. The notion of the judiciary exercising a check or balance on the legislature has given way to a furtherance of the state's will regarding political matters of law and order.

Tocqueville was deeply affected by the plight of "the Negro" and "the Indian." He wastes little time in his final chapter before summarizing their situation. "These two unhappy races have nothing in common, neither birth, nor features, nor language, nor habits. Their only resemblance lies in their misfortunes. Both of them occupy inferior positions in the country they inhabit; both suffer from tyranny; and if their wrongs are not the same, they originate from the same authors" (p. 332).

The treatment of blacks and Native Americans by white people distressed Tocqueville. He feared for their future because he saw the tyranny of the majority in this country was tied to race. Blacks had been uprooted and sold into slavery in another country, and "oppression has, at one stroke, deprived the descendants of the Africans of almost all the privileges of humanity." Native Americans were driven from their lands, "condemned . . . to a wandering life, full of inexpressible sufferings." In observing the role of people of European descent in this process, Tocqueville was clear. "European tyranny rendered them [the minorities] more disorderly and less civilized than they were before" (pp. 333-34).

At the beginning of the American democratic experiment, the relationship between the races infected the entire governmental system. The institution of slavery and the exploitation of the native population were legitimized by all three branches of government. Blacks and Native Americans were treated as a means to an end for white people.

The Constitution of the United States recognized slaves as three-fifths a person. Native Americans didn't even merit mention. Although slavery was to be a factor in the Civil War thirty years after Tocqueville's visit, the laws of "Jim Crow" and segregation would continue in the South with the approval of the government for a century after that war. Native Americans were systematically oppressed and their land appropriated until the whites reached the Pacific Ocean and settled the countryside from shore to shore.

One particular Native American tribe impressed Tocqueville. Although their story is only one of hundreds of stories of the broken treaties that characterized westward expansion, the Cherokee nation stands as a singular example of the humanity and nobility of the Native American race and their oppression by the omnipotence of the majority.

During Tocqueville's visit to America, one of the most debated issues in society and government was the question of Native American removal. As the most powerful tribe in the eastern United States, the Cherokee nation stood at the heart of the matter. Tocqueville comments:

> If we consider the tyrannical measures that have been adopted by the legislatures of the Southern states, the conduct of their governors, and the decrees of their courts of justice, we shall be convinced that the entire expulsion of the Indians is the final result to which all the efforts of their policy are directed.

The Cherokees had sought to adapt to the ways of the whites and still preserve their heritage and land. Many families had taken up farming; Sequoyah created a written Cherokee alphabet, and the nation communicated through writings in its own language. The Cherokee nation newspaper *(Phoenix)* began publication in 1828. The Cherokees were aided in their development by religious missionaries from the North, but their achievements were truly their own. They accepted the words of whites as they would regard their own. They endeavored to learn, to cooperate and to preserve their heritage.[1]

A critical year for the Cherokee was 1828. Although the Cherokee *Phoenix* was publishing and the nation was strong, political developments augured trouble. Andrew Jackson was elected president. Though the Cherokees campaigned with General Jackson against the Creeks (indeed, they saved his army from starvation with their corn through the winter and led the storming of the Creek fortifications), Jackson was a frontiersman and no friend of the Cherokees. Rather than acknowledging any debt to the Cherokees, he lent his support as president to the efforts of Georgians to dislodge the Cherokees from their ancestral land. The Georgia legislature passed a resolution to take the Cherokee land, firing a warning shot of events to come:

> That the policy which has been pursued by the United States toward the Cherokee Indians has not been in good faith toward Georgia . . . That all the lands appropriated and unappropriated,

which lie within the conventional limits of Georgia belong to her absolutely; that the title is in her; that the Indians are tenants at her will . . . and that Georgia has the right to extend her authority and her laws over the whole territory and to coerce obedience to them from all descriptions of people, be they white, red, or black, who may reside within her limits.

In July of 1829, gold was discovered in the north Georgia foothills. The first nugget was discovered near New Echota, home of an expansive Cherokee settlement and the *Phoenix*. The stampede for gold began. Although miners streamed into Cherokee land in the autumn of 1829, the governing council of the Cherokee nation decided to depend on the national influence of their white friends to deflect the greed of Georgians.

On December 8, President Andrew Jackson endorsed the effort to relocate all eastern Indians to the west. Specifically mentioned were the Cherokees. It was clear that the good will the Cherokees had relied upon since the time of President Thomas Jefferson had dissipated.

In mid-December, the Georgia legislature met, encouraged by President Jackson's statements, and greed took over. In actions deemed to take effect in six months, June 1830, the following was issued:

> The legislature acknowledged the critics, but it overcame any and all hesitation. It passed laws forbidding any Indian to engage "in digging for gold in said land, and taking therefrom great amounts of value, thereby appropriating riches to themselves which of right equally belong to every other citizen of the state." They passed a law that further denied Indians rights in a court, declaring that an Indian cannot testify at a trial involving white men; that no Indian testimony was valid without at least two white witnesses; that no Indian contract was valid without at least two white witnesses. They voted through a bill making it unlawful "for any person or body of persons . . . to prevent, or deter any Indian, head man, chief, or warrior of said Nation . . . from selling or ceding to the United States, for the use of Georgia, the whole or any part of said territory." The penalty was a sentence in the Georgia penitentiary, at hard labor, for up to four years. They passed a bill making it illegal for any person or body of persons to prevent, by force or

threat, Cherokees from agreeing to emigrate or from moving to the West. They passed in this same bill a provision outlawing all meetings of the Cherokee council and all political assembles of Indians in Georgia, except for purposes of ceding land. (*Trail of Tears*, p. 225)

The American Missionary Board, appalled at the developments in Georgia directed against the Cherokees, responded with essays by Jeremiah Evarts. Widely circulated and influential, Evarts was most eloquent. One paragraph provides a synopsis of the unfolding events in which the Cherokees found themselves:

> It is now contended by the politicians of Georgia, that the United States has no power to make treaties with Indians "living", as they express it, "within the limits of a sovereign and independent State".
>
> Thus, according to the present doctrine, General Washington and his advisers made a solemn compact, which they called a treaty, with certain Indians, whom they called the Cherokee Nation. In this compact, the United States bound the Cherokees not to treat with Georgia. Forty years have elapsed without any complaint on the part of Georgia, in regard to this exercise of the treaty-making power; but it is now found that the Cherokees are tenants at will of Georgia; that Georgia is the only community on earth that could treat with the Cherokees; and that they must now be delivered over to her discretion. The United States then, at the very commencement of our federal government, bound the Cherokees hand and foot, and have held them bound nearly forty years, and have thus prevented their making terms with Georgia, which might doubtless have been easily done at the time of the treaty of Holston. Now it is discovered, forsooth, that the United States had no power to bind them at all. (*Trail of Tears*, p. 228)

The political mechanism smashed the Cherokees' hopes and future in Georgia and Tennessee. The Indian Removal Bill passed Congress and was signed into law by President Jackson on May 28, 1830.

Yet the Cherokees persisted. The matter was taken through the judiciary to the U.S. Supreme Court. William Wirt and John Sergeant appeared before the Court in March of 1831. Their argument was cogent:

> We know that whatever can be properly done for this unfortunate people will be done by this honorable court. Their cause is one that must come home to every honest and feeling heart. They have been true and faithful to us and have a right to expect a corresponding fidelity on our part. Through a long course of years they have followed our counsel with the docility of children. Our wish has been their law. We asked them to become civilized, and they became so. They assumed our dress, copied our names, pursued our course of education, adopted our form of government, embraced our religion, and have been proud to imitate us in every thing in their power. They have watched the progress of our prosperity with the strongest interest, and have marked the rising grandeur of our nation with as much pride as if they belonged to us. They have even adopted our resentments; and in our war with the Seminole tribes, they voluntarily joined our arms, and gave effectual aid in driving back those barbarians from the very state that now oppresses them. They threw upon the field, in that war, a body of men who descend from the noble race that were once the lords of these extensive forests—men worthy to associate with the "lion", who, in their own language, "walks upon the mountain tops." They fought side by side with our present chief magistrate, and received his personal thanks for their gallantry and bravery.
> (*Trail of Tears*, pp. 241-42)

On July 18, 1831, Chief Justice Marshall read the opinion of the Court. The Supreme Court found the Cherokees "a domestic, dependent nation". . . "in the stage of pupilage." Then he concluded the Court had no jurisdiction over this "domestic, dependent nation."

So, for the Cherokee nation, the tyranny of the majority came full circle. The legislative, executive, and judicial branches had enacted legal fiction to justify theft of the Cherokee lands by white people. The Cherokees must go west or be destroyed.

It was a situation best described by John Ridge, Cherokee leader: "You asked us to throw off the hunter and warrior state: We did so—you asked us to form a republican government: We did so—adopting your own as a model. You asked us to cultivate the earth, and learn the mechanic arts: We did so. You asked us to learn to read! We did so. You asked us to cast away our idols, and worship your God: We did so."

On December 29, 1835, the Cherokees concluded a treaty with the government. In two years' time they agreed to move west. General Winfield Scott arrived in New Echota in May of 1838 to be sure all Cherokees left for the West. He was assigned the task of removing the Cherokees who had not left their land voluntarily. In the preceding six years, approximately six thousand Cherokees had left their eastern lands for the west. General Scott estimated fifteen thousand remained to be moved by the Army.

Throughout the summer, and from July on with cooperation of the Cherokee leader John Ross, the Indians were brought into camp. Ross struck a deal with Scott, reaping financial rewards for getting the Cherokees to cooperate. The avarice of Ross combined with the malevolent actions of the American government culminated on August 28, 1838, with the first Cherokee-administered march west. This and the subsequent marches in the fall of 1838, which arrived in Oklahoma in the spring of 1839, became known by the Cherokees as "The Trail Where We Cried"—or "The Trail of Tears." The loss of life was staggering: "In the detention camps, from three hundred to two thousand died, depending on the authority accepted; on the trail, from five hundred to two thousand" (*Trail of Tears*, p. 391). The government of the United States of America had systematically stolen the homeland and nearly destroyed the Cherokee nation through forced deportation.

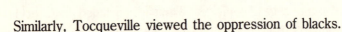

Similarly, Tocqueville viewed the oppression of blacks.

The emancipated Negros [in the North] and those born after the abolition of slavery do not, indeed, migrate from the North to the South; but their situation with regard to the Europeans is not unlike that of the Indians; they remain half civilized and deprived of their rights in the midst of a population that is far superior to them in wealth and knowledge, where they are exposed to the tyranny of the laws and the intolerance of the people. On some accounts they are still more to be pitied than the Indians, since they are haunted by the reminiscence of slavery, and they cannot claim possession of any part of the soil. Many of them perish miserably, and the rest congregate in the great towns, where they perform the meanest offices and lead a wretched and precarious existence. (p. 367-68)

The future of the three races in America was one of oppression and dissolution for the minority and prosperity for the white majority. This inevitable result stemmed from the rule of the white majority through its government. Indeed, the years since Tocqueville's visit have shown systematic oppression by the white majority of blacks and Native Americans. As Tocqueville remarks, "But it is a discovery of modern days that there are such things as legitimate tyranny and holy injustice, provided they are exercised in the name of the people" (p. 417).

The tyranny of the majority has functioned from the inception of democracy in America. It parallels the oppression of other races by the white majority. Yet it is also judged by a higher tribunal. Tocqueville observes:

But the power of the majority itself is not unlimited. Above it in the moral world are humanity, justice and reason; and in the political world, vested rights. The majority recognizes these two barriers; and if now and then oversteps them, it is because, like individuals, it has passions and, like them, it is prone to do what is wrong, while it is discerning what is right. (p. 416)

Clearly Tocqueville discerned a great and inherent danger of American democracy. The exploitation and oppression of minority races by the majority race through a democratic government was exactly the tyranny of the majority Tocqueville described. The question remains whether American government is correcting this omnipotence of the majority at the end of the twentieth century.

At first glance, one would affirm that a corrective course has been charted. Slavery and segregation are now outlawed. "All people are created equal" now applies to Native Americans, blacks, indeed all persons regardless of race, color, or creed. Yet the vast majority of the population is still white, and this majority is reflected in all three branches of government. Events of the 1950s, 1960s, and 1970s revealed a judicial commitment to equality of all people beginning with

Brown v. *Board of Education* in 1954, which desegregated public schools. The civil rights movement was reinforced by judicial and executive branch efforts throughout the 1960s and 1970s. This thirty-year period of minority progress fostered a belief that the system works. However, recent events surrounding the death penalty make clear that although the system works, it does so only at the will of the majority.

The death penalty has served as an instrument of tyranny throughout history. It does so presently in the United States and reflects a racial and class bias in doing so.

There are approximately 20,000 murders in the United States each year. Of that total, 250 or so murderers are sent to Death Row. The mere statistics as to who is on Death Row reveal how racially discriminatory the death penalty is. Although composing less than 20 percent of the population, racial minorities compose 45 percent of Death Row inmates. The true indicator of such discrimination is found in the race of victim. It is exceedingly rare to find a condemned prisoner on Death Row for killing a minority person. Indeed, it is clear white life is valued more because you are most likely sent to Death Row for killing a white person. (The most sophisticated analysis and presentation of this issue was conducted by Professor David Baldus as part of the *McCleskey* v. *Kemp* case, ruled April 22, 1987 by the U.S. Supreme Court). For instance, in the state of Georgia a person is eleven times more likely to be given the death penalty for killing a white person than for killing a black person. If a black person kills a white person, the black person is twenty-two times more likely to receive the death penalty. Even allowing for all conceivable variables affecting the decision of the judge and jury, there is a 4.3 times greater likelihood of receiving the death penalty if you kill a white person. This is twice the established correlation linking cigarette smoking to cancer.

The discrimination by race of victim has been documented in almost every Southern state. The majority opinion in the 5-4 *McCleskey* v. *Kemp* decision of the U.S. Supreme Court accepted this data as valid. But it refused to remedy this rampant discrimination in Georgia because the Georgia legislature enacted the law. Tocqueville's tyranny of the majority, which prevailed in the Supreme Court exiling the Cherokees from their land in 1835 because the state of Georgia expropriated it, persisted in the Supreme Court in 1987 in regard to the state of Georgia's passing a death penalty law discriminatory in its application. In each case, injustice is perpetrated in the name of the will of the majority. The omnipotence of the majority is as terrifying in its oppression of minorities today as in Tocqueville's time. [2]

In addition to race, class is a factor in the application of the death penalty. It is estimated that 90 percent of those on Death Row could not afford their own lawyer at trial. This means the judge appointed a lawyer, usually one who had no experience in a capital case, with a correspondingly poor result for the defendant. Indeed, such work is so poor that as of July 1, 1989, there was a 40 percent reversal rate in capital cases. [3] It should also be understood that in the South, public defender offices on a state-wide basis are the exception rather than the rule, so trained criminal legal help at no cost is not available. So the indigent, unlike the wealthy, must use lawyers who are *untrained* in capital crime.

In considering the politics of the death penalty, it is certainly no historical accident that the Southern states are the death belt states. Over half of all Death Row inmates are confined in the South, a region noted for its shameful treatment of minorities. The exact will of the majority which enforced slavery, "Jim Crow," segregation, and Indian removal targets the poor and killers of whites to be disposed of today just as yesteryear. The imprisonment and killing of minorities and poor who threaten white people is as tyrannical today as in the 1830s. The charade of legal fiction enacted and perpetrated to cover the moral unacceptability of a society killing its citizens is as clear today as the events of the 1830s were to Alexis de Tocqueville.

If anyone remained in doubt that the tyranny of the majority was prevented by judicial action, the U.S. Supreme Court's decisions in June of 1989 dispelled it. In opinions deferential to the authority of state legislatures, the Supreme Court granted permission for states to execute the mentally retarded and teenagers as young as sixteen. The majority opinion bowed to the will of the majority in these areas as it did in racial discrimination in 1987 *(McCleskey* v. *Kemp)* and the reinstatement of the death penalty in 1976 *(Jurek* v. *Texas, Gregg* v. *Georgia* and *Profitt* v. *Florida).*

In the eyes of the majority of the Supreme Court, constitutionality is determined by the power of the vote in the legislature. Since the mentally retarded and children were not protected by specific legislation in a majority of states, there exists no constitutional bar to killing them. The thought (reflected in public opinion polls) of over 60 percent of Americans, that government should not be engaged in killing teenagers and the mentally retarded, did not count because it was not enacted law.

The Psychology of State Killing

In examining the thought process that ensures acceptability of the state's killing its citizens, several writers are of singular assistance. I have benefited from the works of Richard Rubenstein, Hannah Arendt, and Stanley Milgram.[4]

In order to frame the historical times in which we dwell, it is important to recall Richard Rubenstein's reflections on the twentieth century.

> One estimate of the humanly inflicted deaths of the twentieth century places the total at about one hundred million. As fewer men have fallen prey to such natural ills as the plague and epidemic, the technology of human violence has taken up much of the slack. Those whom nature did not kill before their time were often slain by their fellowman. (*The Cunning of History*, p. 7)

As Rubenstein reminds us, we are participants in the most violent time, when states have committed wholesale murder, of any time in history. And the reason for this emerges from the heart of European civilization and is manifested in American culture as well. Indeed, this very process of objectifying our thinking, which lies at the roots of Western philosophy and enabled the Industrial and Scientific revolutions to occur, very easily becomes the objectivity of everything—from nature to people—which enables us to do whatever we will to the people or things that we objectify. In order to fully appreciate the magnitude of this observation, let us examine the society that objectified things and people to the furthest extent in history: the Third Reich of Germany.

The German Third Reich has become so misunderstood it repels people by its mere mention. The real danger of Hitler's Germany, however, is not that it was so unlike us to repel all civilized people, but that it was the apogee of twentieth century civilization at its time.

Indeed, it is in examining the Third Reich clearly that we see how similar America is to it and how frighteningly close we in the United States have come to its psychological and political milieu.

> *The Holocaust was an expression of some of the most significant political, moral, religious and demographic tendencies of Western civilization in the twentieth century.* . . . The Holocaust must be seen against the horizon of the unprecedented magnitude of violence in the twentieth century. No century in human history can match the twentieth in the sheer number of human beings slaughtered as a direct consequence of the political activity of the great states. (*The Cunning of History,* p. 6,7)
>
> One of the least helpful ways of understanding the Holocaust is to regard the destruction process as the work of a small group of irresponsible criminals who were atypical of normal statesmen and who somehow gained control of the German people, forcing them by terror and the deliberate stimulation of religious and ethnic hatred to pursue a barbaric and retrograde policy that was thoroughly at odds with the great traditions of Western civilization.
>
> On the contrary, we are more likely to understand the Holocaust if we regard it as the expression of some of the most profound tendencies of Western civilization in the twentieth century. (*The Cunning of History,* p. 21)

It is in this context of viewing the Nazi Third Reich and contemporary American government that we deal with the process of the state killing its citizens. We begin with a review of the forces that led to Auschwitz.

The German Model of Extermination

The key to the destruction of a minority by the majority is to define the minority in such a manner as to politically deprive its members of all rights and psychologically to regard them as less than human. The political stripping of rights endowed by the state to its citizens, by the majority will of the state, prevents the minority from fighting back through existing political channels because the minority, *by definition,* no longer has the right to oppose the will of the state. This process is concomitant with a psychological view of the minority that regards them as objects. Once the minority is objectified into less than human categories, it becomes possible to dispose of it by whatever means the state selects. The interrelatedness of the political and psychological processes enables laws to be enacted that lead to the extermination of the minority by the majority in an orderly, systematic, and legal manner.

In *The Cunning of History,* Richard Rubenstein brilliantly elucidates the political process of the Third Reich that enabled the Germans to exterminate their stateless people. Beginning with the mentally retarded and political dissidents, the mechanism expanded to include Jews, Poles, and anyone non-Aryan.

After the slaughter of World War I, Europe was faced with persons deemed apatrides or stateless persons. The Nazis denied such persons political rights. Yet it was not just the Germans who regarded these minorities askance. All European countries formed or emerging from World War I except Czechoslovakia protested the treaties they were coerced into signing. These treaties guaranteed political rights to the apatrides created from the geographical and political disunion of the war.

Although various countries in Europe detained apatrides in camps, the Germans of the Third Reich employed the solution to the problem of what to do with such stateless persons: extermination.

In 1933 the Germans proclaimed the denationalization decrees. All citizens granted nationalization from November 9, 1918, until January 30, 1933, could have their citizenship cancelled. All German nationals residing beyond the Third Reich could be placed in this category. The stage was set for the initial concentration camps and an official, available pool of people now existed to fill the camps.

On November 25, 1941, the German Reich issued a decree to dispose of German Jews as it had "nationals" from other countries. The promulgation simply stated that no German Jew had any rights beyond the boundaries of Germany. Thus if the S.S. swept up Jews and delivered them via train to Auschwitz, Poland, the Jews no longer had any rights since they were beyond German borders. In such manner the law enabled Jewish Germans to become objects to be destroyed, courtesy of a train ride to any concentration camp.

In focusing on the society of total domination the Nazis created and maintained at Auschwitz, which exterminated people with Zyklon B in gas chambers and also employed mass crematoria, it is crucial to remember that no crime was committed, no laws had been broken. The people killed were without rights because they had been stripped of citizenship by the state. Before transporting human beings to the concentration camps for extermination, an organizational and consistent technique had been utilized to define the victims as stateless, thus without rights. As Rubenstein states: "They [the Germans] also understood that by exterminating stateless men and women, they violated no law because such people were covered by no law"(p. 33).

A psychological worldview, which undergirded the political mechanics of total domination of a majority over a minority, animated the Third Reich's actions against stateless persons. Hannah Arendt is most helpful in revealing the psychological dimension that created the political structure of mass extermination. Arendt makes it very clear that the Nazis did not merely hate the Jews. Such an emotive reaction was continually brought under control by the bureaucracy, which insisted on rationality and objectivity. Rather, the Germans transformed the minority into an objective category of the subhuman, and thus were able to dispose of them as the rulers saw fit because the minority was not like the majority.

Arendt's pursuit of truth, never resting with stereotypical conclusions, manifested itself in a series of articles for *The New Yorker* magazine about the state of Israel's trial of Adolf Eichmann in 1960. The articles became a book entitled *Eichmann in Jerusalem.*

As both Rubenstein and Arendt reveal, the power of the German Reich was not just the enactment of a political process that legalized the state killing its citizens. Rather, the dangerous accomplishment was the objectification of human beings into non-human categories. This regarding of people as *Tiermenschen,* subhumans, enabled all laws enacted to destroy them to have a cogency, which otherwise would be lacking. You could kill a dissident, a mentally retarded person, or a Jew, once the person was defined as subhuman. This minority was not like the majority and hence could be done away with, if the majority so chose. And in Nazi Germany, the majority clearly chose and endorsed this policy. Of course, such actions are always undertaken for the noblest of reasons. As Adolph Hitler so tellingly phrased it—sounding like a politician in America in 1990 talking about the death penalty or perhaps a member of the U.S. Supreme Court majority—"What is good for Germany is what is good for the Volk [people]."

The fundamental reality in Nazi Germany was that people like Adolf Eichmann, who maintained that his actions in killing millions of people were those of "normal persons," were telling the truth. The Nazi regime did not regard the act of society slaughtering citizens as criminal because German society legislated and approved such behavior. For the Nazis, Auschwitz was perfectly legal, normal, and acceptable.

This legal fiction relied on a person's not thinking of another from the other person's viewpoint. In Germany, except for a few brave individuals whose thinking led to resistance of the Reich, the German people became like Adolf Eichmann. As Hannah Arendt described Eichmann: "The longer one listened to him, the more obvious . . . became . . . his inability to *think*, namely, to think from the standpoint of somebody else" (p. 49).

What characterized the psychology of the Third Reich was the utter ability of the German people to not think, to swallow the government's actions because they wanted to believe ridding society of the subhuman class would make Germany better. This was accomplished by making people objects or things. Once persons are no longer considered human beings, why be concerned about their worth or fate?

Arendt observes: "This 'objective' attitude—talking about concentration camps in terms of 'administration' and about extermination camps in terms of 'economy'—was typical of the S.S. mentality, and something Eichmann, at the trial, was still very proud of" (p. 69). In illuminating the power of such objectivity (*Sachlichkeit*), Arendt recalls the testimony of Dr. Servatius, a tax and business lawyer who never joined the Nazi Party:

> Servatius declared the accused innocent of charges bearing on his responsibility for "the collection of skeletons, sterilizations, killings by gas, and *similar medical matters,*" whereupon Judge Halevi interrupted him: "Dr. Servatius, I assume you made a slip of the tongue when you said that killing by gas was a medical matter." To which Servatius replied: "It was indeed a medical matter, since it was prepared by physicians; *it was a matter of killing, and killing, too, is a medical matter.* (p. 69)

The ability of a whole society to function in exterminating its citizens requires "objectivity," or not thinking of the victim as human. The German Reich accomplished this to a remarkable degree. Industries functioned at concentration camps; trains deported people; and some Jews even helped round up other Jews for deportation, all part of an objective process. It was a societal process of mass murder regarded as perfectly normal by the officials carrying out the killings.

The troops who actually carried out the murders in the concentration camps were aided by the master psychologist of the Third Reich, Heinrich Himmler. Arendt notes:

> Hence the problem was how to overcome not so much their conscience as the animal pity by which all normal men are affected in the presence of physical suffering. The trick used by Himmler—who apparently was rather strongly afflicted with these instinctive reactions himself—was very simple and probably very effective; it consisted in turning those instincts around, as it were, in directing them toward the self. So that instead of saying: What horrible things I did to people!, the murderers would be able to say: What horrible things I had to watch in the pursuance of my duties, how heavily the task weighed upon my shoulders! (p. 106)

The reality of evil in the Third Reich had become so commonplace that it was ordinary. It was "the lesson of the fearsome, word-and-thought-defying banality of evil" (p. 252). In an effort to describe how a society succumbed to such, Arendt reflects:

> Evil in the Third Reich had lost the quality by which most people recognize it—the quality of temptation. Many Germans and many Nazis, probably an overwhelming majority of them, must have been tempted *not* to murder, *not* to rob, *not* to let their neighbors go off to their doom (for that the Jews were transported to their doom they knew, of course, even though many of them may not have known the gruesome details), and not to become accomplices in all these crimes by benefiting from them. But, God knows, they had learned how to resist temptation. (p. 150)

It is tempting to view the Nazi Reich as a relic of a murderous past. If we do so, we choose to ignore the place of the U.S. in the world at the end of the twentieth century. In order to understand the bridge that connects our democratic government to the Third Reich, we must examine the political and psychological milieu of each society. The linkage of the two societies, indeed all modern societies to each other, is described in Stanley Milgram's book, *Obedience to Authority*.

Stanley Milgram is also haunted by the individual's willingness to perpetrate or cooperate in evil. In order to determine if Americans could share in an inclination for obedience to authority that characterized the Third Reich, Milgram conducted a psychological experiment at Yale University. Although eventually including over one thousand participants and conducted in several places, the experiment is essentially simple and designed to determine "how far the participant will comply with the experimenter's instructions before refusing to carry out the actions required of him" (p. 3).

Milgram's experiment involved recruiting two people to participate in a study of memory and learning. One of them is designated as a "teacher" and the other a "learner." The experimenter explains that the study is concerned with the effects of punishment on learning. The learner is conducted to a room, seated in a chair, his arms strapped to prevent excessive movement, and an electode attached to his wrist. He is told that he is to learn a list of word pairs; whenever he makes an error, he will receive electric shocks of increasing intensity.

The real focus of the experiment is the teacher. After watching the learner being strapped into place, he is taken into the main experimental room and seated before an impressive shock generator. Its main feature is a horizontal line of thirty switches, ranging from 15 volts to 450 volts, in 15-volt increments. There are also verbal designations which range from SLIGHT SHOCK to DANGER—SEVERE SHOCK. The teacher is told that he is to administer the learning test to the man in the other room. When the learner responds correctly, the teacher moves on to the next item; when the man gives an incorrect answer, the teacher is to give him a shock. He is to start at the lowest shock level (15 volts) and to increase the level each time the man makes an error, going through 30 volts, 45 volts, and so on (*Obedience to Authority*, p. 3).

It should be mentioned that the "learner" of the study was actually an actor. No shocks are actually delivered.

Much to Milgrim's surprise, "a substantial proportion [60 percent] continue to the last shock on the generator" (p. 5), even though the learner is screaming, demanding release from the experiment, and portraying agony at the greatest level of shock. Adults are very obedient to authority even at the cost of inflicting suffering on another human being.

The conclusion of Milgram's study is not reassuring. After observing individuals inflict suffering on command, over and over again, Milgram reports: "It is the extreme willingness of adults to go to almost any length of command of an authority that constitutes the chief finding of the study and the fact most urgently demanding explanation" (p. 5).

What Stanley Milgram's experiment allows us to see is that obedience to authority is a major characteristic of modern society. Whether in New Haven, Connecticut, in 1970 or Berlin in 1941, modern societies exert enormous control over their citizens. Indeed, in order to please authority, human suffering is willingly inflicted. If anything, with the advent of the computer and increased technological and bureaucratic institutionalization, America in 1990 is far more technologically equipped to ask for and expect obedience than Germany in 1940.

Milgram reveals the willingness of American adults to inflict suffering on command. We too respond to the call of obedience to authority, whether it be electrocuting someone in a psychological experiment at Yale or in the electric chair in the death house at the Florida State Prison in Starke. The question now becomes is such suffering being inflicted in society itself rather than confined to a psychological experiment? And if such obedience is carried out on orders from authority, how is it possible in a democratic government?

As of September 1, 1989, 121 people have been officially murdered in American death chambers since 1976. On Death Row approximately 2,600 await a similar fate. The process of selecting, labeling, and exterminating those condemned by the state is a bureaucratic, legal, and accepted mechanism of society. American society is quite willing to murder selected citizens for the greater good.

Tocqueville pointed out the inherent danger of a democratic government. The tyranny of the majority was a reality in his day inflicted on Native Americans and blacks. This tyranny has manifested itself throughout American history, usually defined racially, and does so today in the institution of the death penalty. "The will of the majority" (U.S.

Supreme Court opinions, 1976) desires elimination of a class of people, defined as murderers. But the classification can be expanded easily, as the Nazis did in moving from the mentally retarded and euthanasia to dissidents and Jews, and finally outright slaughter.

One might argue that Holocaust victims, slaves, and Native Americans were innocent and that the victims of capital punishment, criminals, are guilty. This is obviously true, but this argument misses the central issue of the state assuming the authority to take human life. The state has engineered a legal mechanism against humanity itself. The power of the state has become a threat to humanity through its use of capital punishment. After all, was a slave less of a human being because the law decreed him chattel? Was a Native American less than human because the state defined him in such a manner that made it legal to take his land? Or was a victim of the Holocaust less of a human being because the Third Reich decreed him subhuman? Is a murderer less of a human being because the state objectifies him in order to kill him?

In each of these cases, the person is uniquely gifted with life and does not forfeit that gift even if the state seeks to take it. The state lawfully took life in each category of victims listed above because it gives itself the authority to do so, but the essential humanity of each person remains. The state is engaged in mere legal artifice to accomplish its objective.

In the United States of America, the natural inclination is to view treatment of criminals as different from the way we treated blacks and Native Americans. Such an observation is obviously true to the extent that we, the state, do not discriminate by enslaving blacks, nor by exiling Native Americans. Yet the reality is that the discrimination is manifested in a more sophisticated manner than in the last century or even in the racial segregation of this century. The social factors of race and poverty have an inescapable impact on determining who goes to Death Row. As I have pointed out, the people who are sentenced to Death Row are the poor who cannot afford lawyers, and the killers of white people.

The majority of Americans are inflamed about crime. The legitimate fear of crime is a subjective but real phenomenon. When political leaders manipulate this fear by calling for the death penalty, they are able to attract cheap votes even though the death penalty does nothing to solve crime or murder rates.[5]

Alexis de Tocqueville was prophetic when he feared the tyranny of the majority. When the majority decides to eliminate those whom it fears, the objective machinery of government implements the subjective desire of the people. Whether it is treating the blacks as property through slavery, Native Americans as expendable in order to take their land, or murderers as subhumans to satisfy a mythical notion of self-preservation, the objective realities are driven by the subjective will of the majority. It matters not whether this majority will is moral or just. What matters is that it achieves what it wishes. And the frightening reality in the United States in 1990 is that many people will be exterminated because they have been slated as disposable by the majority.   Hannah Arendt hauntingly elucidates the banality of evil that pervades the majority consciousness. In her postscript to *Eichmann in Jerusalem,* she is still searching for words to convey the ordinariness of evil.

> The expression "administrative massacres" seems better to fill the bill. . . . The phrase has the virtue of dispelling the prejudice that such monstrous acts can be committed only against a foreign nation or a different race. There is the well-known fact that Hitler began his mass murders by granting "mercy deaths" to the "incurably ill," and that he intended to wind up his extermination program by doing away with "genetically damaged" Germans (heart and lung patients). But quite aside from that, it is apparent that this sort of killing can be directed against any given group, that is, that the principle of selection is dependent only upon circumstantial factors. It is quite conceivable that in the automated economy of a not-too-distant future men may be tempted to exterminate all those whose intelligence quotient is below a certain level. (pp. 228-89)

By using the term *administrative massacres* the societal cooperation, the routine nature of the state legally killing its citizens is forcefully brought out. The bureaucracy, the government, the religious, all factors of society cooperate to achieve this result. As Richard Rubenstein stated, "One of the least helpful ways of understanding the

Holocaust is to regard the destruction process as the work of a small group of irresponsible criminals who were atypical of normal statesmen."

As of this writing, the tyranny of the majority is completely effective in implementing the destruction of the minority in the United States. All branches of government and society as a whole cooperate in the process. But presently we are not at the point of massacring thousands of people. Rather, it is an administrative process, which at this time kills singularly. Indeed, in order to convey the reality of killing machinery, let us recall the words of a Death Row prisoner: Jerry Wayne Jacobs of Alabama.

In a visit to Death Row at Holman Unit in Atmore, Alabama, I conversed with a man who described the process of condemnation, confinement, and killing, he told the following story: "I once worked at a slaughterhouse in Bartow, Florida. We would pen up the livestock, then send them down the chute one by one and kill 'em. That's what they're doin' with us here. They've got us penned up and one by one, they lead us down to that yellow electric chair and kill us. Ain't a bit of difference between here and there."

So it is from the condemned on America's Death Row and the wisdom of Hannah Arendt that I offer another description of the process we call the death penalty. It is administrative, truly a bureaucratic process of the technological society. For now, it is not a massacre; rather, it is a slaughter. The American government is slaughtering its citizens administratively and legally.

It is an irony of administrative killing, be it massacre or slaughter, that the orchestrators of the process believe their actions actually make it easier for the victims. Arendt notes: "Eichmann claimed more than once his organizational gifts, the coordination of evacuation and deportations achieved by his office, had in fact helped his victims; it had made their fate easier. If this thing had to be done at all, he argued, it was better that it be done in good order" (p. 190).

This precise reasoning has been offered by such administrators of slaughter as Florida's Governor Bob Graham, former Chief Justice of the U.S. Supreme Court Warren Burger and current Chief Justice William Rehnquist. To kill people expeditiously is really the slaughterer's great favor to the victim!

The Nazi leaders realized the power of language. They invoked "language rules" to cover the reality of their deeds. Arendt reports: "It is rare to find documents in which such bald words as 'extermination,' 'liquidation,' or 'killing' occur. The prescribed code names for killing were 'final solution,' 'evacuation,' and 'special treatment.' "

In a similar manner, language is corrupted by the functionaries of killing in America. All human feelings are cloaked under the guise of doing one's duty. The person to be killed is referred to as objectively as possible. When actually killed by the particular instrument of slaughter, the dead person is said to have "expired." The executioner's anonymity is usually preserved to maintain the "professional" nature of the proceedings. Much emphasis is placed on carrying out the killing "professionally." Indeed, each member of the death squad is assigned specific instructions. The completion of one's duty is the actual strapping of the arms into the electric chair or other designated "procedures." Indeed, examination of an operations chart for an official killing in Florida leaves the reader feeling all precautions imaginable have been taken to dehumanize the events of killing a human being. This attitude is exemplified by the guard who asked me to tell Tim Baldwin that there was "nothing personal" intended in the guard's actions to help kill Tim. So, the focusing on the task at hand enables the member of "the team" to become lost in the successful completion of detail and not be disturbed by the total picture of how he cooperates in killing a person. Indeed, no humanity or compassion is allowed in the effort to be an objective professional.

Yet even the most professional killings sometimes go awry. At such times the role of the medical community, always in attendance at a state-sponsored killing to verify death, becomes even more questionable.

For example, when a heartbeat is discovered after the initial thrust of killing is administered, a doctor pronounces the presence of life. Despite allegiance to the Hippocratic oath to preserve life, such determination of life in a person results in the state's administering further doses of the killing device. It is repeated until the person is killed and the doctor pronounces death. The doctor, paid by the state to render a service in killing a citizen, does so obligingly despite taking a solemn oath to preserve life. Just as willingly the chaplain, usually a

Christian minister, serves the state in expediting the execution. Indeed, the integration of every profession into the societal mechanism of killing is accomplished quite easily.

Observing the process that the American government utilizes to kill its citizens, the similarities with the Third Reich are chilling. The tyranny of the majority offers up minorities for killing in a legally prescribed, socially approved fashion. The death chambers and the death houses churn out their victims with the cooperation of all elements of society. It is easily done because it is merely the disposal of society's trash; subhuman specimens. Unlike the majority, their behavior hinders and offends the will of the majority. This is no accidental product of government but the result of an inherent flaw in democracy itself—the crushing of the minority.

When the record of Western Europe's abolition of the death penalty is examined, the ancient roots of civilization are often noted as a reason for discarding the death penalty. Perhaps a closer historical encounter provides a better explanation.

In World War II, Europe experienced tyranny firsthand through the Nazis. The Germans occupied Europe, part of Scandinavia, and reduced much of Britain to rubble through bombing. Europeans were oppressed and slaughtered. The experience of such tyranny leads the survivor to want to ensure that no one else experiences such suffering again. As a German government official expressed to me after I visited him in Berlin: "We've seen quite enough of the death penalty in our society. We know what it is about." Europeans had experienced so much horror during the war that the idea of the government killing its citizens was repulsive to them. This is why there is no death penalty in Western Europe.

The United States had the opposite experience in World War II. The country was a liberator, not subjected to war on its own soil. Indeed, the country has always viewed itself as opposed to tyranny and the champion of the oppressed. So it has a difficult time viewing itself as a tyrant, which utilization of the death penalty shows it to be. And, of course, reading the story of any tyrant in history reveals the despot never perceives itself as doing anything but good.

The question arises, to what standard do we hold states that slaughter their citizens? The internal laws are inadequate because they guarantee the victims for the death chambers. Is there an ethical dimension beyond the laws of a respective state that protects human rights beyond the provincial boundaries of a country?

This is the ultimate issue Arendt and Tocqueville wrestle with in their work.

Tocqueville mentioned "two barriers . . . the moral world [of] humanity, justice and reason; and in the political world, vested rights" (p. 416). Arendt dwelled in depth on "the inadequacy of the prevailing legal system and the current judicial concepts to deal with the facts of administrative massacres organized by the state apparatus" (p. 294).

The twentieth century teaches a simple and powerful lesson: Do not give the state authority to take human life. The state is an imperfect mechanism, dedicated to its own survival and certainly not an arbiter of who should live or die. Whether it be John Spenkelink in Tallahassee, Florida, or any citizen before any governmental tribunal, the human right to life is a metaethical one that should be protected by existing authority, not threatened by it. Each country in the world should strive to protect this right to life of every citizen.

In order to ensure this, the United Nations or the World Court should create a special international tribunal to deal with countries that seek to kill their citizens. If countries insist on officially slaughtering their citizens, despite efforts of the international court to redress the cause of such state action, two levels of sanctions should be available to be imposed: 1. Economic sanctions by the world community against the offending state, and 2. Political asylum granted in other countries to the designated victims that the state seeks to kill.

We can only overcome administrative massacre and slaughter by investing the right to life in the international court of "humanity, justice, and reason." Each individual in the world has a right not to be killed by his own government. It is only an international forum, armed with the power of economic boycott and political asylum, which can lift a standard for the protection of individuals above and beyond provincial bounds. Without such a cooperative, international effort, the twenty-first century will see states continue to administratively slaughter their citizens, providing endless victims for death chambers throughout the world.

The Religious Community and the Morality of Murder

I was once told a story about Elie Wiesel, survivor and writer of the Holocaust experience. Wiesel was asked by a member of the audience at the conclusion of one of his lectures, "Mr. Wiesel, where were the Christians during the Third Reich?" Wiesel is said to have responded: "They were running the concentration camps."

This one episode concisely portrays the role of Christians in Hitler's Germany. Aside from the confessing church, led by people such as Dietrich Bonhoeffer, official Christianity capitulated to the state's slaughter. (Eberhart Bethge's remarkable rendering of Dietrich Bonhoeffer and his times is most insightful.) Stanley Milgram's research reveals not one person who stopped the proceedings of inflicting suffering for religions reasons. Indeed one woman who responded as Milgram hoped all participants would, ceased administering the electric shocks when the victim showed significant pain. The woman, Gretchen Brandt, "grew to adolescence in Hitler's Germany and was for the great part of her youth exposed to Nazi propaganda. When asked about the possible influence of her background, she remarks slowly, 'perhaps we have seen too much pain' " (*Obedience to Authority*, p. 85).

The total societal assimilation of the religious community cannot be underscored enough. The irony that the Christian Church, founded on the executed Jesus of Nazareth, is unable to prevent the state from continuing its administrative massacres and slaughters reveals that the true obedience to authority is to the state, not to the Lord who calls for a cost of discipleship. As Arendt so tellingly puts it, the family man, "for the sake of his pension, his life insurance, the security of his wife and children . . . was prepared to do literally anything. The family man became the mob man and finally the hangman."[6]

The Judeo-Christian heritage has been consistent over the centuries in teaching that murder is an immoral act. Although the tradition has been ambivalent on capital punishment, a consensus has emerged among virtually every major religious body with a position on the issue that the death penalty contravenes the tradition and should be abandoned. Thus, an evolving standard of morality in the religious community has coincided with the official position of every Western democracy except the United States to move toward an abolition of the death penalty.

One of the reasons for the evolving standard of morality in the Judeo-Christian tradition has been the realization that each person is a child of God. If each soul is endowed with the image of God, then society would do well to respect such a reality and not destroy it through the process of state-sanctioned killing.

The problem of modern society is that the techniques of execution have made it possible to destroy human beings with a rapidity and effectiveness unknown in human history. As such methods become available the discussion becomes one of how to implement the method to destroy people, and not whether such action should be undertaken. The morality of state-sanctioned murder is sustained by the ability of the state to kill its citizens as a solution to a problem (that is, the Jewish problem, the mentally ill, the dissident, the criminal).

In each instance of designating and exterminating the citizenry, the state assumes its morality from the efficacy of being able to accomplish the act. This places the state in the incongruous position of arguing that murder is a moral act, so long as it is the state that commits the murder and it is done for the good of the people. Translating this into the language of the 1990s in the United States of America means that the state may place a human being into a cage, approximately 6' x 8', for years. The condemned person is under surveillance with a highly restricted routine, perhaps one that goes something like this: a shower twice a week, exercise two to three times a week, and food brought to the individual in the cell. The condemned person otherwise remains in the cell, except for a visit, which can occur only twice a week. Then on a designated day or night, the condemned individual is removed from the cell and prepared for execution. After waiting, anticipating such fate for years, the killing is accomplished with either an electric chair, gas chamber, poisoned needle, hanging rope, or discharged rifle(s).

It is clear that if any individual endeavored to recreate the state's mechanism for killing, the individual would be charged with premeditated and cold-blooded murder. The thought of removing a fellow citizen from the community, confining this person in an area the size of a closet for years, informing the individual when and how death will occur, then carrying out the killing of the designated person, strikes most citizens as an outrageous horror. Yet, this is precisely what the state does with the death penalty. Such an action performed by the state is just as immoral as an action taken by an individual citizen. Sanitizing the process, labeling the killing an execution, does little but obscure the reality that a cold-blooded murder is committed.

Once the question of technique—how the state kills its citizens—is overcome, and the morality of the state killing its citizens is exposed for the deliberate process of slaughter it truly is, the only remaining defense for the state is the dubious one of assuming the morality of its action. In light of the abandonment of the morality of this official murder by the Judeo-Christian community and every other Western democracy, the state is reduced to proclaiming the killing process allowable because it deems it so, in the name of the people.

The hypocrisy of the state's position, committing murder to show murder is wrong, is clear. The death penalty is not an act of restoration. It does not bring back the life of the victim. Rather, it adds one more victim and victim's family to the grieving circle. The death penalty is an act of retribution, which is simply a state-sanctioned murder.

There is nothing inherent in the act of murder that demands the vengeance of taking the life of the murderer. Indeed, the Bible shows us that some of the most favored people of Yahweh were murderers, from David to the apostle Paul. The Bible teaches that God has always been able to separate the act from the person. This is clearly shown in the fourth chapter of Genesis, the account of the first murder, where Yahweh punished Cain with exile for the murder of his brother Abel.

The immorality of murder, whether committed by the individual or the state, lies at the heart of the Judeo-Christian faith. Human life is to be husbanded, not eradicated. The moral response to murder demands that the state not compound murder by committing murder itself. Capital punishment must be abandoned because it is merely an exercise in vengeance.

When the state's cloak of morality is removed and the politics of the death penalty is revealed, it becomes clear that the only way to eliminate the catastrophes such as Auschwitz and the Florida State Prison is for the state to be prevented from taking human life. Once the state begins to play God and determine who lives and who dies, mass slaughter is lurking around the corner. The state is the arbiter of life and death only through wanton abuse and discrimination, because of the manner in which it functions. In pursuit of accomplishing the will of the masses, the tyranny of the masses emerge, and minorities and individuals become expendable. The entire machinery of government is marshalled in a legal process to destroy designated citizens for the good of the whole. Justice, mercy, forgiveness, and reconciliation are unknown elements in a system designated for extermination. Rather, revenge and the public good become the euphemism for the state's entry into the act of destroying life.

It would be easier if I could believe that murderers, or whomever we deem worthy of the death penalty, had to forfeit their right to life. But I know society is concerned about the subjective exorcism of its fear of crime. Establishing a mechanism for achieving this goal, even if it is a racist charade, is what the death penalty is truly about. It is not about an individual commiting a murder as much as it is about society deciding to exterminate a segment of the population that the majority fears. There are many punishments for criminal behavior, and the European nations have managed to do quite well without the death penalty. We could do so as well, if we so chose.

But that is the point, we do not choose to do so. The majority clings to this vestige of a way of attempting to control the minority, and so this subversive form of discrimination will continue to be manifested through the government until the day this barbarity is seen for what it is: a systematic killing process that is unworthy of a democratic people and that shames us in the eyes of the civilized world and in the sight of God.

NOTES

1. For the chronicling of the Cherokee nation, I am indebted to John Ehle's excellent book *Trail of Tears: The Rise and Fall of the Cherokee Nation* (New York: Doubleday, 1988).
2. For incontrovertible evidence of racial bias in capital punishment see David C. Baldus, George G. Woodworth, and Charles A. Pulaski, Jr., *Equal Justice and the Death Penalty: A Legal and Empirical Analysis* (Boston: Northeastern University Press, 1989).
3. Information on the reversal rate in capital cases provided by NAACP Legal Defense Fund.
4. Richard L. Rubenstein, *The Cunning of History* (New York: Harper & Row, 1978); Hannah Arendt, *Eichmann in Jerusalem: A Report on the Banality of Evil*, rev. and

enlarged ed. (New York: Penguin, 1965); Stanley Milgram, *Obedience to Authority: An Experimental View* (New York: Harper & Row, 1974).
5. For a thorough examination of how the death penalty fails to accomplish any goal it purports to achieve see Ronald Tabak and Mark Lane, "The Execution of Injustice: A Cost and Lack-of-Benefit Analysis of the Death Penalty," *Loyola of Los Angeles Law Review,* vol. 23 (November 1989).
6. From "Organized Guilt and Universal Responsibility" as quoted by Leslie Epstein in "Atrocity and Imagination," *Harper's,* vol. 271 (August 1985): pp. 13-16. This article is an adaptation of an address originally delivered by Leslie Epstein at a conference on the Holocaust at Millersville University, Millersville, Pennsylvania.